Psychoanalysis
AND
Psychotherapy

Psychoanalysis

AND

Psychotherapy

DEVELOPMENTS
IN THEORY,
TECHNIQUE,
AND TRAINING

By FRANZ ALEXANDER, M.D.

DIRECTOR, CHICAGO INSTITUTE FOR PSYCHOANALYSIS

CLINICAL PROFESSOR OF PSYCHIATRY, UNIVERSITY OF ILLINOIS

W · W · NORTON & COMPANY · INC · New York

First Edition

TO THE MEMORY OF

Sigmund Freud

ON THE HUNDREDTH ANNIVERSARY

OF HIS BIRTH

Contents

Preface

THIS BOOK is an attempt to present in a comprehensive manner some contributions of my own and of others made during the last two decades to the theory and technique of psychoanalytic treatment and to the utilization of psychoanalytic knowledge in various methods of psychotherapy. I am particularly interested in the application of psychoanalytic principles to that type of psychotherapy which differs from traditional psychoanalysis mainly in its quantitative aspects. This form of therapy in recent years has become known as "psychoanalytically oriented psychotherapy" or "dynamic psychotherapy."

It was suggested that my articles on this subject be published in a book in their original form. Because of certain controversial issues concerning both the theory and the practice of psychoanalytic treatment, which these publications occasioned, it appears to me advisable to present these contributions in a comprehensive text, in which some of these issues will be discussed. Most of the controversies pertain to the question of how to differentiate between "classical" psychoanalysis and "psychoanalytically oriented psychotherapy."

My interest in this borderline field developed from recognizing the great therapeutic possibilities of psychoanalytic knowledge which have remained unexploited in the standard approach, suitable only to a limited and relatively small number of psychiatric patients. Two large groups of patients are not suitable for the standard approach: (1) those severe ones whose basic deficiency in ego functions makes them unable to face their conflicts; (2) those milder, acute, and incipient cases who can be helped adequately by less complete and less intensive treatment. Both groups, the very severe and the mild cases, require modifications in treatment procedures, using, however, the same psychodynamic principles as the standard procedure.

The application of psychoanalysis to the severe cases, particularly the major psychoses, offers a great therapeutic challenge. This topic, however, is not dealt with in this book and the reader is referred to *Principles of Intensive Psychotherapy* by Frieda Fromm-Reichmann (54).

The treatment of acute and incipient neuroses has great social significance. The trend in the whole of medicine is toward prevention. The intermediary step to this ultimate goal is the early discovery and treatment of cases while they are still treatable because they progress into a chronic phase which often resists the most intensive therapy.

Neurosis can be looked upon as the result of a positive feedback mechanism. In a negative feedback the response to a stimulus elicits a third process which is fed back as a message (information) to the source of the stimulus and either reduces or increases it so that a steady state is insured. It is a kind of automatic control mechanism. In a positive feedback the response changes the original stimulus always in one direction which in turn changes the response in the same direction and thus a vicious circle is established. The whole circular process is out of control.

Neurotic symptoms develop as responses to failures in the ego's integrative function and serve as substitutive but not adequate gratifications of subjective needs. They detract from the available free cathexes and reduce the free motivational powers of the person. Moreover, they lead to secondary conflicts which in turn require defenses, further diminishing free available cathexes for realistic gratifications in life. As a result the individual loses more and more of his capacity to deal with his actual life problems successfully. This requires new symptom formation. Through early treatment this spiraling type of vicious circle can be avoided. Therapeutic interventions can be considered as negative feedback mechanisms which make the maintenance of a steady state possible.

The experiences of war psychiatry demonstrated this fact. It is erroneous to assume, however, that such incipient cases do not require expert management. Inadequate treatment not only fails often to arrest the neurotic process but may even contribute to its progression to chronic neurosis by mobilizing the latent neurotic potentialities which are well-nigh universal in our contemporary Western civilization (72).[1] Because of the social significance of reaching a great variety of patients, I see herein the most important therapeutic possibility of psychoanalysis.

While the standard procedure in psychoanalysis is the best tool for research since it aims at a complete reconstruction of the patient's personality development, its therapeutic range is limited. The preponderance of Freud's interest in research is to a large degree responsible for the scant interest of his followers, until very recently, in the systematic exploration of all the therapeutic possibilities of our theoretical knowledge. For Freud the emphasis on research, that is to say, the wish to increase his knowledge, was the only logical attitude. How could he expect to help the neurotic without better understanding the nature of the disease? The time has come, however, to explore the wider therapeutic applications of our basic knowledge which has been accumulated during the last fifty years.

If psychiatrists, particularly psychoanalysts, and the psychoanalytic institutes do not consider it their task to explore systematically the whole range of therapeutic applications of psychoanalytic knowledge and to teach these applications to their candidates and other residents of psychiatry, the current situation will continue: the majority of patients will be left to unsystematized, intuitive, sometimes brilliant but as a whole unreliable treatment. All this points to the need for greater exploration and teaching of the techniques of dynamic psychotherapy. Herein at present lies the greatest possible con-

---

[1] While using the expression of Kubie, "neurotic potential," I do not follow entirely his definition of the "neurotic component" (see Chapter I).

tribution of psychoanalysis to mental health, second only to its general influence upon the outlook of contemporary man, modifying his interpersonal relations, his educational and child-rearing practices.

Some of the views presented in this book have been previously published in periodicals and symposia. Some new contributions to problems of treatment are added and recent developments from a historical perspective are evaluated.

This book contains also a prognostication of the future of psychoanalytic training and practice. So far as the history of training is concerned I am in the fortunate position of an eyewitness. I matriculated as the first student of the Berlin Psychoanalytic Institute, which was founded in 1920 as the first psychoanalytic institute to come into existence. A few years later I was appointed a teacher at the same Institute and I have continued to be active in psychoanalytical practice and training.

The present book does not aspire to resolve all conflicting views or to say the last word about them. It attempts to state my position clearly so that views will not be attributed to me and my collaborators which we do not hold.

More important, however, than the clarification of these particular controversial issues for me is to take stock and evaluate the potential contribution of psychoanalytic knowledge to the treatment of disturbances of personality functions, to mental health, and to the general outlook of Western culture. From the evaluation of the past and the present I shall try to visualize the direction which the psychologic approach to personality may take in the future.

FRANZ ALEXANDER

Center for Advanced Study in the
    Behavioral Sciences
Stanford, California
August 8, 1955

Acknowledgments

FIRST OF all I wish to recognize the help and stimulation I received from my collaborators at the Chicago Institute for Psychoanalysis. Working in daily contact with them both in research and in teaching made it possible to approach the problems of psychoanalytic technique in a more objective manner. Exposing the same recorded material to a number of observers is possibly the most important methodological advancement I witnessed in my thirty-five years' practice of psychoanalysis. This allows a constant exchange of evaluations of the same material and criticisms of abstractions and generalizations by individual therapists. This makes for what is characteristic of science: cumulative knowledge constantly subjected to the observations and reasonings of independent workers.

I am most grateful to Drs. Kenneth E. Appel, Karl Bowman, C. H. Hardin Branch, Henry Brosin, Joan Fleming, Frieda Fromm-Reichmann, Francis J. Gerty, Roy R. Grinker, George C. Ham, Heinz Hartmann, Lawrence S. Kubie, Maurice Levine, Sandor Lorand, Karl Menninger, Sandor Rado, F. C. Redlich, Norman Reider, John Romano, Leon J. Saul, and John C. Whitehorn for their invaluable help in stating their views and practices concerning teaching psychoanalytic concepts to residents in psychiatry in response to a questionnaire I sent them.

I wish to express my appreciation in particular to Drs. Thomas M. French, Ralph Gerard, Gerhart Piers, Helen Ross, and Morris Stein, who read the manuscript, for their suggestions and criticisms.

Chapter I is based on an address delivered on May 9, 1954, at the joint meeting of the American Psychoanalytic and Psychiatric Associations' annual convention. Parts of Chapter II have been published in the transactions of the Congres International de Psychiatrie, Paris, 1950, based on my address, "The Evolution and Present Trends of Psychoanalysis." Parts of Chapter III are contained in a paper, "The Problems of Psychoanalytic Technique," published in the *Psychoanalytic Quarterly*, 1935. The two case histories and part of the discussions and conclusions contained in Chapter IV have been published in two papers, "The Analyses of the Therapeutic Factors in Psychoanalytic Treatment" (*Psychoanalytic Quarterly*, 1950), and "Some Quantitative Aspects of Psychoanalytic Technique" (*Journal of the American Psychoanalytic Association*, II, 4, October 1954). Chapter V is based on an address which I delivered before the San Francisco Psychoanalytic Society, February 14, 1955. Parts of Chapter X are contained in my article, "Psychoanalysis and Psychotherapy," published in the *Journal of the American Psychoanalytic Association*, II, 4, October 1954. I wish to thank the editors, Dr. John Frosch and Dr. Raymond Gosselin, and Dr. John C. Whitehorn, Chairman of the Editorial Board which published the report of the 1952 Conference on Psychiatric Education held at Cornell University, and Librairie Scientifique Hermann et Cie, for permission to make extensive quotations and republication of parts of the original articles.

The completion of this book would have been delayed considerably without the opportunity of spending a year at the Center for Advanced Study in the Behavioral Sciences, where ideal conditions were created for the Fellows for continued and uninterrupted concentration.

Psychoanalysis

AND

Psychotherapy

Introduction

THE COMPLEX field of psychoanalysis deals with so many imponderabilia that it is not an easy undertaking to express views and opinions in a way which avoids interpretations different from what the author tries to convey to his readers. This difficulty has in part semantic reasons. It comes from the vagueness of some of our technical expressions. Partly it has emotional origins. Many of our terms are "loaded." The brief history of psychoanalysis is full of emotionally highly charged issues. Freud for many years had to face an almost universal rejection of his views, a rejection which in the beginning had, primarily, not intellectual but emotional foundations. It became necessary for him and his followers to defend novel insights into personality against misunderstanding and distortion. Most, if not all, of these early polemics were motivated by emotional "resistance" due to the fact that psychoanalysis aims at making conscious that psychological material which is excluded from consciousness because of the person's unwillingness to recognize and admit it. This led then to an inclination among us to reject criticisms coming from outsiders and to consider deviation from what was supposed to be the "official" view as signs of "resistance." There was a readiness among analytical authors not to deal, in the first place, with the intrinsic merits of a criticism or a new formulation or technical deviation but instead to interpret the author's psychology, remarking, for example, that the author had not been fully analyzed, or wanted to be original at any cost, or had an unresolved conflict with authority, or was a compromiser ready to sell out to the enemy. Of course such contentions were not infrequently justified and it would

3

be easy to cite examples for each one. On the other hand, no matter what an author's motives may be—the urge to contradict or the quest for originality—the validity of his statements cannot be questioned on the basis of his motivations. The urge to contradict might have led him to valid criticism and his urge for originality may have contributed to his acquiring some genuinely new insight.

The inclination to seek the author's motivation is a legitimate problem in psychology but if not kept in its proper place can easily vitiate scientific criticism. This introduces into scientific discussion something scientists have always frowned upon, and justly so: the "argumentum ad personam." Deviation from what is considered as well-established in theory or in practice puts the deviationist on the defensive. He has not only to demonstrate the validity of his position but he must defend himself against the tacit or open charge that he proposes his views not because of factual evidence or intellectual conviction but because of some ulterior, although unconscious, motives. This puts a premium on conformity and an odium on independent thought and can become a serious impediment to the advancement of knowledge.

A new emotional complication has arisen more recently as a result of the growing official acceptance of psychoanalysis by universities and the medical community in general. In the earlier days, to become a psychoanalyst meant to accept a minority status and extraterritorial existence at the borderline of medicine and quite outside of academic institutions. The psychoanalyst was deprived of the aura which goes with academic status. Mostly, even in the past, he was an M.D., yet when he became a psychoanalyst his first allegiance was to the International Psychoanalytical Association. He wanted to be identified in the first place as a psychoanalyst and only secondly as a physician. Gradually as psychoanalysis has found recognition as a medical specialty the tendency has become stronger among psychoanalysts to liquidate the traditional isolation of psychoanalysis and to become fully accepted members of the medical fraternity. This issue was particularly significant in the United States, where psychoanalysis gained a profound influence upon psychiatry. Now it is only a question of time until psychoanalysis, which actually has become, along with neuroanatomy and neurophysiology, one of the basic sciences of psychiatry, will become fully absorbed in medical training and practice. No one can validly oppose this trend provided psychoanalysis does not need to sacrifice its essential principles of theory and treatment for the sake of more ready acceptance. One can easily emasculate a theoretical concept by admitting certain elements of truth in it while refuting its essential implications. This danger is what motivated Freud to declare that his theory could only be accepted or rejected as a whole.

The growing acceptance of psychoanalysis, on the other hand, is opening new avenues for development. More and more psychiatrists and psychoanalysts are becoming aware of the great possibilities of applying basic psychoanalytical knowledge to psychotherapy in general. Owing, however, to the traditional insistence on the autonomy of psychoanalysis as a discipline separate from the rest of psychiatry, efforts to extend the therapeutic applications of psychoanalysis beyond the original so-called "classical" procedure, without differentiating them radically, have been looked upon with reservation by a number of psychoanalysts who consider this a new attempt to compromise with official medicine and academic psychiatry. For these psychoanalysts, the merits of the new efforts to expand the therapeutic scope of our field was a secondary consideration. Their first concern was to protect psychoanalytical practice and treatment from dilution, to preserve it in its pure, unadulterated form, and to protect the identity of the psychoanalyst as distinct from that of other psychiatrists.

It can easily be seen that this consideration of practical

policy makes it difficult to evaluate in a detached manner some newer developments. From a broad historical perspective, the most significant contribution of psychoanalysis has been to place psychological techniques for giving help to patients on a sound and reasonable basis. Before the advent of psychoanalysis, psychotherapy, no matter whether it took the form of hypnosis, suggestion, persuasion, or consolation, was crudely empirical in nature. There was no systematized knowledge about the structure and functioning of the human personality, and psychotherapeutic procedures were fortuitous, magical, or at best, intuitive. The term "psychotherapy" consequently acquired the connotation of something primitive and unscientific. This connotation has been carried over to the present and any alliance between psychoanalysis and psychotherapy creates an immediate emotional distress in the well-trained psychoanalyst. The word psychotherapy is an example par excellence of a "loaded" expression. The cumbersome term "psychoanalytically oriented psychotherapy" is only partially successful in counterbalancing the effect of the "loaded" portion of the term: psychotherapy.

There are other such "loaded" concepts and expressions in our field, such as "manipulation." Psychoanalysis attempts to restore mental health by affording the patient an insight into the nature of his difficulties accompanied and made meaningful by a highly controlled type of emotional experience. This experience enables him to extend the integrative faculty of his ego over impulses which he excluded from his consciousness because he was unable to bring them into harmony with the rest of his personality. It is an extension of insight and control over one's self obtained through re-experiencing in the transference situation conflictful situations of the past. In this highly methodical procedure it is the therapist's role to serve as a target for the patient's preformed emotional reactions and to help the patient to understand these reactions in the light of his past experiences. To make this process effective the therapist restricts his function to interpretation and avoids any active guidance of the patient in his everyday life. Preanalytic psychotherapy was in sharp contrast to this type of procedure. The therapist's first inclination was to function as an adviser, to help the patient with his practical problems. The therapist "manipulated" the patient's environment and gave positive guidance and assistance. This function he carried out mostly on the basis of common sense. This "common sense," however, did not know anything about unconscious motivations, about the complexity of the contradictory trends, desires, and values existing in the patient. It knew nothing about transference reactions. In fact, pre-Freudian common sense did not know anything in a systematic way about the nature of personality functions. The only exception to this is seen in the genius of great authors whose perceptiveness enormously surpasses the common-sense understanding of the average person. The psychotherapist's effectiveness, consequently, was quite limited, since he could not reach the patient's real, though hidden, motivations. It was a hit-or-miss procedure. The chance for his manipulations to be effective depended mostly on vague intuition, which—although universally present in every person—has great limitations because of the therapist's own emotional resistance, blind spots, and emotional involvement in the treatment.

The expression "manipulation," referring roughly to all active and practical intervention in the patient's life situations, came into ill repute after the advent of psychoanalysis. And yet a certain amount of "manipulation" is inherent in every psychoanalytic treatment, as has been recently pointed out by Bibring (19). To advise the patient not to make any important decision during the treatment is in itself important advice, imposing upon the patient a kind of moratorium for the duration of the treatment. Moreover, in many treatments, the analyst, either at the beginning or during the treatment, often has to insist on certain external conditions under which the treatment can be carried out successfully. He may advise the patient to move away from his home for the duration of the treatment. He may advise continuation or cessation of certain occupational activities. True, he makes his recommendations on a rational basis and not merely following his hunches or impressions.

Freud's abstinence rule, although no longer routinely applied, is another example for active advice concerning the patient's conduct of life during the treatment. His recommendation that phobic patients should be encouraged in a certain phase of treatment to expose themselves to situations which they have avoided because of their neurotic fears is still another example of overt "manipulation." It certainly is a highly undesirable policy to shun or decry as "unanalytic" technical innovations based on analytical insight, only because the founder of psychoanalysis is no longer with us and cannot give such newly proposed techniques his approval. All this explains why so little attention has been given in the theory of treatment to any type of active intervention. Ferenczi's active technique never gained wide popularity. Active intervention was called "manipulation," a term which retained the highly negative, deprecatory connotation reminiscent of the prescientific phase of psychotherapy. In the meantime our knowledge has advanced and it now appears that we are able to introduce certain well-planned active devices, which not only do not interfere with the psychoanalytic process but may enhance its effectiveness. Yet anyone who attempts to deal with these aspects of therapy may easily appear to be abandoning pure psychoanalytical principles and reverting to a crude manipulation which was practiced in psychotherapy in former days.

The most undesirable result of the loaded term "manipulation" is that there is a tendency to overlook these latent manipulatory devices present in every "classical" analysis. Instead of recognizing their role in treatment and either eliminating them entirely or utilizing them knowingly, there is a tendency to disregard them. In this way the gap between the actual practice of psychoanalysis and its theory is becoming wider and wider.

In addition to these emotionally loaded terms and concepts the development of psychoanalytic thought and practice faces another difficulty: the evaluation of therapeutic results. The feeling of futility which one often has when listening to or reading arguments about treatment procedures comes from the fact that these arguments of necessity remain mostly deductive. Their correctness cannot be tested against observations as required in all other fields of knowledge. Even the theory of probability, which is based on rigorous logical reasoning, must still face the test of the actual experiment. This methodological principle which no science can dispense with is extremely difficult to apply in the field of psychoanalytic treatment.

In all fields of medicine the effectiveness of a therapeutic measure is evaluated by the statistical analysis of results. Such an evaluation in the field of psychotherapy—using the term in its comprehensive sense referring to all psychological methods of treatment including psychoanalysis—encounters unusual difficulties. Everyone who has tried statistical evaluation of results of psychoanalytic treatments knows the enormity of this problem. The Berlin Psychoanalytic Institute in 1929 published a statistical review of the therapeutical results of its clinic. The Chicago Psychoanalytic Institute in 1938 published a five-year report of results. I cooperated in both of these undertakings and know the difficulties from first-hand experience.

Psychoneuroses often manifest themselves in symptoms about which only the patient himself has knowledge. For instance, many patients suffering from compulsion neurosis may go through life without even their nearest associates knowing about the symptoms. In fact it is a common experi-

ence that such a patient, only after several months' analysis,
confesses to his own analyst the details of his obsessions and
rituals. The external, observable behavior and manifestation
of psychoneurotic difficulties is often not conspicuous at all.
The disease consists of a kind of subjective suffering with
only slight and indirect behavioral manifestations. In such
cases the patient is the ultimate judge whether or not he has
been helped. The best example is a "hysterical" pain super-
imposed upon an organic lesion which persists after the organic condition has been remedied. Some of the exasperations
and latent resentments of physicians against the hysteric patient, which in the past greatly impeded the development of
psychiatry, were due exactly to this fact. The physician who
found no objective, demonstrable cause for the hysterical
pain or other hysterical symptoms when the patient persisted
in complaining about his suffering reacted with resentment
and was inclined to call it malingering.

In this respect, even the psychoanalyst is not in a much
better position. He may know a great deal about the origin
of such symptoms and their meaning and the emotional use
the patient makes of them. He may feel that during a certain
period of treatment the symptoms should have disappeared
according to the textbook. Yet he, just like the less well-
informed physician, is dependent upon the patient's own
statement. This is, of course, not true in those cases where the
symptom manifests itself in overt behavior, as in the case of
a character neurosis.

Also other criteria of improvement and cure are less definite
than in other fields of medicine. It is not uncommon that a
patient feels more comfortable after treatment but his environment may consider him a greater problem than ever
before. To estimate the disappearance of subjective complaints is a thorny problem in itself. To estimate the desirability of the results from the framework of adaptation to
the external environment is something which depends upon

the value system of the evaluator. A crude example of this has been the study of Hyman, et al., who in evaluating thirty-three cases of patients treated by psychoanalysis counted all treatment that resulted in divorce as failures (67).

It is obvious that every psychoanalytic or psychotherapeutic treatment aims to bring about a change in personality functioning. Such changes are extremely manifold and mostly inaccessible to precise measurement. Some of these changes, however, can be precisely described. For example, a child suffering from a learning inhibition may show after analytic treatment a marked improvement in his scholastic record. He may advance from the worst to the best student in arithmetic. At the same time he may show some other changes which cannot be so simply evaluated. By losing his intellectual inhibitions he may become more aggressive and less compliant. This may be regarded by the therapist as a definite improvement, in contradiction to the parents' and teacher's evaluation.

Mental health, in ultimate analysis, can be considered as a measure of adaptation. It is most important to realize that this is not an adaptation to a given external environment alone but also to the internal environment—the patient's basic personality. It is a combination of two kinds of adaptations: to the limitations and possibilities of the patient's own personality and the limitations set by a given environment.

Speaking of a given environment, I include also the possible environments which the patient can choose to enhance his satisfaction and efficiency as a human being. The naïve idea that the well-psychoanalyzed personality has unlimited possibilities is nothing but a new edition of old concepts of magic. Psychoanalytic treatment may enhance to a very great extent the adaptability and flexibility of a person and by eliminating inhibitions may free the way to a fuller utilization of the patient's talents and abilities. Nevertheless, it has its natural limitations.

The many-faceted nature of personality functions and the complex meaning of adaptation, including adaptation both to the internal and the external environment, makes it extremely difficult to evaluate the results of a treatment as a whole, although it may be quite possible to define partial changes in restricted areas.

The complexity of the problem may explain why the American Psychoanalytic Association's effort to induce its members to participate in a project to evaluate therapeutic results has not yet materialized in a satisfactory manner. Many psychoanalysts came to the conclusion that the time is not yet ripe for such a grand-scale evaluation experiment and that we should be satisfied to establish the effectiveness of the psychoanalytic process by restricting our study to a more limited goal. One should try to account for certain changes in the patient's personality functions that can be observed during a selected phase of the treatment, and try to explain, as precisely as one can, how these changes came about under the influence of the treatment.

In spite of these difficulties the practitioners of psychotherapy, and particularly psychoanalysts who have a long and continued contact with their patients, have a justified conviction about the effectiveness of their therapeutic endeavors. To regard this conviction as merely subjective is not valid. The psychoanalyst observes in his daily contact with his patient a continuous process and is in the position not only to observe the process in detail but also to account to a considerable degree for the course it takes. He observes how with his interventions and attitude he influences the therapeutic process and can explain reasonably how changes come about.

It is true that there are almost no detailed reports of this kind in existence at the present time. Far the greatest part of the observations of the therapeutic process are made in private practice. The exigencies of private practice are not favorable for exact recording. Few day-by-day accountings and evaluations of psychoanalytic sessions over a period of time have been published. A rigorous evaluation of what exactly takes place both in the patient as well as in the analyst's mind would require records which can be restudied by the analyst himself as well as by others. A project of this kind has been worked out by Drs. Gill, Hilgard, and Shakow, with the cooperation of an advisory committee, (57) and accepted by the Ford Foundation for consideration for support. The realization of this plan may become a landmark in the development of psychoanalysis. The value of such a detailed report of representative samples of psychoanalytic treatment is probably of much greater significance than large-scale statistics of many cases. The effectiveness of any form of psychotherapy can be evaluated only by a record which not only shows the initial state of the patient and his condition after the termination of treatment but also gives a precise account step by step of the psychological processes which have taken place in the patient in response to the therapist's interventions. Lacking such records, we can support our belief in the effectiveness of treatment only by selected examples and general reflections. The present volume does not claim to do more than to offer this type of material. It would be deplorable in the face of the difficulties of precise evaluation to throw up our hands and declare a moratorium until we are able to document our conclusions in a more complete and reliable manner.

Chapter I

PSYCHOANALYSIS IN WESTERN CULTURE

AFTER ABOUT three hundred years of extroverted interest in the surrounding world, Western man has arrived at the phase of self-scrutiny. Following his spiritual awakening in the Renaissance he began to explore the globe, then the solar system and the human body. Man's place in the animal kingdom was recognized as late as the middle of the nineteenth century. Around the same time increasing interest in understanding society signaled a gradual shift of scientific curiosity from the cosmos to man himself. The last step in this turning toward the self was Freud's theory of the human personality.

Once before in the history of thought a similar sequence of shifting interests took place. In ancient Greece a long period of cosmological speculation was followed by an increasing interest in psychology, ethics, and politics. It appears that this withdrawal of interest to the self marks a critical point in cultural development. It occurs when the traditional social mechanism no longer functions smoothly because of rapid changes in the social structure and when the first signs of decline appear. Socrates, Plato, and Aristotle came on the scene when Athenian democracy began to show the first signs of crisis. In our present era, too, and coinciding with the crisis of our free societies, interest in psychology is in the process of replacing the naïve and carefree preoccupation

14

with the world around us. This shift is preceded by a beginning of self-criticism, skepticism toward absolute truths, and epistemological relativism. Protagoras in Greece, Hume and Kant in modern times are precursors of a trend which recognizes the relativity of knowledge dependent upon the nature of the perceiving apparatus, man himself. Among contemporary social scientists Mannheim has postulated the same correlation between social crisis and introspective interest. He considers social change and particularly the ascendancy of new social classes to be the source of skepticism and relativism arising out of the "mutual destruction and devaluation of divergent political aims." And he adds, "in personal life, too, self-control and self-correction develop only when in our originally blind vital forward drive we come upon an obstacle which throws us back upon ourselves" (77).

This historical coincidence of social crisis with awakening interest in the self is not surprising to the psychoanalyst. A person becomes aware of himself when the automatic gratification of his subjective needs is interfered with. Self-awareness is a result of the interruption of automatic gratifications which do not require any cognitive effort. Consciousness is neither an unmixed pleasure nor a futile luxury of nature. It is the result of frustration which mobilizes those complex processes we call thinking. The function of the ego is to gratify subjective needs which are not gratified automatically but require specific adaptive responses. As long as previously acquired and stabilized automatic patterns work well we do not need to take cognizance of our internal processes. We breathe without being aware of it; only the lack of oxygen will call our attention to the respiratory function. As soon as social change becomes rapid and old adaptive cultural patterns no longer fit into the altered conditions, man becomes conscious of the social process itself.

A burst of interest in social theory accompanied the industrial revolution. It influenced the ideas of Malthus, Adam

Smith, Bentham, Ricardo, Marx, and others. As a final response to the rapidly changing society psychoanalysis appears as a self-protective measure for man when his reliance on automatic, traditional behavior patterns fails him. To paraphrase Freud, where superego was, now conscious ego ideals must be. Self-knowledge becomes imperative and the bliss of self-forgetful curiosity in the surrounding world belongs to the past.

Another response to stress caused by the changing social scene—in a sense an opposite response—is a trend away from individual freedom to what Toynbee calls the universal state, toward increased central planning and control, toward the type of social system which relieves the citizen of the increasingly difficult free choice, and takes care of him but at the same time prescribes his activities, his social functioning, and even his thoughts. Whether this is an unavoidable phase of cultural development, as Toynbee assumes, is an open question. Even if history repeats itself, it does not repeat itself precisely. Whether or not free societies can remain free and can solve the problems which they themselves have created by rapid change, rendering individual choice more and more unreliable, no one can tell. The dilemma in which contemporary man of the West finds himself, however, is unmistakable. Free societies recognize and favor individual differences. These are considered the sources of all progress. The center of gravity in free societies is the individual person. Society's function is to provide maximum opportunity for self-expression and at the same time to guard the members of society from infringing on one another's interest by insisting that everyone keep the accepted rules of the game. It represents a kind of optimal equilibrium between the initiatives of free men and the interest of the group. This type of system under favorable conditions, such as during the last three hundred years of Western culture, by encouraging individual expression in the sciences, arts, and technology can be highly productive. At the same time, because it accelerates social change and as a result complicates the problems of individual adjustments, it creates insecurity. Self-regulating mechanisms, such as the supply and demand principle in economics, no longer function smoothly and the urge for central planning appears. The failure of such automatic regulations, however, is not restricted to the field of economy. Traditional value systems lose their categorical force and this throws individuals back to their own choice. This results in a flight from free choice and enterprise toward the security of steady jobs, preferably in large, depression-proof companies, or in state employment.

The social behavior of man is always governed by two trends: one toward stability and security; the other toward adventure, exploration of the unknown and creation. The trend toward security is the manifestation of self-preservation which we define today more precisely as the homeostatic principle. It is expressed in man's striving to secure the basic necessities for survival with a minimum expenditure of energy. The trend toward new ventures into the unknown is the manifestation of an equally basic biological principle, that of growth and propagation. Neither of these two trends is more fundamental than the other. They constitute life. Growth and propagation result from that surplus which remains over and above what is needed to survive. Whatever is left of that amount which is needed for maintaining the homeostatic equilibrium is retained in the form of growth. Growth, however, has its limitations when maturity is reached. After maturity the surplus energy is expended in the form of creativity—both biological and social. A great deal of this surplus is discharged playfully or for the sake of meeting the challenge of obstacles in adventurous pursuit. Both motives, the quest for security and the lust for adventure and mastery, are always present in the social aspirations of man, although they do not always have the same distribution. In certain historical periods, like the Middle Ages, the security motive dominated. Other periods are characterized by an experimental spirit. American democracy, particularly during the pioneer era, is one of the most dramatic examples of a rapidly changing free society driven by the spirit of mastery of challenges. It is an extreme case of a dynamic free society whose spiritual origins go back to the Renaissance.

In the last twenty years we have witnessed a reversal of this trend in this country, a reversal which began several years earlier in Europe. Public-opinion polls have shown that the overwhelming majority of American youth prefer jobs which pay low salaries but offer continuity, and only a very small percentage still prefer to take the risk of depending upon personal ability to make a great success. Elliott Cohen describes the young intellectual: "Culturally he feels himself the survivor of a long series of routs and massacres. Insecurity is his portion, and doom and death are to him familiar neighbors. . . . There is very little in him of that lust for life and experience, of the joy of living for its own sake, of a sense of wide horizons or worlds to conquer, or much of that early curiosity that drove his older brothers expansively over the realms of knowledge" (21). Such vivid statements as well as the result of polls state the fact without explaining it. A number of contemporary sociologists, anthropologists, and psychoanalysts have not only recognized this profound personality change in our present generation but have indicated some of its deeper psychodynamic background.

Margaret Mead impressively describes the difficulties which the American youth today has to face to find his own formula of life (78). The contemporary young man or woman cannot learn from his or her parents because from generation to generation the patterns of behavior change to fit the ever-changing conditions. They must learn from each other and in groping experimentation find their own principles of behavior.

Erik Erikson came to similar conclusions in describing the

difficulties of contemporary youth in finding what he calls their ego identity (27).

David Riesman refers to the same transition when he speaks of a change from the "inner-directed" personality structure of the past to the "other-directed" personality of the present (87).

A closer scrutiny reveals that the difficulties of social adaptation which these authors describe in different terms are the same ones to which psychoanalysts attribute etiological importance in neuroses. Neurosis is a condition in which the ego fails in its task of harmonizing subjective needs with each other and with the internal standards of the personality which are the imprints of the prevailing social value system. Neurosis indeed is the characteristic disturbance of our age as were infections and plagues in past periods when people began to congregate in large cities before they knew how to master the biological hazards of such close coexistence. Psychoanalysis fulfills the same function today that bacteriology did in the past. The greatest health problem of our time is the increasingly difficult task of the individual to adapt his subjective needs to an ever-changing world, to replace traditionally sanctioned patterns with ad hoc adaptive responses.

From this perspective psychoanalysis appears as a self-curative reaction of Western society to the immense complexities of adjustment. Psychoanalytic treatment aims to replace the individual's automatic, traditional internalized patterns with the ability to find his own formula of life based upon a fuller understanding of himself.

One of the conventional arguments against psychoanalysis has been that analysts consider it their task to help the patient adjust himself to the environment no matter what this environment may be. It has been argued that this must hamper development and lead to stagnation. Discontent of people with their environment is the source of change and progress. Since neurosis consists in the inability to accept the environment without conflict—both the external environment and its internalized, incorporated value system—helping the neurotic to adjust himself to existing conditions amounts to making a conformist of a protester. The analyst may relieve such a patient from his neurotic suffering but at the same time the patient pays the price of giving in to society and sacrificing his individuality. Since the range of human adjustability is tremendous, as is exemplified by the great variety of existing cultures, each offering a different pattern for community life, it is not impossible for psychoanalysis to make people accept the solution which their own society offers to them.

According to this argument psychoanalysis is a conserving factor opposed to change. But the argument collapses if one considers that the basic feature of our heterogeneous Western culture is the individual's opportunity to change his own environment by participating actively in the social process. Moreover, it is a culture characterized by "social mobility." In fact psychoanalytic treatment often results in helping a patient to choose an environment more suited to him than the one in which he developed his neurotic difficulties. As a result of treatment he may change his occupation, his human contacts, he may divorce his spouse, and he may even emigrate to another country which has a different ideology.

American civilization started with the emigration of discontented elements who did not find a place in their native environment. Viewing the role of psychoanalysis as helping adaptation to a given environment raises a theoretical question. Suppose psychoanalysis had existed in the days of the Pilgrims? If applied successfully to the protesters, it would have helped them to accept the conditions under which they lived and the great experiment, "The American Dream," would not have come about.

Considerations of this kind may suffice to illustrate the complexity and the ambiguity of the concept of mental health. The thesis that psychoanalysis is a method which helps the individual accept his environment is worse than an over-simplification. It is erroneous because it neglects one fundamental aspect of psychoanalytic treatment. Psychoanalysis aims at something more than merely helping the patient to adjust himself to the social system in which he lives. Psychoanalysis is a true product of that phase of Western civilization which had deep respect for individual differences. It aids a person in the integrative task in which he failed: in reconciling his own basic personality with his environment without sacrificing that intangible something which makes him a person different from all others. Psychoanalysis is the most individual type of treatment ever produced by medical science. Each case is a unique problem. What primarily concerns the therapist is not the nosological classification of a person, not in what way he is similar to others but in what way he differs from them. Every person has his own potential formula of adjustment. Psychoanalysis aims at an adjustment which takes cognizance not only of a given social environment but also of the uniqueness of every person. From this perspective psychoanalysis gives reality to the expression, "the respect for the dignity of the individual," a term which is often used in a vague and well-nigh meaningless fashion. This respect for individual differences explains why psychoanalysis is unthinkable and prohibited in totalitarian societies. The psychotherapist who sees the salvation of the patient in re-creating him according to his own image, even if such a thing were possible, certainly does not practice anything which is even similar to psychoanalysis.

This is the reason why the countertransference problem is of such profound significance. It is by now generally recognized that the analyst is not a blank screen upon which the patient reflects his own transference reactions. Even though the therapist himself has been thoroughly analyzed, he remains an individual in his own right. The important fact, however, is that he, too, has been analyzed with respect for his own individuality. Both analyst and patient belong to the same culture which believes in and values individual differences. This belief translated into therapeutic practice means that patient and therapist are allied in a joint venture to find a solution for the patient which might be similar to solutions of many others but still is designed to emancipate his unique potentialities. Environment is not considered immutable in all its aspects but as something which can itself be changed. A nonconformist solution might be the best therapeutic result for a given person. Neurosis and nonconformism are not identical. Neurosis is a self-crippling ineffectual way of expressing and trying to realize one's highly individual aspirations.

If psychoanalysis were a procedure which merely helps a person adjust himself to existing conditions, it would be most desirable and favored in totalitarian societies. That the opposite is true shows that the policy makers know intuitively that its underlying philosophy by no means promotes conformism. Stated in a somewhat oversimplified form, psychoanalysis tries to help a person to remain an individual in a complex society and to express his individual inclinations on a realistic and socially constructive level by creative participation in the social process.

In this connection one is reminded of the profound formulation of Ferenczi, contrasting social with biological development, the former being alloplastic, the latter autoplastic in nature. Biological development consists primarily in producing changes within the organism which fit the environment. In distinction from the rest of the animal kingdom man creates his own environment.[1] The thesis is hardly tenable that psychoanalysis attempts to induce a person to accept a static system and to give up his unique asset, the ability to

[1] Bird nests and spider webs can hardly be compared with the creation of a cultural environment. These are strictly predetermined, inherited performances.

create his own world. This misinterpretation of psychoanalysis has its foundation in the fact that the therapeutic procedure utilizes the introspective faculties of the ego to achieve a change in personality structure. This change, however, consists in the realignment of the personality's original resources in order to use them for outward-directed action. Neurotic symptoms, as Freud succinctly formulated it, are substitutes for full-fledged action. In neurosis, internal processes in fantasy are substituted for adequate outward-directed action suitable for gratifying basic and derivative needs. This definition implies that psychoanalysis aims at the reversal of the neurotic process by enabling the patient to use alloplastic instead of autoplastic means of gratification.

In this light psychoanalysis and the social sciences, attempting a better understanding of himself and of the social process, appear as possibly the last efforts of Western man to save his individuality from yielding to increasing insecurity which drives him toward the universal state. If this effort fails, the only remedy left is a social system in which individual choice is reduced and responsibility for biological and spiritual survival is transferred from the individual to the community. No one can predict the outcome of this race between the increasing trend toward the universal state and the valiant effort of the social and psychological sciences to help man remain master of his fate.

The proponents of the universal state argue that a highly differentiated industrial society does not necessarily increase insecurity. They like to offer the biological organism as an example of a highly differentiated system in which the cells have no doubts or uncertainties about their functions or their survival so long as the total organism functions properly. The cells' biological role is restricted to a particular function and their supply of energy is secured by automatic regulatory processes. The only organ which has to worry is the highest coordinating center of the organism. Theoreticians who play with these analogies conclude that in the universal state the central government in a similar fashion takes over all the chores and problems of human society. The rest of the people do not have to worry about anything but performing their specialized and prescribed functions.

If this analogy were correct, the inevitable conclusion would be that our present insecurity stems from the fact that we are victims of a cultural lag, still living in the past, adhering to what Mannheim called the "liberal-democratic, bourgeois ideology," worshiping the false gods of individualism introduced into Western history through the northern Italian cities in the early Renaissance (77). It was then perpetuated and further developed in the hero worship of the explorer, the scientific discoverer, the artist, the protestant who makes man the ultimate arbiter of his values; in the adoration of the laissez-faire free-trader and the creative but often unscrupulous entrepreneur. Their argument continues as follows: All these basically narcissistic but admittedly imaginative and gifted individuals were useful in their own times. They may have helped us to explore our habitat, to master time and space. They are certainly responsible for the tremendous rapidity of social change. But they outlived their usefulness. In their creative or predatory fervor they built up such a thoroughly novel cultural environment that our present task in the West is to bring order into the chaos created by this unregimented if imaginative flight of ideas. Not only is self-expression for its own sake outdated but at present it is disruptive, dangerous, contributing to further chaos. The social tasks of our culture have changed. They consist in consolidation and in the rational use of the achievements of the creative genius of our forefathers. This is the next logical and inevitable step in social evolution.

Some of the theoreticians who propose these views are ready to abandon the dogma of historical materialism and to admit that the last three centuries' development is due primarily to such psychological factors as improvement of scientific observation and reasoning. They concede that ideas may change the material substratum of society. They claim, however, that no matter how these material, technological, and economic changes came about, our ideological outlook and values must be adapted to them and the individual must yield his place to the mass man.

It is true this sequence of events—periods of creative self-expression followed by a period of consolidation in which the previously exalted individual yields his place to the ex-alted state—has occurred repeatedly in the course of history. Yet the question arises whether this is an inevitable sequence of events. Is this the only possible outcome of the fact that man through his creative abilities has so radically changed his environment that for a time he must busy himself with learning how to live in it? Is this blind dialectic of history, the swing of the pendulum between periods of creative change followed by consolidation and finally by decline, a universal law or only one among other possibilities?

When I confronted Freud with this question, as to whether the wave of the future lies in the direction of the totalitarian state, he gave another reply: "Why do cells organize them-selves into higher units? Only in order to survive and become more effective in defending themselves against external dangers. Termites are the weakest creatures on earth. They have not even a protective hard shell like ants. No wonder they seek to survive by cooperation and sacrifice their freedom for the sake of mere existence. But man is the crown of crea-tion, the master who dominates the world. Why should he give up his freedom to the same extent as the weak and help-less termites? Against what enemy must he organize himself in so rigid a fashion?" [2] The obvious answer is: against his only serious enemy, his fellow man. And from here on the

---

[2] Whether or not external danger and pressure are the only factors promot-ing collaboration, which of necessity always requires some curtailment of individual freedoms, is not a point for discussion here.

This is quoted from memory. It was first published in my book, *Our Age of Unreason* (2).

argument may go like this: Because of his alloplastic genius man constructs machines and other labor-saving devices which greatly relieve him of the greatest part of the burden of procuring the necessities for survival. Extrapolating this trend toward the utilization of labor-saving devices into the future, we may reasonably expect that the economic problem of supplying food, shelter, and locomotion will be relegated to the machine and man will have to face the problem of what to do with his liberated energy. There is no logical reason why such a development should require an increased restriction of man's freedom of expression and degrade him to an insectlike automaton. That technology creates insecurity and through it a trend toward the universal state in which man's self-determination is abolished is obviously a paradoxical phenomenon which requires specific explanation. By no means is it self-evident that industrialism must necessarily lead to an unproductive phase of human history, a return to a kind of tribal society in which each individual's place and function are rigidly predetermined. I do not propose a full explanation for this paradoxical phenomenon. Its solution might give us the way out of the throes of the crisis which manifests itself in the ideological split between Western culture and the rest of the world.

I do not claim to have an answer and should like only to emphasize one more or less obvious contributing factor. Man made the machine but instead of remaining its master he is gradually becoming its slave. Under the impact of machine civilization, man becomes more and more machinelike himself. Instead of leaving to the machine those functions which can be performed with automatic repetition, he is in the process of automatizing and routinizing those functions which require choice and inventiveness. In his admiration of the calculating machine, he proposes to rewrite Hamlet with a machine which can reshuffle all the words of the English language in all permutations until it finally ejects an immaculate copy of the story of the Danish prince. Instead of evaluating a person as a unique combination of his constituent elements he tends to disregard the unique features for what is common and measurable. He deals with his fellow man on the basis of crude categories such as race, social group, height and body weight, number of credits which he received in his classes, man hours and all the data which can be counted and put on a punch card. Instead of using the machine for the purpose for which it was invented—to give him freedom to use his creative faculties—he wants to organize society taking the machine as a model. It must be obvious that technology need not lead to the loss of spiritual freedom, loss of respect for individual differences, and to increasing insecurity. On the contrary, it could be used for increasing freedom and encouraging the luxury of individuality. The universal state is by no means a logical, inevitable outcome of industrial civilization.

My lament that man is shaping his own personality to become machinelike is not an explanation but simply a statement of fact. The motivational background of this social trend still awaits explanation.

One of the customary answers is that the destructive utilization of technology for conquest and exploitation creates precisely the type of emergency situation in which social control and rigid organization of society become imperative. The atmosphere of the cold war and the constant preparation for the ultimate showdown of power require strict organization of material and human resources and prohibit the luxury of individual freedoms. In our times the expectation of the day of doom, of the last judgment, has been replaced by the expectation of the atomic war. The abuse of the machine for destructive purposes at a time when it could be used to relieve the struggle for existence for all inhabitants of the earth is obviously one of the factors.

This view consists essentially of applying the psychoanalytic concept of fixation to sociology: the phenomenon of cultural lag. In spite of our potential abundance we behave as if we were still living in a world of scarcity in which the competitive struggle for natural resources is the only answer for survival. We still adhere to the old method of war for solving conflicts of interest. We have not yet adjusted ourselves to the new situation which our rapid conquest of natural forces presents. We do not recognize all the potential peaceful utilizations of our technological knowledge, which could solve constructively all those problems we now try to solve by mutual destruction. This, however, is a partial answer which considers only the economic factors. Of equal or greater significance are ideological issues which are more or less independent of our basic vegetative needs.

The materialist theory of history which explains all the human profiles in unilinear fashion as emanating from the economic structure of society, which explains from economic structure the ego ideals, basic personalities, ego-identities or ego-representations characteristic for an era or for a culture, is one of the great and dangerous fallacies of the past, a fallacy from which not all contemporary social scientists have extricated themselves. The influence of the economic substratum is, of course, powerful and conspicuous, and therefore more readily recognized. However, it is well known that traditional value systems, social attitudes and institutions, which once came into being largely under the influence of economic factors, exert their influence even after the conditions which produced them have changed. In the past these social attitudes and institutions might have been adaptive reactions to existing conditions, but through tradition they retained their dynamic power long after they outlived their adaptive usefulness.

This temporal lag, however, is not the only noneconomic determinant of personality formation. No one to my knowledge has stated the fallacy of this narrow economic determinism more convincingly than one of the few true philosophers of our aphilosophical era, Jose Ortega y Gasset (81a). He believes that necessity for survival does not explain man's whole behavior. It explains only what is least interesting and least characteristic of man as a culture-building species. Behavior for survival is more rigidly determined by the specific survival problems than behavior which takes place after the basic needs are fulfilled. Adaptive responses to basic necessities leave less choice open than those self-expressive modes of behavior which are not dictated by immediate survival needs. In other words, man shows his human qualities more in his leisure than in his struggle for survival.

There is a tendency among some psychoanalytic authors to equate rational behavior, in other words, behavior well adapted to existing conditions, with mental health and to consider as "neurotic" all behavior which is largely determined by unconscious motivations. This is how Kubie, for example, defines the omnipresent "neurotic component" in human behavior (72). Accordingly, the "unconscious" assumes for him an undesirable connotation even though he recognizes its significance for creativity. I consider more adequate another definition of neurosis: a failure of the integrative functions of the ego. Inasmuch as unconscious psychological content is "repressed" content, Kubie's definition equating neuroticism with the preponderance of unconscious motivations applies because all that the ego cannot integrate harmoniously in its own system becomes repressed and therefore remains excluded from the learning process and later adjustment. As such, repressed motivations constitute what Kubie calls the "neurotic potential." It is, however, by no means necessary to assume that everything which is unconscious is the result of repression. Early patterns which are the results of previous adjustments can remain unconscious as long as new adjustment is not required. Consciousness, as has been stated before, is not a luxury but a necessity. Subjective needs become

conscious when they are frustrated because their gratification requires new adaptive changes. On such occasions conscious cognitive processes are needed.

All nonadaptive (nonutilitarian) behavior, such as play and
the free flow of creative fantasy, retains its unconscious
motivations without necessarily being the source of neuroses.
Play and creativity are functions not subjected to survival
needs and can therefore remain unadjusted to the serious
exigencies of life. Because they disregard the pressing exigencies of reality they retain their ability to shape reality.
Hence their culture-building value. Here is the source of man's
creative ability to change the environment according to his
own dreams and desires. Instead of adjusting to reality, with
these creative faculties man can adjust reality to himself.
This is the essence of what different authors refer to as the
"creative unconscious," the source of art, science, social
Utopia, etc. What man does with his faculties after he has
secured his basic needs—how he plays, how he daydreams,
how he uses his creative capacities—distinguishes him as a
personality. In his routine, utilitarian, economic performance,
whether he is pushing a button or tilling the soil, he is like the
next person. His behavior is determined by his social role
and function. By this I do not imply that behavior in leisure,
in play and fantasy, are not determined, but they are determined by other than survival needs; they are more varied and
characteristic for the person as an individual. The homeostatic, or self-preservative functions of the ego are less characteristic of a person as an individual than the manifestations
of his libido. What makes man different from all other species
is that he uses his creative forces not only for biological
growth and propagation but alloplastically for building different forms of cultures which are not solely determined by
survival needs. On the contrary, in his playful, nonutilitarian,
but libidinous and exuberant exercise of his faculties man

makes discoveries the utility of which is only later discovered. Anthropologists, particularly Roheim, have shown that such practical occupations as agriculture, gardening, and cattle raising, which marked the beginnings of human civilization, originally were not developed planfully for a utilitarian purpose. On the contrary, these useful occupations developed from playful activities of man, from idle hobbies, and were exploited only secondarily for economic purposes.[3] While playfully acting out primitive fantasies concerning propagation, he discovered gardening. Cattle raising stems from the totemistic rites in the religious practices of the primitives. Domestic animals served at first as the representation of father, mother, and children, and not until later was their practical usefulness discovered. This is true even for the later technological discoveries. Flying was originally the playful whim of adventurous persons who never dreamed of the future practical significance of their hobby. Utility was certainly not the primary motivation of their experimentation but the yearning to rise toward the skies, which often appears in our dreams to express our wish for mastery, power, and freedom. Flying originally was invented neither for the sake of future passenger traffic nor for throwing bombs at our enemies.

We come then to the seemingly paradoxical conclusion that culture is the product of man's leisure and not the sweat of his brow. His productive abilities become liberated when he is relieved of the necessities of the struggle for survival. Without being familiar with the psychoanalytic theory of ego and libido, Ortega y Gasset, with the visionary intuition of the true philosopher, came to similar conclusions. He writes: "The ancients divided life into two spheres. The first they called *otium*, leisure, by which they understood not

[3] See also the historian Huizinga, who in his Homo Ludens (66a) takes a similar position, namely, that play has a primary role in cultural development.

the negative of doing, not idling, but the positive attitude of seeing to the strictly human obligations of man, such as command, organization, social intercourse, science, arts. The second, consisting of those efforts which meet the elemental necessities and make *otium* possible, they called *nec-otium*, with apposite stress on the negative character it has for man" (81a).

It is a sad commentary on our times that man, when technology potentially and to a degree actually relieves him from the chores of his homeostatic or life-preserving burdens, loses his raison d'être, cannot find new goals, cannot find new values, a new ego identity. As Ortega y Gasset says succinctly: "Desiring is by no means easy" (81a). He reminds us of the quandary of the newly rich man. "With all wish-fulfilling means at his command he finds himself in the awkward situation of not knowing how to wish. At the bottom of his heart he is aware that he wishes nothing, that he himself is unable to direct his appetite and to choose among the innumerable things offered by his environment. . . . If it is so difficult to wish for objects which are already available, one may imagine how difficult the properly creative wish must be, the wish that reaches out for things yet nonexistent and anticipates the still unreal. If a man is unable to wish for his own self because he has no clear vision of a self to be realized, he can have but pseudo wishes and spectral desires devoid of sincerity and vigor." One cannot help thinking of our contemporary youth—whom Riesman calls "other-directed"—devoid of an internalized system of values. Ortega suggests that "it may well be that one of the basic diseases of our time is a crisis of wishing and that for these reasons all our technical achievements seem to be of no use whatever."

In a previous publication I came to the same conclusion in saying that in this technological era we are so exclusively busy raising our living standards that we do not know what to do with ourselves after we have achieved this goal (2).

It appears as if Western culture were suffering from something like a "retirement neurosis."

Many feel that our crisis consists basically in losing faith in science, a faith which has animated us in the last three hundred years. Some thinkers, such as Niebuhr or Maritain, want to fill this gap with a return to supernaturalism and mysticism (23). Is this loss of faith in scientific method justified, however? We may well have recognized by now that the methods and concepts of the natural sciences cannot resolve the social dilemma of our times. But we have taken the first steps toward the scientific exploration of man's complex motivational dynamics and the nature of his specific culture-building potentialities. Sociology and psychology are the emerging sciences of our times. Auguste Comte, the father of sociology, was born 234 years later than Galileo; Freud, 288 years later. The natural sciences have over a two-hundred-year head start on the social sciences. Closing this gap is a worthy goal. The specific cultural significance of psychoanalysis lies in helping Western man to find his ego identity. I do not have in mind only psychoanalytic therapy and its derivatives but the over-all influence of psychoanalytic thought and knowledge about child-rearing, educational practices, parent education; its influence upon contemporary literature and art, transmitted rapidly through all the new channels of communication. I refer particularly to the fact that psychoanalysis is becoming before our eyes an integral part of the collective consciousness of the West.

The all-pervasiveness of this influence offers hope that through understanding himself and the society in which he lives, the poor-rich man of the West may find new aspirations for the future.

The understanding of the dynamic interaction of the self with the social environment is in itself a goal so stupendous that it could occupy the productive capacities of many generations to come. Faith in the progress achieved through the

natural sciences of the last centuries may be duplicated by
a new faith—in what the social sciences may do for the
further progress of man.

The mechanical philosophy of the *vis-a-tergo* which explains *what is from what was* is not sufficient for an understanding of man. Man has the unique ability to create something which is not yet existing. He does not live *from* his
past alone but he lives *for* his future. Although past, present,
and future represent a dynamic continuum, a person best
reveals his unique identity in what he strives for. Technology
has relieved him at least potentially of a great part of the
effort needed for mere existence. We have no reason to
doubt that the new social sciences, and psychology in particular, will give him guidance in finding what to live for,
a content for wishing what is appropriate to his own individuality and to the world in which he lives, or better said,
in which he wants to live.

Chapter II

DEVELOPMENT OF THE THEORY
OF PSYCHOANALYTIC TREATMENT

In the following brief résumé an attempt is made to follow step by step the evolution of concepts which led to the present theory and practice of psychoanalysis. This will require the restatement of well-known and often described facts and details; it is hoped that the reader will have the patience which is necessary to appraise a complicated thought process. It is hoped also that making explicit certain tacitly accepted conclusions will elucidate the foundations of our present theoretical beliefs and the controversies and differences in emphasis which prevail among the practitioners of psychoanalysis.

The development of psychoanalytic therapy and its theory are closely interwoven. The principles of therapy evolved both from the underlying theory and from actual experience; the observations made during the therapeutic process contributed to the development of the theoretical concepts.[1]

The basic discovery was the existence of unconscious processes and their dynamic influence both on overt behavior and on conscious thought processes.

There is no doubt that the study of hypnotic phenomena

---

[1] A thoughtful discussion of the reciprocal influence of theory and therapy is found in Kris's paper on "Ego Psychology and Interpretation in Psychoanalytic Therapy" (70).

gave the first inducement to postulate the workings of unconscious psychological processes. Cathartic hypnosis was
an experimental demonstration that forgotten events can be
recalled and that the affects which originally accompanied
these forgotten events can be brought into consciousness. In
cathartic hypnosis the therapeutic factor apparently consisted in an intensive emotional discharge induced by the
dramatic revival of repressed traumatic events of the past.

What the patient felt as a trauma in itself was often a quite
trivial occurence. For example, Anna, Breuer's patient, originally developed her aversion to drinking water when she
saw her English governess's little dog drink from a dish used
by the family. When she recalled this trivial episode in
hypnotic trance, she burst out with violent hatred against the
governess and abused her profanely. After this, her symptom
—the aversion to water—disappeared (20).

From similar observations Freud concluded that hysterical
symptoms are caused by emotional experiences of the past
which on account of their painful nature have been eliminated
from consciousness by the fundamental mechanism, repression. The discharge of these repressed emotions gives relief
from symptoms. The fact that this relief was of only a temporary nature necessitated further research. Moreover, the
most important pathogenic factor was not the traumatic experience which was revived in hypnosis in itself, but those
preceding experiences which made the patient vulnerable to it.

Freud correctly concluded that such a trivial event—
observing the little dog drinking from a dish used by the
family—could not in itself account for the symptom. Anna
must have been sensitized by previous experiences in order
to react so violently to that episode. Today with our knowledge of the typical tragedies of childhood it is not difficult
to conclude that the dog for Anna meant another child with
whom she had to share the governess's attention. Her hatred
for the governess was due to her inability to share love, a

quality which she must have acquired in her early development.

After Freud recognized the importance of the genetic exploration of the earlier history for the understanding of the immediate factors in neurosis, his main therapeutic efforts became focused on the reconstruction of early emotional development. This required filling in the gaps of memory caused by repressions.

The next basic insight in the development of psychoanalytic thought was that the hypnotic state does not eliminate the patient's readiness to deal with the repressed events. Hypnosis is a measure by which the controlling functions of the ego are temporarily set aside because the patient regresses in relation to the hypnotizer to the dependent and obedient attitude of a child. After consciousness is regained the patient's conscious ego's capacity to face and deal with repressed impulses is not enhanced.

The next step consisted in the search of a method by which the ego's ability to handle the unconscious mental content could be increased. To increase this capacity requires two changes: (1) overcoming the ego's resistances against facing the repressed content and (2) increasing the ego's integrative capacity, the capacity to coordinate, modify, and harmonize the hitherto repressed impulses with each other and with the existing environmental conditions.

Before a suitable technique was found a brief period followed in which Freud experimented with "waking suggestion," that is, urging the patient to try to remember the events which introduced his illness. Only after this frontal attack to reach that type of psychological material which the patient was not capable of dealing with, and had therefore repressed, proved futile did Freud work out an effective procedure.

The significant step was the discovery of the method of free association. Free association in the emotionally permissive atmosphere of psychoanalytic interviews was an ideal device for the systematic study of the patient's past. In freely associating the patient abandons the conscious control over his train of thought and gradually reveals material which has been repressed before. This procedure includes, however, an even more important factor, and this is the emotional relationship existing between physician and patient. The physician assumes an objective, nonevaluating attitude which encourages the patient's freedom to express himself frankly.

A period followed in which the genetic reconstruction of personality development became the aim of therapy. Only later, after the structural dynamic theory of the personality had been conceived, did the therapeutic process become better understood. The original repressions take place, in childhood to a large degree at least, under parental influences. Those impulses which find disapproval, punishment, loss of parental love are the ones which the child represses. The main factor is that the child's ego is weak and has no other means of defending itself against the onslaught of his own impulses than to exclude them from consciousness. He is incapable of control, postponement, or modification of his impulses and desires. He cannot withstand temptation and cannot tolerate suspense. All impulses and desires which are perceived are immediately carried out in motor action. Repression is, if not the only, the most important defense mechanism of the child. This whole process of repression can be reversed in the emotional atmosphere prevailing between patient and physician using the method of free association. The physician reacts differently from the way the parents did—he does not evaluate and judge. The patient gradually recognizes—although not necessarily in explicit verbal terms—that when he expresses something which he himself would condemn, this does not meet with disapproval on the physician's part. The effect of his freedom to express thoughts and desires without reprisal gradually takes hold and the patient's self-revelations become more and more frank. Not only those things which the patient concealed from other persons but even those which he had concealed from himself gradually become verbalized.

One essential part of the therapeutic process appears in this light to consist in becoming conscious of psychological content which has been unconscious because it was repressed. No disagreement exists today concerning the basic thesis. Helping unconscious material to become conscious is an indispensable part of the therapy. How this process of self-revelation effects a therapeutic result is the next problem to deal with.

We may start from Freud's discovery that repressed attitudes of the patient in the course of the treatment are gradually directed toward the therapist, or, in other words, the psychoanalyst becomes the target of the patient's unconscious attitudes. This phenomenon he called transference and recognized very early that this "emotional experience" is the dynamic axis of the curative process. In the transference the patient's ego is given an opportunity to face those emotional situations which it could not manage in childhood when the ego was weaker. The weak ego of the child had to repress these emotions which, therefore, remained excluded from the ego's integrative activities. The emphasis was on the difference in the integrative powers of the adult and the immature ego of the child. The rationale of this method is to give the ego a new opportunity to deal with an old conflict.

The other important fact according to Freud is that the repetition of an old conflict in the transference is of lesser intensity than the original. The intensity is reduced because the emotions involved in the transference are reactions to previous experiences and not to the actual patient-physician relationship. The only actual relation between patient and physician is that the patient comes to the physician for help and the physician tries to fulfill his expectations. His job is not to evaluate his patient's reactions but to understand them and to help the patient recognize precisely their nature. It is

only in the patient's mind that the therapist assumes the role
of the father or mother, or of an aunt or younger sibling.
This offers an opportunity for the patient to discriminate
between the old conflicts which were real and the transference
conflicts which are repetitions of the old conflict but directed to a person who has not the same role as those toward
whom the original feelings were directed. In this connection the important consideration is that the neurotic patterns
did not develop in a vacuum, but were reactions to parental
attitudes and the totality of the family situation. This is the
meaning of Freud's contention that once neurotic reactions
had a sense, in the past situations in which they arose, but
appear in the present as irrational, because they are in-
congruous with the actual life situation and also with the
patient-therapist situation.

The crucial therapeutic factor implicit in this formulation consists of the fact that the analyst's reactions are different from those of the parents or siblings. For the sake of
simplicity we speak here of only the most common and
significant past experiences, namely those of the child in the
family, his sole universe in the first years of life. It is understood, of course, that the parental role may be taken over by
a nurse, by an uncle, by an aunt, who then can be considered
parent substitutes. The simplest examples of the working of
this therapeutic factor are seen in self-assertive and aggressive
attitudes which may have been repressed in the past due to
parental intimidation. It is obvious that if the therapist wants
to revive these repressed and self-assertive impulses during
the treatment, he must reverse the intimidating influence of
the parents. The mere fact that the patient's slightest expression of aggression, self-assertion, or resentment are met objectively without any emotional response or retaliation on
the part of the analyst corrects the original intimidating influence of the parents. In other words, the parental intimidation is undone and the tolerant attitude of the therapist has

now replaced the parents' role in the patient's mind. If the patient realizes that his modest self-assertion will not be criticized or punished, he will experiment more boldly and express himself more freely toward the analyst. This change often goes hand in hand with a change in the patient's behavior in his daily life. He may now express himself more freely toward persons in authority in his actual life situation. In this way his adult ego has an opportunity to deal with aggressive attitudes which, because of his anxiety, his fear of parental repudiations, he had previously repressed. Actually a much more complicated process goes on, but this simple example may serve to explain the dynamic pattern underlying this whole process. Parental intimidation, of course, is not the only form of pathogenic experience. Parental overindulgence, emotional rejection, and ambivalence are of similar importance.

The essence of this whole process consists then in the difference between the physician's reaction and that of the parents. The objective, nonevaluating attitude with the connotation of helpful interest is the most significant factor in allowing the emergence of repressed material and its revival in the transference situation. Equally important, however, is the recognition on the patient's part that these reactions are no longer suited to the present situation. They are not suited to the situation between him and the therapist and they are equally unsuited to his extratherapeutic, interpersonal relationships. He is no longer a child, and the persons with whom he has to do are not his parents. This recognition is not merely intellectual insight but is at the same time an emotional experience. At the same time recognizing and experiencing this discrepancy between the transference situation and the actual patient-therapist relationship is what I call the "corrective emotional experience" (14). This is not the discovery of a new therapeutic factor; it is only an explicit recognition of the essential therapeutic agent in the psychoanalytic process, as formulated by Freud himself, though he did not use the term. The corrective emotional experience is, therefore, the central therapeutic agent in the original and now standardized psychoanalytic procedure.

The course of the treatment consists in a long series of corrective emotional experiences, which follow one another as the transference situation changes its emotional content and different, repressed (pathogenic) childhood situations are revived and re-experienced in the relationship to the therapist.

Other authors have dealt with this central phenomenon under different terms. Sterba in a lucid article recognized the same principle, stressing not so much the emotional aspect as the intellectual counterpart of the phenomenon which I called the corrective emotional experience (90). He refers to it as "disassociation within the ego." The transference situation is interpreted and this shows the patient that his attitude toward the therapist is rooted in his childhood and is not an adequate reaction to the physician. It is neither adequate to the therapeutic situation nor to the patient's conscious adult personality. Such interpretations help to eliminate the so-called transference-resistance, which results from the fact that the attitudes the patient expresses toward the therapist, due to their infantile origin and ego alien content, are rejected by the patient's ego. Sterba points out that "through this interpretation there emerges in the mind of the patient, out of the chaos of behaviour impelled by instinct and behaviour designed to inhibit instinct, *a new point of view of intellectual contemplation.*" The disassociation within the ego results because the patient's ego identifies itself with the analyst and accepts the analyst's interpretation, which points out the past determination of the transference feelings. The contrast between present reality and repetition of a past, no longer existing, situation becomes evident. This introduces a double attitude in the ego—the automatic repetition of past feelings and a realistic attitude of observation supported by identification with the therapist. Sterba validly compares this process with the superego formation, which also introduces into the personality identification with adult "judgments and evaluations" from the outside world. He recognizes, however, the important difference between superego formation and ego-disassociation during therapy, in that the latter takes place in an "Ego which is already mature." Accordingly it is not quite accurate to ascribe the patient's acceptance of interpretations to his identification with the analyst. Understanding of a geometrical thesis does not require anything like an identification with the teacher. Naturally, a positive transference is helpful; the patient will be inclined to accept the analyst's point of view even before he is thoroughly convinced of its validity. In superego formation the type of "intellectual cognition" to which Sterba refers in describing ego-disassociation in therapy is not operative. The attitudes and value judgments incorporated in the superego are taken over wholesale, not on the basis of intellectual conviction but exactly by the process we call identification. In this, intellectual conviction plays no significant role. Had Sterba followed through consistently the difference between superego formation and what he calls ego-disassociation, he would have recognized that *identification with the analyst* and the *cognitive recognition of the discrepancy between the present situation and the transference attitude* are two different phenomena, though both may be present at the same time. The identification based on positive transference has only a transitory value and alone would have no permanent effect; it only introduces and facilitates the patient's own differential judgment which is no longer dependent upon anyone in the outside world. It is what we may call real conviction. The fact that Sterba speaks interchangeably of identification and intellectual cognition brought about by interpretations shows that he was aware of the fact that there are emotional factors, in addition to correct interpretations, which are necessary for such an "intellectual cognition" to develop in the patient. This is precisely where the concept of the corrective emotional experience enters.

It is evident that the analyst's interpretation, pointing out the infantile situation in which the transference attitude is rooted, is effective only because the therapeutic situation is actually different from the infantile one. Otherwise the transference reaction would not be unrealistic. If the analyst actually took over the father's authoritative or overindulgent attitude or the brother's rivalrous feelings, the transference reaction which develops would be nothing but a repetition of an old situation in its totality. The fact that the analyst is uninvolved, objective, and merely interested in understanding and thus helping the patient makes for the contrast between present reality and transference. This "experiencing" of the difference between the two is the most important factor, more important even than interpretations which but spell out in words what the patient feels. Such a corrective experience can be helpful in itself, while the best interpretation will be ineffective if the analyst's attitude belies his interpretations. This is why the effect of the countertransference is so powerful. Were the concept of the analyst as a blank screen valid, the problem of countertransference never could assume the significance it actually has in the therapeutic process. We shall return to this problem in a later chapter.

Strachey, in an article published at the same time as Sterba's, also emphasized the significance of the patient's recognition of the difference between the "archaic phantasy object" (transference attitude) and "the real external object" (92). Under the influence of interpretations, "if all goes well, the patient's ego will become aware of the contrast between the aggressive character of his feelings and the real nature of the analyst, who does not behave like the patient's 'good' or 'bad' archaic objects." This is the essence of what Strachey called "mutative interpretation." "For the patient, having become aware of the lack of aggressiveness in the real external object, will be able to diminish his own aggressiveness; the new object which he introjects will be less aggressive, and consequently the aggressiveness of his super-ego will also be diminished." Strachey did not consider the complications of this process by countertransference, a factor which only later received more explicit recognition. He attributes the effectiveness of interpretations to a fact which I described in an earlier publication, namely that during the treatment the patient ascribes to the analyst the functions of his superego (3). In contrast to my formulation, however, according to Strachey the modified image of the analyst is reintrojected into the patient's mental apparatus in the form of a more permissive superego and this facilitates further expression of repressed material. According to my view the analyst's interpretations help the patient to replace the older automatic superego functions with conscious judgment, or, in other words, superego functions are replaced by ego functions. Strachey's wide use of projection and introjection mechanisms in describing the therapeutic processes in treatment of adults appears to me questionable. Interpretations appeal to the cognitive functions. They are not introjected but understood. Understanding of an interpretation is not introjection or identification in the precise meaning of these terms. The differential judgment which recognizes the difference between past interpersonal relations and the actual patient-physician relationship is based on insight; it is, however, reinforced by the actual experiencing of the difference between transference attitudes and the actual patient-physician relationship. Strachey's description of the treatment process applies more to child-analyses or to the treatment of psychoses than to that of adults. He underestimated the significance of well-developed ego-functions in adult analysis, something which Sterba emphasized. That is why Strachey objected to my earlier formulation, accord-

ing to which analysis tries to substitute for automatic and unconscious superego regulations, ego-functions allowing greater
discrimination and ad hoc responses.

In summary, the essence of psychoanalytic therapy consists in exposing the ego in the treatment situation to the
original emotional conflicts which it could not resolve in the
past. This revival of the pathogenic emotional experience
takes place in the patient's emotional reactions to the analyst,
and is called the transference neurosis. It consists in an irrational emotional involvement of the patient with the therapist
to whom he attributes the role of important persons in his
past life. The original neurotic conflict which consisted once
in a disturbed relationship of the child to his family environment now appears in a disturbed relationship of the patient to
the analyst. The irrationality of this emotional involvement
stems from the fact that the responses had sense only in the
past situation, and now they are repeated in the therapeutic
situation without the analyst's giving any provocation. This
revival of the original conflict in the transference situation
gives the ego a new opportunity to grapple with the unresolved conflicts of the past. Of course, the totality of the past
situations cannot always be revived in the transference. Experience shows, however, that the central conflict situations
of the past are always repeated in the transference. According to this view, the fundamental therapeutic factor consists
in transference experiences which are suitable to undo the
pathogenic experiences of the past. In order to give the new
experience such a corrective value, it must take place under
certain highly specific conditions. How to establish these
conditions is the main technical problem of the psychoanalytic
treatment.

In most chronic cases the re-experiencing of the injurious
interpersonal relationships of the past under more favorable
conditions in the transference situation is not alone sufficient.
The patient must also obtain an intellectual grasp and recog-

nize the past sense and the present incongruity of his habitual emotional patterns. The relationship of emotional experience and intellectual grasp is probably the most difficult and most controversial part of psychoanalytic treatment. Later I shall take up this problem in greater detail.

This formulation of the standard procedure represents a summary of Freud's views contained in his five articles on psychoanalytic technique published between 1912 and 1915 (40, 41, 42, 43, 44). What is added is only the explicit recognition and detailed description of what I call the corrective emotional experience, which is implicitly recognized in Freud's original theory as the central therapeutic factor.

Chapter III

SOME EARLIER MODIFICATIONS
OF TECHNIQUE

The general principles of psychoanalytic technique, as formulated by Freud in his five articles between 1912 and 1915, have been subjected to careful reconsideration by various authors. In this chapter I shall discuss some of the earlier modifications without attempting to give a complete review of all of them. Many of the modifications suggested by various authors are essentially similar. They can be grouped according to the emphasis which is given to the different factors inherent in the standard treatment. These modifications consist mostly in changes in emphasis rather than in basic innovations or modifications. Some of the authors in developing their ideas of technique did so with the honest conviction that they were suggesting radical improvements over the standard technique. Others, more modest, maintained that their discussion called attention to certain principles developed by Freud which for some reason or other had been neglected by the majority of analysts in their practical daily work.

There is an obvious reason for this constant urge to improve upon the analytic technique. Psychoanalytic therapy is extremely cumbersome, consumes the time and energy of patient and analyst, and its outcome is difficult to predict on the basis of simple prognostic criteria. The desire to reduce these difficulties and to increase the reliability of psychoanalytic treatment is only too understandable. The difficulties, the time-and-energy-consuming nature of psychoanalytic therapy, are by no means disproportionate to its ambitious aim: to effect a permanent change in an adult personality, which has always been regarded as something inflexible. Nevertheless, a therapist is naturally dissatisfied, and desires to improve upon his technique and to have precise and definite technical rules in place of indefinite medical art. The unremitting attempt to reform the technique, therefore, needs no special explanation; what needs explanation is the frequency with which pseudo reforms are presented by their authors, under the illusion that they are discovering something new.

This illusion originates in the complex nature of the psychoanalytic method. Psychoanalytic technique cannot be learned from books. The psychoanalyst must, so to speak, rediscover in his own experience the sense and the details of the whole procedure. The complex behavior of the patient as it is presented to the therapist simply cannot be described in all its details, and the understanding of what is going on emotionally in the patient's mind is based on an extremely refined faculty usually referred to as intuition. In a former article I tried to deprive this faculty of the mystical halo which surrounds it by defining it as a combination of external observation with the introspective knowledge of one's own emotional reactions (4).

Freud's articles on technique were published at least fifteen years after he began to treat patients with the method of free association; they may therefore be considered a résumé of some fifteen years of clinical experience. These technical discoveries, for which a genius needed fifteen years, must be recapitulated by every student of psychoanalysis on the basis of his own experience. Though his study is now facilitated by general and simple formulations and by the precise description of those psychological processes which take place during the treatment, nevertheless the material which presents itself in every case is so complex and so highly individual that it takes many years for the student to achieve real mastery of the technique. Transference, resistance, acting out, removal of the infantile amnesia—these things he learns to appreciate only gradually. In consequence, he will be especially prone to emphasize those particular points of technique whose validity and importance begin to impress him. This alone can explain so many tedious repetitions and reformulations of the principles of technique—reformulations which are usually one-sided and much less judicious and clear than Freud's original formulations.

The general principles of the standard technique are evolved from the psychological processes observed during treatment: the phenomena of transference, resistance, the patient's increasing ability to verbalize material previously unconscious, and the gradual removal of infantile amnesia. In the procedures that deviate from the standard, either one or another of these phenomena is emphasized from the standpoint of therapeutic significance and is often dealt with in isolation from the others. The controversy is always centered around the therapeutic evaluation of (1) *emotional abreaction*, (2) *intellectual insight*, (3) *appearance of repressed infantile memories*. Those who believe that the best permanent therapeutic result comes from the patient's complete insight into the nature of his emotional conflicts will stress technical devices which have this aim; they will concentrate upon precise interpretations of content. Those who consider the most effective therapeutic factor to be the removal of infantile amnesia will be inclined to stress the reconstruction of the infantile history. In reality all these therapeutic factors are closely interrelated and dependent upon one another. For example, the occurrence of infantile memories is often, though not always, connected with emotional abreaction; intellectual insight, on the other hand, may prepare the way for emotional abreaction and recollections; and emotional experience, if not overwhelmingly intense, is the only source of real insight. Without emotional abreaction, intellectual insight remains theoretical and ineffective. The close interrelation of these factors is clearly recognized in Freud's papers on technique, and his technical recommendations are based upon knowledge of these interrelationships.

The majority of the innovations overemphasized one or another of these factors.

One can roughly differentiate three trends in technique and in its modifications: (1) neocathartic experiments, (2) reconstruction and insight therapy, and (3) resistance analysis. It should be stated, however, that none of the innovations or technical procedures which stress one factor and neglect the others has ever found general acceptance, and I suspect that the actual techniques used by most of the innovators themselves in their daily work remain closer to the original than one would assume from their publications. I shall try to evaluate critically some of these technical suggestions in the perspective of the development of the technical concepts of psychoanalysis.

TWO MAIN TRENDS: EMOTIONAL EXPERIENCE—
EGO ANALYSIS [1]

A brief and by no means complete survey will illustrate our point that divergence from the standard procedure usually is a one-sided overemphasis of one of two basic therapeutic factors. So far as one can reconstruct the evolution of analytic technique, Freud, after he gave up hypnosis, began to lay more and more stress on insight and the reconstruction of the infantile history. This was quite natural. He tried to reproduce in the waking state the phenomenon he and Breuer had observed during hypnosis, namely the patient's

[1] On page 54 it will be explained why only two main trends are distinguished and why emphasis on recollection is not treated separately as a third trend.

recollection of forgotten traumatic situations. The main goal was to make the patient remember through the process of free association, and so far as this was not fully possible to complete the gaps in memory through intellectual reconstructions. Around 1913, however, when Freud first formulated systematically the principles of the technique as we use it today, we see that he was already fully in possession of the dynamic concepts described above and considered analysis by no means a merely intellectual procedure. Yet once he had recognized the importance of the patient's intellectual insight as a precondition of the integrating activity of the ego, in contrast to some of his followers, he never lost sight of its significance.

It seems that at some time between the introduction of the method of free association and the technical recommendations of Freud in the early 'teens there must have been a period in which analysts overrated the importance of an intellectual reconstruction of the infantile history. Even after Freud's publications on technique, many analytic pioneers seem to have persistently overintellectualized the analytic process, and stressed the interpretation of content and reconstruction of infantile history, overlooking the importance of the dynamic handling of resistance and transference. This explains the joint publication by Ferenczi and Rank of *Entwicklungsziele der Psychoanalyse*, which may be regarded as a reaction against this overintellectualized procedure (34). In a review of this publication I attempted to show that the authors went to another extreme (5). According to them the whole analysis consists in provoking transference reactions and interpreting them in connection with the actual life situation. It appeared that the old abreaction theory had begun to emerge from the past. Ferenczi and Rank thought that after the patient had re-experienced his infantile conflicts in the transference neurosis, there was no need to wait for infantile memories; they believed that insight was possible without recollection merely through the re-experiencing of the different transference situations which are modeled after the forgotten conflictful childhood experiences. They believed that much of the originally repressed material had never been verbalized in the child's mind, and therefore one could not always expect real recollection of the situations upon which the transference reactions are modeled. If Ferenczi and Rank's contention had been right, namely that one need not wait for the lifting of infantile amnesia, this would have justified the hope for a considerable abbreviation of the treatment. In general, the most time-consuming part of the treatment is believed to consist of what is called the working through. Working through means the tedious task of helping the patient bring his transference manifestations in relation both to his actual life situation and also to his former experiences. It appeared that Ferenczi and Rank might have neglected this phase of the treatment. The working through is synonymous with helping the ego's integrative function through persistent interpretation; it belongs to that category of therapeutic factors which we have designated as insight. The practical conclusion which Ferenczi and Rank drew from this theory was the setting of a termination date to the treatment. After the patient's past conflicts have been clearly repeated and expressed in his transference behavior and these have been thoroughly understood by him, even though the connection with the original events is not established, the analysis, they said, can be terminated on a date set by the analyst.

The further developments are well known. Rank more and more centered his attention on the life situation, and considered insight into the infantile history as merely a research issue with no therapeutic significance whatsoever. Ferenczi, however, soon discovered that the artificial termination of the analysis did not work out therapeutically; he dismissed it from his technique, and tried to enhance the effectiveness of the therapy by increased emphasis upon the abreaction factor. Though he did not return to the method of cathartic hypnosis, he frankly admitted that he considered abreaction, as it takes place during cathartic hypnosis, to be the really effective therapeutic factor, and he tried to reproduce it in the method of free association by creating artificial emotional tensions, at first through his active technique, later through his relaxation method. With the help of the ingenious technical device of relaxation, sometimes he succeeded in creating semihypnotic states, in which the patient repeated his infantile emotional conflicts in a dramatic fashion (30, 31, 32, 33).

These technical reforms represented a renewed emphasis upon the significance of emotional experience and a relative neglect of intellectual integration, the working through. In this sense, Ferenczi's techniques can be classified as new forms of abreaction therapy.

Considering that recollection of repressed events is a part of the extension of the ego's integrative function, one can see that insight and recollection belong to the same category of therapeutic factors. Recollection connects the present with the past. This connection is interrupted by repression. Obviously recollection is an important factor in that process which might be called learning from past experiences. The view that repression interrupts the learning process seems well substantiated and is generally shared by all psychoanalytic authors. Yet the direct therapeutic value of the mere process of recollection is not quite clear. If the patient succeeds in understanding and resolving a transference relationship which itself is the repetition of previous repressed interpersonal conflict situations, one might question why it is necessary for him to remember the original events. On the other hand, if the ego, during the treatment, was capable of dealing with the repressed conflict situation, we might ask what prevents the ego then from remembering the repressed event, which was only repressed because the ego could not handle it in the past. Freud—at least once—considered the removal of infantile amnesia the consequence of making the transference situation conscious, a view which I have later proposed in more explicit terms (44, 6). The removal of infantile amnesia can be considered as one sign of a successful analysis rather than an absolute prerequisite of it. The recovery of memories is a sign of improvement rather than its cause. As the ego's capacity to cope with repressed emotions increases through experience in the transference, the patient is able to remember repressed events because of their similar emotional connotations. The ability to remember shows the ego's increased capacity to face certain types of psychological content. This change in the ego is achieved through the emotional experiences of the treatment, although it cannot be denied that remembering and understanding the origin of neurotic patterns has a therapeutic influence in itself and helps the reintegration of repressed psychological content in the total personality.

Since recollection is a part of insight, and is also a re-experiencing of the past, we can reduce the fundamental therapeutic factors to two: an intellectual and an emotional (experiential) factor. Accordingly, in the development of the theory and practice of treatment two major trends can be distinguished, one toward utilizing the therapeutic value of the patient's emotional experiences during treatment and the second toward increasing his insight, or, in other words, helping the ego in its integrative task. Generally it has been recognized that these two processes are really indivisible and the therapeutic process consists in insight which accompanies emotional experience. Only in extreme techniques is one or the other factor largely neglected.

In his later work Ferenczi became more and more interested in intensifying the emotional experience. One of Reich's contributions is essentially in the same direction (86). He concentrated on analysis of the resistances to allow, by their removal, the emergence of highly charged emotional experience.

Reich's resistance and layer analysis, however, also contained views pointing toward a trend which later became known as ego analysis. According to Reich, the aim of therapy is the transformation into orgastic genitality of energy bound up in neurotic symptoms and character trends. The discussion of this narrow theoretical concept does not lie within the scope of this study. Our present interest is his stress on certain hidden manifestations of resistance, which, he believed, are not recognized by most psychoanalysts, and his strict distinction between interpretation of resistance and interpretation of content. According to Reich certain hidden manifestations must first be analyzed and only afterwards can the analysis deal with the content which the patient's ego is resisting. The important things are not the familiar open manifestations of resistance, but those secret manifestations which the patient expresses only in a very indirect way in characteristic behavior, for example, in pseudo cooperativeness, in overconventional and overcorrect behavior, in affectless behavior, or in certain symptoms of depersonalization. The emphasis on hidden forms of resistance is unquestionably of great practical value. Glover mentions, in his treatise on technique, the importance of these hidden forms of resistance which one easily overlooks, and Abraham, in one of his classical contributions, described the pseudo-cooperative attitude of certain patients as a specific form of hidden resistance (59, 1). Reich's emphasis on understanding the patient's behavior apart from the content of his communications is a typical example of the rediscovery of one of the many therapeutic revelations that every analyst encounters during his development, as he gradually becomes more and more sensitive to the less obvious, more indirect manifestations of the unconscious. However, Reich's distinction between resistance which is expressed verbally and that ex-

pressed by gestures and general manner of behavior is somewhat artificial. All of these expressions complement each
other and constitute an indivisible unity.

Reich's other principle of the primacy of resistance interpretation over content interpretation is based upon a similarly artificial and schematic distinction. As Fenichel has
pointed out, the repressing tendencies and repressed content
are closely connected (28).[2] They constitute one psychic
entity and can be separated from each other only artificially.
The patient's resistance, for the careful observer, always dis-
plays at least roughly the content against which the resistance is directed. There is no free-floating resistance. At least
the general content of the repressed material can be recognized at the same time as the resistance itself. The more the
analyst is able to help the patient understand his resistance
in connection with what it is directed against, the sooner
the resistance itself can be resolved. The verbalization of what
the patient is resisting usually diminishes the resistance itself.
Strachey has convincingly described the reassuring effect of
correct and timely interpretations, which can best be witnessed in child analysis (92). It is true, as Fenichel states in
his critical discussion of Reich's technique, that in the interpretation of the content the analyst can go only slightly
beyond what the patient himself is able to see alone, at any
given moment (28). Yet every resistance should preferably
be interpreted in connection with what it is directed against,
provided of course that the content interpretation is timely.

Reich's concept of layer analysis is similarly a product of
an overschematizing tendency. That unconscious material appears in layers is a familiar and well-established observation.

---

[2] As a matter of fact, Fenichel mentions this argument as expressing not
his own views but those of the advocates of content interpretation, including Freud. He writes: "They (these advocates) think that because of the
persistent interweaving of defensive forces and rejected tendencies, it is impossible to verbalize the ones without at the same time verbalizing the others."
(Author's paraphrase.)

Freud dealt with this concept as far back as "The History of an Infantile Neurosis," and in *Totem and Taboo* he showed that the primary aggressive heterosexual phase is as a rule concealed by an overdomestication of these tendencies, by a masochistic passive homosexual phase (45, 46). Following Freud's lead, I tried, in an early paper, "Castration Complex and Character," to reconstruct the history of a patient's neurosis as a sequence of polar opposite phases of instinctual development (6).

The existence of certain typical emotional sequences is generally known, for example early oral receptivity leading under the influence of deprivations to sadistic revenge, guilt, self-punishment, and finally to regression to a helpless dependence. The validity of such typical emotional sequences, which make the material appear in "layers," is sufficiently proven, and every analyst uses this insight as a useful orientation in the chaos of unconscious reactions. This, however, does not change the supreme rule that the analyst cannot approach the material with a preconceived idea of a certain stratification in the patient, for this stratification has individual features in different patients. Though certain general phases in the individual's development succeed others with universal regularity, the different emotional attitudes do not necessarily appear during the treatment in the same chronological order as they developed in the patient's past life history. Moreover, the pathogenetic fixations occur at different phases in different cases, and the fixation points determine what is the deepest layer in any given case. Often we find an early period of sadism leading to anxiety and covered consecutively by a layer of passivity, inferiority feelings, and a secondary outbreak of aggression. In other cases we see that the deepest pathogenetic layer is a strong fixation to an oral dependent attitude, compensated by reaction formations of overactivity and aggressiveness, which in turn are covered by a surface attitude of helpless receptivity. It is not uncommon for a patient, in the course of the first two or three interviews, to reveal in his behavior and associations a sequence of emotional reactions belonging to different phases of his development. As Abraham emphasized during a discussion at the Berlin Psychoanalytic Society, it is not advisable to regard the different emotional reactions as they appear during the treatment in a too literal, too static sense, as though they were spread out one layer over the other, for in the unconscious they exist side by side.[3] During development, it is true, they follow each other in temporary sequences, one emotional phase being the reaction to the preceding one. During treatment, however, due probably to as yet unknown quantitative relationships, they do not exactly repeat their historical chronological order. I have often observed in more advanced stages of an analysis—sometimes even in the early stages—that patients during one analytic session display almost the whole history of their emotional development. They may start with spite and fear, then take on a passive dependent attitude, and end the session with envy and aggression again. The analyst can do no better than follow the material as it presents itself, thus giving the lead to the patient. Reich's warning against premature deep interpretations is correct, to be sure; Freud emphasized this point in his technical recommendations, and it is implicit in the general principle that interpretation should always start from the surface and go only as deep as the patient has capacity for experiencing it emotionally. But in Reich's overschematic procedure, the danger resides in the fact that the analyst, instead of following the individual stratification of emotional reactions in the patient, approaches the material with an overgeneralized diagram of layers before he is in a position to decide which emotional attitude is primary and which should be considered as reaction. The chronological order of the appearance is by no means a reliable criterion. An observation of Roy Grinker

[3] Unpublished discussion.

and Margaret Gerard clearly demonstrates that the order in which the transference attitude of a patient appears is determined also by factors other than the chronological order in which it developed in the patient's previous history.[4] As an interesting experiment they had a female schizophrenic patient associate freely for a few days alternately in the presence of a male and a female psychoanalyst; they observed that the patient's attitude was influenced by this difference of the analyst's sex. When the male analyst conducted the session, the patient was constantly demanding and aggressive; to the female analyst she complained and was more confiding, seeking reassurance. This experiment shows that the chronological sequence of transference attitudes does not always follow a historically predetermined stratification of infantile attitudes, but is also determined by other factors.

Reich's principle of the primacy of resistance interpretation over content interpretation found its most consistent expression in an extreme distortion of the analytic technique, in Kaiser's resistance analysis, from which every interpretation of content is pedantically eliminated. The analysis is reduced to an extremely sterile procedure of pointing out to the patient his resistance manifestations (69).

There is little to be added to Fenichel's critical analysis of this technique (28). Its most paradoxical feature consists in Kaiser's limitation of the therapeutic agent of analysis to dramatic abreactions, which reminds us of some experimentations of Ferenczi, who for a while attempted to achieve such abreactions by a merely intellectual procedure by convincing the patient of the irrationality of his resistance behavior and resistance ideas. This intellectual insight, Kaiser thinks, can break down the resistance itself and allow the repressed material to appear in a dramatic fashion. In order to create strong emotional tensions, he carefully avoids every interpretation of content and goes so far as to condemn every

---

[4] Personal communication.

indirect allusion of the analyst to preconscious material, even if this is so near to consciousness that it needs only verbalization in order to appear on the surface. It is not the intellectual insight into the resistance, but the avoidance of all content interpretation, that creates in the patient the tensions which provoke dramatic abreactions. The reassuring effect of verbalizing preconscious material, which encourages further expression of repressed material, has been mentioned above. To call the child by its name removes much of the patient's fear of the uncanny tension that comes from the pressure of preconscious material when it is merely felt as some unknown danger. The analyst's objective discussion of such material eliminates the infantile fear of the condemning parents and of their inner representative, the harsh superego. Verbalization of repressed content has for the patient the meaning of a permission; careful avoidance of it means condemnation.

Obviously here the analyst's fascination with the emotional fireworks is what leads to such a distortion of the analytic technique. The ideal of the standard technique is just the opposite—a permanent, steady, uninterrupted flow of repressed material, undisturbed by sudden dramatic advances that necessarily lead to new regressions, and which often neutralize the effect of many weeks' or many months' work. This steady flow can, however, only be obtained by a judicious and economic use of resistance and content interpretations in the connections in which they appear, by helping the patient connect the emerging material with the rest of his conscious mind and with his past and present experience.[5]

In the late 1930s a period followed which is often referred to as the time of ego analysis. In practice this consists in a greater emphasis on what is traditionally called working through. In theory this is an attempt at a judicious considera-

[5] In Chapter IV this generalization will be qualified by describing the effect of intense emotional experiences occasionally observed both in standard psychoanalysis and dynamic psychotherapy.

tion of both of the basic therapeutic factors: emotional experience and insight, including the revival of forgotten memories as a part of insight. This trend was stimulated by Freud's publication of *The Ego and the Id*, a cornerstone in the development of psychoanalytic thought (47). Under the influence of this publication interest in isolated unconscious mechanisms of the primary process (as best exemplified in the imagery of dreaming) gradually gave place to an effort to understand the kaleidoscopic picture of unconscious processes from the point of view of the ego, whose task consists in bringing the manifestations of subjective needs (instinct) into harmony with each other and with the environment.

One of the first comprehensive attempts to apply Freud's then new theory of the ego to the understanding of clinical material was my publication, *The Psychoanalysis of the Total Personality* (7). In this work I tried to explain the manifold symptomatology of compulsion neurosis as an attempt at equilibrium, an attempt of the total personality to reconcile ego alien tendencies with the demands of the superego, in a fashion similar to Freud's explanation of the function of the dream work. The dream work's function consists of transforming the ego alien content into a distortion which evades the censorship of the superego, satisfies its claims, and at the same time gives a covert expression of the repressed content. By the concept of the bribery of superego I proposed to resolve the seeming contradiction which Freud formulated, in saying that the compulsion neurotic is at the same time more moralistic and less moralistic than the healthy individual. In his rituals the compulsion neurotic complies with the values inculcated into him during his development (superego). He is more cleanly, more orderly, gives more consideration to other persons' needs than the average individual. He has to put his shoes at his bedside in a symmetrical fashion, neither one of the pair sticking out. He must put his dresser drawer in perfect order. He behaves like an overconscientious schoolboy under his compulsion to recount from time to time all the names of the presidents in correct chronological order. His obsessional symptoms on the other hand most blatantly express ego alien tendencies. He may have recurrent frank, incestuous fantasies. He may have the obsessional idea of hitting people over the head with an ax, or putting disgusting material like feces in his mouth. In fact his obsessional ideas may be a complete repertory of all those trends which he learned to deny himself during the early period of his superego formation. I tried to explain that his need to repress these primitive tendencies is diminished because the repressing agency, the superego, is bribed by excessive compliance.

In the manic-depressive psychosis the same balance can be observed in a biphasic manner. The manic phase of uninhibited expression of ego alien tendencies during which the patient may behave in a sexually licentious and extremely aggressive manner is followed by the depressive phase of contrition in which the inhibitory and self-accusatory trends of the superego prevail. This theory originally proposed by Freud and Abraham fitted well with the equilibrium seen in compulsion neurosis, if one considers the one as a simultaneous and the other as a biphasic attempt at equilibrating between the expressive force of the unconscious ego alien tendencies and the inhibitory force of the repressing agencies. Furthermore, I proposed that in conversion hysteria the two trends are condensed into a single symptom. The hysterical symptom has a Janus face. It expresses the ego alien trend and at the same time its denial.

This emphasis on the total personality influenced the therapeutic procedure only at a later period. Nunberg was the first to emphasize that the process by which unconscious content becomes conscious consists in an integrating act of the ego (79).

In the light of Nunberg's analysis of the psychoanalytic process, the function of psychoanalytic interpretations is

the establishment of new correct connections and the breaking up of old overgeneralized and more primitive connections. The emergence of preconscious material into the
conscious was long considered by Freud to be the establishment of a new connection: that between object-images and
word-images. Obviously what we call abstract thinking represents a still higher grade of synthesis between word-images.
Although we do not yet know much about its detail, what
we call conscious thinking consists mainly of the establishment of new connections between conscious contents. It
must be remembered, however, that these new, higher-grade
connections cannot be established arbitrarily by the ego. The
connections must be correct, that is to say they must be in
conformity with the results of the ego's reality testing. Therefore generalization, the establishing of connections between
different conscious elements, is permanently counteracted by
the critical or distinguishing faculty of the ego, which it uses,
however, only under the pressure of reality. Without the
pressure of the reality testing functions, the synthesizing
function would run amuck as it does in many philosophical
systems. Nunberg convincingly demonstrated all this and
considered the delusional system in paranoia to be the result
of such a faulty overstressed effort of the ego to synthesize,
by which it desperately tries to bring order into a personality
chaotically disorganized by the psychotic process.

Nunberg also called attention to the fact that every neurotic symptom and most psychotic symptoms are synthetic
products. In fact all unconscious material, as it presents itself
to us during the treatment in the process of becoming conscious, appears in certain synthetic units; fear together with
guilt and hate, receptive wishes and dependence overreacted
to by aggression, appear to us as two sides of the same unit.
We discover the synthetic nature of the unconscious material also in generalizations which connect or identify the
objects of sexual impulses in the unconscious. The extension

of the incest barrier over all individuals of the other sex is the simplest and best-known example of this generalizing tendency of the mental apparatus. The process by which an unconscious content becomes conscious therefore consists in the disruption of primitive synthetic products and the reassembling of the elements in the higher synthetic system of consciousness, which is more complex, more differentiated and consequently more flexible.

Thomas M. French's studies of consecutive dreams clearly demonstrate that during the course of treatment a progressive breaking up of primitive emotional patterns takes place, together with a building up of new, more complex relationships between the elements (36). This new synthesis allows more flexible behavior than the rigid automatic behavior which is determined by unconscious synthetic patterns. It is the ego's function to secure gratifications of instinctive needs harmoniously and within the possibilities of the existing external conditions. Every new experience requires a modification of the previously established patterns of instinct-gratification. The unconscious consists of psychological units, expressing more primitive, usually infantile connections between instinctual needs and external observations. These primitive units as we know are not harmonized with each other, nor do they correspond to the external conditions of the adult. Therefore they must undergo a new integrating process into higher systems: a new adjustment must be found between instinctual needs and external reality, in which process the ego plays the part of mediator. The establishment of these new patterns, however, necessitates the breaking up of the old units—in other words, of symptoms or fixed behavior patterns which correspond to earlier phases of ego development. What must be emphasized, however, is the fact that all unconscious material appears in synthetic units, which constitute certain primitive patterns that connect instinctual demands with the results of reality testing.

According to this concept, the process by which an unconscious content becomes conscious corresponds to a recapitulation of ego-development, which also consists in a gradual building up of more and more complex and flexible systems of connections between different instinctual needs and sense perceptions. In this light the therapeutic process appears as the continuation of the learning process, which has been interrupted by repressions.

The effect of interpretation can most simply be compared with the process of the child's learning to connect and differentiate objects. At first, when the child learns the word "stick," it begins to call every longitudinal object a stick, and then gradually learns to differentiate between stick, pencil, poker, umbrella, etc. When a neurotic patient learns to differentiate between incestuous and nonincestuous objects, that is to say to react differently toward them, he repeats essentially the same process.

In his systematic study of patients' consecutive dreams and parallel sequences during analysis, French subjected this learning process to a thorough investigation and described the therapeutic process as a progressing type of discriminatory learning (36, 37).[6]

In the light of the above discussion it is obvious that our interpretations must fulfill both purposes: they must break up the primitive connections and help to establish new, more differentiated ones that are in harmony with the reality which confronts the adult, and also in harmony with the adult ego's standards. What we call "working through" has the function of aiding the integrating process. Its therapeutic value is sufficiently proven by experience. Every correct interpretation serves both purposes: mobilization of unconscious material and its integration into the system of consciousness.

[6] The elaboration of French's theoretical concepts and their relationship to the psychoanalytic technique will be published in his Volume III of *The Integration of Behavior* (University of Chicago Press).

The *synchronization* of the two functions of interpretation into one act, including emotional experience and insight at the same time, may be considered a fundamental technical principle, which might be called the *integrative principle of interpretation*. It is not possible to isolate these two processes artificially, as Kaiser tried to do, because the best means of overcoming a resistance is the correct interpretation of its not yet verbalized unconscious background at a time when the ego is ready for it. I don't know of any more precise rule for the correct evaluation of the right moment than to follow the spontaneous process of self-revelation and be, as Fenichel suggests, just one step ahead of the patient. The basis of the ego's resistance is its inability to master or assimilate unconscious material. Everything which the patient can understand, that is, everything which he can connect with other familiar, already mastered psychological content, relieves fear. In other words, every new synthesis within the ego, by increasing the ego's ability to face new unconscious material, facilitates the appearance of new unconscious material. The longer the patient is exposed to material which puzzles him, which seems strange, and appears to him as a foreign body, the longer the analysis will be retarded and the appearance of new unconscious material blocked. The ideal we strive for in our technique is the connection of unconscious material with what is already understood by the patient. This makes of the analysis a continuous process. Therefore, whenever it is possible, interpretations should refer to previous insight. To be sure, interpretation does not consist merely of the creation of new connections but also of the breaking up of primitive infantile connections. This can be done only if the material, as it appears in its totality, is exposed to the patient's critical judgment. Umbrella, walking cane, poker, lead pencil, must be demonstrated together in order to break up their faulty identification and generalization as a stick. The interpretations must point out these connections, formed by the mind in infancy, as they appear in the presenting material. We know that these connections, as they occur in symbols for example, often seem strange to the mind of the adult, who has forgotten and overcome this primitive language of the unconscious. It is perhaps too much to expect that the patient will be able without help to recognize the infantile generalizations as something self-evident. I do not doubt, however, that after the old primitive connections are broken up, the patient, because of the integrating power of his ego, would in time establish the new syntheses alone.[7] Here, however, is the place where the analyst can help and accelerate the integrating process. Interpretations which connect the *actual life situation* with *past experiences* and with the *transference situation*—since the latter is always the axis around which such connections can best be made—are called *total interpretations*. The more that interpretations approximate this principle of totality, the more they fulfill their double purpose: they accelerate the assimilation of new material by the ego and mobilize further unconscious material (7).

This principle of totality should not be misunderstood and used in a different sense than is meant. Totality does not mean, for example, that all deep overdeterminations in a dream should be interpreted. Totality does not mean an unlimited connection of material which, though in fact related, is still far from the surface. It implies totality not as to depth but as to extension—the connecting with each other and with previous material of elements which belong together. It cannot be emphasized too much, however, that these connections should center around the emotionally charged material, usually the transference manifestations. French refers to this dynamic center as the focal conflict, focal at the moment it is observed (38).

[7] See later the discussion of the question as to when the ego can take over the process of reconstruction and does not need the therapist's help (Chapter VIII).

The supreme requirement for the correct handling of the technique, more important than any principles and rules, is the precise understanding in detail of what is going on at every moment in the patient. It is needless to say that all the formulations here given should be considered not as rules but as general principles to be applied always in accordance with the individual features of the patient and the situation.

The isolation of resistance and content in interpretation is not a desirable aim though at times it is necessary, in particular when the material against which the patient has resistance is not yet understood by the analyst. Probably the most effective way of permanently overcoming resistance consists in helping the ego to integrate, that is to say to understand, new material. Therefore in the long run those technical experiments which aim at sudden abreactions of great quantities of unconscious tendencies often fail, although this may be successful in individual cases. These techniques expose the ego not to a continuous flow but to sudden eruptions of new material, and often cause new repressions, repression being a phenomenon which Freud has explained as resulting from the infantile weak ego's inability to deal with certain instinctual needs. The reproduction of such an inner traumatic situation, in which the ego is exposed to overpowerful stimuli, cannot be a universal principle of our technique. In analytic therapy our main allies are the *striving of unconscious forces for expression and the integrating tendency of the conscious ego.* Even if we do nothing else but not interfere with these two dynamic forces, we will be able to help many patients.

It has often been maintained that psychoanalysis consists mainly in the mobilization of unconscious material and that the integration of this material must be left to the patient's ego. The standard current technique, based on Freud's technical recommendations, and consisting in interpretations centering around the transference situation, involves an active

participation of the analyst in the integrating process. Through
our interpretations, we do help the synthetic functions of the
ego. How much such active help each patient needs is one
of the most timely issues and will be discussed in connection
with psychoanalytically oriented psychotherapy.[8] Understanding this integrative function of our interpretations and
evaluating how much the patient's ego can perform without
our help may contribute to developing the art of analysis
into fully goal-conscious, systematically directed procedures.
Always keeping in mind the function which our interpretations fulfill in the treatment may help eventually to bring us
nearer to the ultimate goal, the abbreviation of the psychoanalytic treatment.

As has been said before, in the thirties definite progress
was made in defining the functions of the ego, which had
more and more influence on psychoanalytic therapy, particularly that phase of the treatment called working through.
The contributions of Nunberg, Anna Freud, French, Hartmann, Kris, and Lowenstein to ego-psychology are representative of this trend (79, 39, 36, 37, 38, 61, 62, 63, 70,
71, 76). We may turn now to some recent contributions
which deal with the emotional experiences of the patient
during treatment and their therapeutic value.

[8] See Chapter X.

Chapter IV

LATER DEVELOPMENTS IN THEORY AND TECHNIQUE

I. THE PRINCIPLE OF FLEXIBILITY

As HAS been shown in the previous chapters, two trends can be clearly distinguished in the development of the theory of psychoanalytic treatment. The one consists in the preoccupation with the integrative process within the ego as a result of insight which the therapist aids by his interpretations. He supports the ego's function to connect the different elements of past experiences with his current difficulties in resolving his actual life situation. The other is concerned with the nature and intensity of the emotional experience in the transference situation, without which intellectual understanding remains therapeutically ineffective. Ferenczi and Rank's controversial monograph, "Developmental Trends of Psychoanalysis," published in 1925, remained until the late thirties the last comprehensive publication which explicitly re-emphasized the significance of the emotional experience in the transference situation as the major therapeutic factor (34). They maintained that this re-experiencing of old conflicts in itself suffices to achieve therapeutic results.

In 1937, in the Institute of Psychoanalysis in Chicago, we undertook a systematic study of the therapeutic process in which we experimented with certain quantitative variations of the therapeutic factors (14). After seven years of col-

71

laborative study there resulted a renewed emphasis upon the emotional experience, neglected since Ferenczi and Rank's much contested brochure. Our study was motivated mainly by the extreme unpredictability of therapeutic results and also by the discrepancy between the length and intensity of the treatment and the degree of therapeutic results. Patients frequently improve after a relatively short period of analysis. Traditionally improvements were considered to be transference results if they were not based on a systematic working through of the patient's past and present conflicts with as complete a genetic reconstruction of the personality development as possible. It was held that the patient's improvement was due to the emotional experience in the transference which cannot persist unless followed by insight; it was assumed that the patient would soon relapse if the treatment were interrupted at this point. The common argument was— and this, even today, is held by many—that quick therapeutic results cannot be based on deep, thoroughgoing changes in the dynamic structure of the personality. To achieve the latter, years of continuous treatment are required. At the same time the lack of results after many years of consistent psychoanalytic treatment is often explained by assuming that the patient's ego is weak and is not capable of resolving the conflicts, even after they are brought into the integrative scope of the conscious ego. In our studies we focused interest on this quantitative problem which has never been satisfactorily answered. We formulated the problem in this way: Is it true (1) that the depth of therapy is necessarily proportionate to the length of treatment and the frequency of the interviews; (2) that therapeutic results achieved by a relatively small number of interviews are *necessarily* superficial and temporary, while therapeutic results achieved by prolonged treatment are *necessarily* more stable and more profound; and (3) that extreme prolongation of an analysis is justified on the grounds that the patient's resistance will *eventually* be overcome and the desired therapeutic results achieved (14)?

The results of this study were published in 1946. This publication raised many controversial issues centering around a variety of therapeutic problems, such as: (1) The significance of the corrective emotional experience. (2) Technical measures by which the emotional re-experiencing of the past can be influenced in order to have an optimal intensity. Among these measures, particularly the changes in the frequency of interviews and temporary interruptions of the treatment occasioned a great deal of controversy. (3) Also questioned was the suggestion that spontaneous countertransference attitudes should be replaced by conscious planned attempts to create an interpersonal climate favorable for corrective emotional experiences. (4) The relationship between the patient's extratherapeutic experiences and those which he has in the transference situation. (5) The principle of flexible application of the different therapeutic factors to different types of patients (14).

The last issue, that of flexibility, initiated the current controversy concerning the question as to whether one can draw a sharp line between psychoanalysis proper and other analytically oriented forms of psychotherapy.

Our contention was that the patients who are treated by the psychoanalytic technique constitute an extreme variety of personality types who suffer from a great variety of neurotic conditions. If this is true one can hardly defend the thesis that every patient should be subjected to the same type of therapy.[1] This contention led to heated arguments concerning the relationship of psychoanalysis proper and psychoanalytically oriented psychotherapy. The thesis that different patients need different types of treatment was not con-

[1] See also E. Weigert, "The Importance of Flexibility in Psychoanalytic Technique" (94), and Leo Stone, "The Widening Scope of Psychoanalysis" (91).

tested. It was long recognized that psychoanalytic knowledge can be applied in all forms of psychotherapy. What remained controversial was where to draw the line between psychoanalysis proper and psychoanalytically oriented psychotherapy. Some analysts believed that a sharp line could be drawn. Others doubted the possibility of drawing such a sharp line and doubted the desirability of making an artificial distinction. In this chapter some of these controversial issues will be discussed, particularly the nature and significance of the corrective emotional experience and suggestions as to technical measures of a quantitative nature by which this emotional experience can be influenced so that it reaches an optimal intensity. This problem requires a re-examination of the psychoanalytic technique from the point of view of its quantitative aspects.

2. QUANTITATIVE ASPECTS OF THE CORRECTIVE EMOTIONAL EXPERIENCE

Concerning the essential nature of the treatment there seems to be little disagreement among psychoanalysts today. We all agree that the essence of psychoanalytic therapy consists in exposing the ego in the transference to the emotional conflicts which it could not resolve in the past.

The new settlement of an old unresolved conflict in the transference situation becomes possible not only because the intensity of the transference conflict is less than that of the original conflict—as Freud expressed it, the transference is only a shadow-play of the original conflict—but also because the therapist's actual response to the patient's emotional expressions is quite different from the original treatment of the child by the parents. The therapist's attitude is understanding but at the same time emotionally detached. His attitude is that of a physician who wants to help the patient. He does not react to the patient's expression of hostility either by retaliation, reproach, or signs of being hurt. Neither does he gratify the patient's regressive infantile claims for help and reassurance. He treats the patient as an adult in need of help, but this help consists merely in giving the patient the opportunity to understand better his own problems. He does not assume the role of an adviser nor does he assume practical responsibility for the patient's actual doings. He does not give the patient an opportunity for any realistic blame or gratitude for anything but rendering a professional service. In the objective atmosphere of positive helpful interest the patient becomes capable of expressing his originally repressed tendencies more frankly. At the same time, he can recognize also that his reactions are out of date and are no longer adequate responses to his present life conditions or to the therapeutic situation. Once, of course, in the past they were, if not adequate, still unavoidable reactions—the reactions of a child to the existing parental attitudes. The fact that the patient continues to act and feel according to outdated earlier patterns whereas the therapist's reactions conform to the actual therapeutic situation makes the transference behavior a kind of *one-sided shadowboxing*. He has the opportunity not only to understand his neurotic patterns, but at the same time to experience intensively the irrationality of his own emotional reactions. The fact that the therapist's reaction is different from that of the parent, to whose behavior the child adjusted himself as well as he could with his own neurotic reactions, makes it necessary for the patient to abandon and correct these old emotional patterns. After all, this is precisely one of the ego's basic functions—adjustment to the existing external conditions. As soon as the old neurotic patterns are revived and brought into the realm of consciousness, the ego has the opportunity to readjust them to the changed external and internal conditions. This is the essence of the corrective influence of those series of experiences which constitute the transference. There is no disagreement that this is the essential nature of psychoanalysis.

In his criticism of the classical procedure, Rado recently claimed that the power of insight into neurotic patterns obtained by their repetition in the transference situation is overrated (82). By his "adaptational technique" he aims to induce the patient to modify his behavior and replace the old patterns with new ones adapted to the actual life situation. I do not think that an adult neurotic patient needs the exhortations of the psychoanalyst to accomplish this task. His most powerful motive to accomplish new adaptation lies in the corrective emotional experience afforded by the transference situation. One of the ego's basic functions is adaptation to ever-changing situations. Once the patient experiences the infantile origin of his transference reactions, and at the same time faces a new interpersonal situation in the transference, to which the old pattern does not fit, this alone activates the ego to find a new adequate adaptive response.

Rado in his criticism of the classical technique overlooked this most powerful therapeutic factor, and in my opinion much of the active guidance in the new adaptation which he offers by his adaptational technique is not needed. All this is much less effective than the corrective influence of the emotional experience inherent in the classical technique.

As will be elaborated later, the standard procedure can be improved by rendering the corrective influence of the transference situation more effective by giving increased attention to the interpersonal climate of the treatment situation.

In the above formulation one fundamental fact was stated but no attempt made to explain it. I refer to the fact that the patient in the objective, encouraging attitudes of the analytical situation spontaneously expresses his basic neurotic patterns in relationship to the analyst; in other words, he develops that transitory artificial neurosis which Freud called the transference neurosis. At this point I shall not discuss the question of why and how the transference neurosis unavoidably develops in all cases of chronic psychoneurosis if the analyst's attitude is appropriate. In Chapter V this question will be taken up in some detail. Now it might suffice to state that the analytic situation encourages a temporary regression to infantile attitudes because all evaluative reactions on the analyst's part are consistently absent. It is under the normative influence of the parents that the inhibitions or repressions developed. Neurotic patterns are maladaptations to the standards which the parents represent. In most cases they can be traced to more extensive repressions than is common in normal people. These old behavior patterns become conserved because their exclusion from consciousness did not allow the continuous adaptive modification which is required for normal development during emotional maturation. Neurotic symptoms are a combination of substitutive outlets for non-adjusted impulses and are at the same time defenses, such as denials, compensations, and self-punitive reactions to these ego alien impulses. The permissiveness and the lack of evaluations in the psychoanalytic situation have a tendency to counteract repression and mobilize the original impulses which were repressed under the influence of parental intimidations. Thus a freer expression of the original neurotic patterns is encouraged. This process is complicated by the fact that, in the case of chronic neurosis, much of the original parental-child relationship has become internalized. The external struggle between child and parents, the expression of hostility and sexual impulses, of guilt, expiation by suffering and punishment—all this complex interplay between the child and his environment has been transformed into an internal struggle. The parental images become incorporated as part of the personality in the form of the superego, and the external battlefield of emotional interplay becomes transplaced into the internal arena of the personality. The emotional interplay between the child and parents becomes an internal conflict between differentiated parts of the personality. During psychoanalytic treatment the intrapsychic conflict becomes again transformed back into its original interpersonal form as an interaction between the patient and the physician in the transference situation. Only after this externalization of the intrapsychic conflict has taken place and the transference neurosis has developed can the real therapeutic task be undertaken—the treatment and cure of the transference neurosis (9, 10). The full development of the transference neurosis often takes place after a brief period of time, sometimes within a few days, sometimes after several months of treatment.

After the transference neurosis is fully established the analytic task becomes: (1) to keep the intensity of the emotional participation of the patient at an optimal intensity, (2) to give insight by interpretations, and (3) to create an emotional climate in the treatment situation which will favor the patient's need to correct his reaction patterns appropriately to the new interpersonal and intrapsychic situation. The nature of this interpersonal rapport is what I refer to as the emotional climate of the treatment. After the transference neurosis has developed, the analyst's own attitude becomes of paramount significance for the intensity of the emotional experience as well as for its corrective effect.

3. THE COUNTERTRANSFERENCE

As early as 1910 Freud introduced this expression referring to the physician's emotional involvement in the treatment (48). It took about thirty years, however, before the analyst's unconscious and conscious, spontaneous and studied, reactions toward the patients were further explored as to their significance upon the course of the treatment.

In spite of the extensive interest manifested by the numerous articles devoted to the problem of the countertransference, there is still not full agreement concerning the definition of this phenomenon. Orr in a recent publication described the different interpretations of countertransference

(81). In general the authors of studies on this subject hold one of three types of definition. There are those like English and Pearson, and also P. Heimann, who regard as countertransference all of the analyst's possible attitudes toward the patient (26, 64). Others, like Sharpe, differentiate between conscious and unconscious countertransference reactions (89). Berman defines countertransference more precisely as a phenomenon parallel to transference, when the analyst reacts to the patient not according to the actual patient-physician relationship but repeats toward the patient emotional attitudes which were formed in the past toward important figures in his earlier life (18). Glover differentiates between positive and negative countertransference and counterresistance. Since all the definitions offered by the different authors belong to one of these categories or combinations of them, no special reference will be made to a number of excellent contributions.

Little similarly classifies the different meanings of the term countertransference as it is used by different authors: regressive revival in the analyst of reaction patterns toward the patient which have been formed in the past, specific reactions of the patient's transference, and the totality of the analyst's attitude toward the patient, which contains both unconscious-repressive and conscious responses (75).

Gitelson distinguishes between total reactions to the patient as a person and reactions to particular psychodynamic situations, especially transference attitudes of the patient as they develop during the treatment (58).

Some authors separate the different reactions of the analyst more rigidly than others who approach the problem of the patient-physician relationship as a changing dynamic interplay between two personalities which consists of conscious and unconscious elements: partially realistic responses to the actual patient-physician relationship, partially repetitions of the therapist's earlier fixed reaction patterns.

Most authors define countertransference in the same way as transference has been defined: it is that portion of the analyst's reaction to the patient which is not appropriate to the patient-physician relationship but which is an addition to or distortion of a realistic attitude toward his patient determined by the analyst's own characteristic preformed reaction patterns.

Making this distinction one must bear in mind that all interpersonal relations are a composite of reactions: highly differentiated and adequate responses to the actual situation and admixtures of more or less prestabilized conscious and unconscious reaction patterns. This view is clearly expressed by Berman (18).

All interpersonal attitudes constitute a continuum in which these components are present in different degrees. They are the end products of a developmental process during which early child-parent and child-sibling attitudes are gradually transformed into adult attitudes. In normal development the original patterns are flexibly modified and lose their rigidity. Accordingly adult attitudes have a wider range. A healthy adult reacts to other persons individually and has much less rigid and unalterable categories of behavior, such as rebelling against or being fearful of any person in authority, or feeling protective or guilty toward everyone who is weaker than he is. On the other hand, his later interpersonal attitudes remain influenced by his early experiences in his family and retain, although in a modified form, some of the early reaction patterns. Moreover, every person may regress to earlier patterns and lose later-acquired, more flexible attitudes under the influence of excessive conflicts.[2] Most people, even if psychoanalyzed, will retain certain sensitive spots and will react in a more predetermined fashion to some emotional situations than to others. Therefore, it is difficult

---

[2] Panic reactions are a common example.

to separate precisely early predetermined patterns from later-adopted modifications. These constitute a continuum.

Countertransference may be defined then as the grossly regressive, fixed patterns which are largely determined by the past experiences and are transferred to the patient not as an individual but as the representative of a person who played a role in the therapist's early years. Such fixed patterns, together with modified and more flexible attitudes, are present in everybody and characterize him as an individual.

When persons are engaged in a collective task, the fact that they have a common goal helps all of them to assume attitudes which are determined more by the task than by the individual personalities of the participants in the task.

Accordingly for every human interrelationship in which two persons enter into a common effort, such as for example therapy, an optimum model of collaboration can be theoretically constructed. One can devise an ideal model of mutual attitudes between patient and physician best designed for the success of the therapeutic enterprise. If two persons ally themselves to accomplish a goal, to erect a wall for example, there is an optimal type of behavior for both by which this goal can be best achieved. The one might hand the bricks and the other place them, or whatever division and integration of work of the participants might be best suited for the goal. A similar but more complicated ideal model could be devised for the psychotherapeutic situation. The patient will behave in a way which is required for the therapist to help him. He will freely associate, that is to say, he will reveal himself without controlling the train of his ideas and will consider the therapist only as an expert who is trying to help him. The therapist, on the other hand, will have only one reaction to the patient, the wish to understand him as an individual and give him an opportunity for readjustment through insight offered by the analytical process. He will help this procedure by using what he has learned about human personality and the technique of treatment without being disturbed by any of his personal and subjective (pre-formed) reactions.

No matter what discrepancies may be present among the different authors commenting on this subject, there is today universal agreement that this ideal model does not, and can-not, exist in reality. So far as the transference phenomenon is concerned, it is generally recognized that the transference, in spite of the fact that it deviates from the original ideal model (therapy as progressively developing insight), is not only a hindrance to therapy but also its most effective in-strument. The patient's predetermined emotional distortions of the patient-physician relationship, which repeat toward the analyst early fixed patterns, is not only the material from which the patient's neurotic structure can be best understood, but the very repetition of these patterns, their emotional re-experiencing, is the axis of the therapy. Only by re-experiencing the neurotic patterns can their unsuit-ability to the present situation be discovered, and only the recognition of this unsuitability can serve as a motive for resolving the transference reactions and replacing them with attitudes which are in harmony with the patient as an adult person in a given life situation. Resolving the transference neurosis is equivalent to changing the patient's habitual way of handling the actual interpersonal situations in his life, including the transference situation.

So far as the countertransference is concerned, the pre-vailing view is that the analyst's own emotional reactions to the patient should be considered as a disturbing factor. It is a kind of unavoidable impurity.

Some authors, among them Weigert, Frieda Fromm-Reichmann, Heimann, and Benedek (94, 53, 64, 17), however, mention certain therapeutic assets of the countertransference;

they point out that the analyst's understanding of his countertransference attitudes may give him a particularly valuable tool for understanding the patient's transference reactions.

Tower, recently, in an unpublished address on countertransference, postulates that in every "truly deep analytic
procedure something in the nature of a countertransference
neurosis develops, which may be of crucial significance in
the sense of a catalytic agent for the beneficial or unfavorable final development of the treatment." According to her,
every successful analysis consists of the resolution of both the
transference and "countertransference neurosis." She supports her thesis with a uniquely frank and detailed self-
analysis of her own emotional involvements in four cases
(93). Tower's position sharply contradicts an earlier paper
of Balint and Balint (15). In this the authors recognize the
fact that analysts do not represent blank screens but are
perceived by the patients as individuals with their own characteristic traits. Yet they consider this impurity as negligible
for the therapeutic process.

In spite of these different evaluations, all authors believe
that in order to minimize this impurity in the treatment situation the therapist should be aware of his own emotional reactions and keep them under control. (Glover speaks of the
"analyst's toilet" [60].) One of the most important objectives
of the analyst's own training analysis is just this: it helps him
to know, to control, and possibly even to change his spontaneous countertransference reactions. In this way he can at
least approach the original ideal of representing a blank screen
upon which the patient can reflect his own reaction pattern
without being influenced by the analyst's personality, and
can attribute to the analyst the roles of the originally important persons of the patient's past. It is obvious that the
more neutral the analyst's attitude is the less will he interfere
through his actual personality and actual behavior with the
patient's tendency to attribute to the analyst whatever role

suits his needs. This concept, though internally consistent, does not precisely describe the phenomena which actually take place in treatment. The analyst remains a real personality for the patient no matter how neutral he tries to be. As soon as the transference relationship is well established, the analyst's own spontaneous responses to the patient are of great significance in hastening or retarding the process of readjustment.

The theoretical significance of the conception of the analyst as a blank screen can hardly be exaggerated. It supplied the theoretical model of the therapeutic process. Such a basic model is the essence of every theoretical construction. Deviations in nature from the theoretical model are the starting points toward new knowledge which leads to an improved model. An unavoidable "impurity" in the treatment process became more and more recognized, an impurity which introduces a significant discrepancy between the theoretical model of the psychoanalytic process and what actually takes place between patient and analyst. The latter's reactions toward the patient—no matter how well he may control them—are sensed by the patient. These countertransference reactions constitute an important factor and eventually have to be recognized in the theory of the treatment.

As has been pointed out above, the countertransference is generally considered something which is undesirable and disturbing, because it interferes with the patient's free expression of his transference reactions, which according to the theory should be determined solely by the patient's past experiences. The countertransference reactions of the analyst introduce stimuli which are not determined by the patient's past but by the analyst's own personality. Therefore the analyst should be aware of his countertransference leanings, should have them under full control, and substitute for them the basic attitude of objectivity and detachment, the only attitude which does not disturb the process of gradual self-revelation. This detached objective attitude is, of course, studied and not quite spontaneous because even the well-analyzed therapist retains certain characteristic reactions to other persons.

This was clearly stated by Glover when he referred to the state of being "thoroughly analyzed" as a hypothetical state (60). We may add that even if the therapist is "thoroughly analyzed," he remains a person in his own right, with his own characteristic reaction patterns, different from other "thoroughly analyzed" persons.

Recognizing this fact Benedek concludes her paper on countertransference with the statement that "the therapist's personality is the most important agent of the therapeutic process" (17). Obviously the crucial issue in this statement is the definition of the "therapist's personality." It may be defined as the aggregate of the interpersonal reactions which are characteristic for a person as an individual. Benedek describes the psychoanalytic process as the "unfolding of an interpersonal relationship in which transference and countertransference are utilized to achieve the therapeutic aim." I believe, however, that Benedek would agree that some of the spontaneous countertransference reactions are disturbing factors and must be controlled. What the therapist cannot change, of course, is his individual personality as a whole.

It has been argued that a detached objective attitude comes naturally to the therapist whose orientation toward the patient is to understand him and through understanding help him. An experienced surgeon does not react toward the physical disfiguration of a diseased body by evaluating it from the aesthetic point of view; a boil to him is not ugly or beautiful. He is interested only in what causes it and in the means by which he can remove it. There is no doubt that the experienced analyst's prevailing interest is to understand the patient, and consciously he certainly does not evaluate him. However, nature is always more complex than theory. Advancement in most fields of knowledge comes when the discrepancy between the theoretically conceived picture and the actual happenings becomes clearly and explicitly recognized. It is needless to quote many examples from the history of science. The Boyle-Mariotte Laws concerning the behavior of gases was modified by the Van der Waals theory which included and accounted for the observed deviations. The concepts of modern physics arose from the fact that the simple Newtonian laws did not obtain precisely for phenomena of too large or too small dimensions. It is an irrefutable fact that no matter how well the analyst is analyzed —in other words, how well he knows and controls his own characteristic interpersonal reactions—there is always an admixture of highly personal attitudes which are characteristic for him as an individual person. If every analyst could remain a pure, detached intellect, we would have no explanation for the stark fact that some patients do better at treatment with one type of analyst than with another. In practice we do recognize this fact, particularly in our teaching practices. We soon discover in our supervisory work that certain students can handle certain patients better than others—for example, men better than women, compliant persons better than rebellious natures. In training analyses one of the most important aims is to reduce the influence of this "personal equation." Our ideal is to make the student able to deal equally well with all kinds of patients. This goal is never reached because, as I stated before, even after the most painstaking analysis, the trainee will still remain an individual in his own right.

In pre-Freudian psychotherapy the therapist was quite naïve about how his own personality, his own values, entered into the treatment situation. In fact each therapist tried to reform the patient by imposing upon him his own orientation. One of the fundamental advancements in psychotherapy is the recognition that this is exactly what should be avoided, that the patient's problem must be solved quite independently of the particular tastes and values of the therapist. Some values, of course, we all share, patients and analysts equally, if we belong to the same culture. This basic value system can be considered at least roughly constant. Psychoanalysis, however, aims at an adjustment which takes cognizance of individual differences existing between people. Individual emotional patterns survive even in psychoanalyzed persons, and consequently the therapeutic process, which is an inter-action between two individualities, can never be reduced to an equation in which the only variable is the patient's preformed patterns and the analyst is always the same objective intellect. How to deal therapeutically with this fact is a crucial problem of psychoanalytic technique.

An example will make this complex problem more concrete.

Let us consider one of the frequent occurrences in the transference. The patient repeats toward the analyst a combination of the hostile rivalry and guilt which he entertained toward his father and which he could never resolve. Let us assume further that the original conflict developed because of the extremely permissive attitude of the father toward his son to whom he could not deny anything. This occurs often when the father himself has been brought up without understanding by rejecting parents. This makes him so sensitive toward the helplessness of a child that in order to save his son from the suffering to which he was subjected he leans over backwards and tries to gratify all the son's wishes. Yet, in spite of his father's generosity, the son becomes involved in the oedipal rivalry with him as a result of his strong attachment to his mother. As a result, an intensive conflict develops between hostile rivalrous feelings toward the father and his feeling of love, admiration, and gratitude. This is an impasse which is difficult to solve even for a fully mature person. The child often succumbs to this emotional impasse and chooses one of many possible neurotic solutions. One of these is to provoke the father into hostile behavior by irritating and tantalizing him. Should he succeed in provoking the father to express anger and hostility, he will be relieved of his guilt feelings. Then he can feel hostile without intense conflict. With an overindulgent father such victories, however, are extremely rare, and he will have to repress not only every aggressive impulse but every other form of self-assertion. Such a patient will attempt to repeat the same behavior toward the analyst. He will develop toward him a hostile competitive attitude which will take some specific form depending upon the actual life situation. He will envy the analyst's success and will resent the analyst's position of authority. At the same time, he will feel the same guilt toward the analyst who tries to help him. If the analyst's attitude is sufficiently neutral, the patient will attribute to him the role of the father. As the treatment progresses and the defenses are weakened, the patient's hostility will be mobilized. The problem of countertransference must be considered at this point.

The analyst remains a person in his own right. The blank screen is an abstraction which does not correspond exactly to reality. The analyst has his own emotional reactions toward the patient whether he expresses them overtly or not, and it is not easy to conceal them without special effort. These emotional reactions are determined by his own past history. He may react to the patient's rivalry and provocation with some resentment. Another analyst might be unaffected by this and will react more as the patient's own father did, with indulgence and sympathy. Then the patient will face the same situation he faced in his childhood. Since his hostility does not elicit any reprisals from the analyst, his own guilt feelings will mount and require further repression of every aggression. He may continue for a while with his attempts to elicit some sign of rejection on the analyst's part. After a while the situation may become intolerable, and he must either leave the analyst and find a less sympathetic one or repeat his own neurotic adjustment to the indulgent father figure—inhibition and turning his hostility against himself in the form of depression. It is obvious that the more the analyst's unconscious countertransference attitude (which in a well-trained analyst will never find drastic expression,) resembles that of the patient's father, the less chance there is that the patient will feel the need to correct his own pattern. He will utilize his own neurotic pattern, which in this case is nothing but an adaptation to parental overindulgence.

Since analysts have become interested in the elusive phenomenon of countertransference, it has become a particular issue in the training of analytic therapists in the so-called supervised analyses. In observing the student's attitude toward the patient many teachers have discovered that quite often the analytic process becomes stymied on account of the inexperienced student's lack of ability to control his spontaneous countertransference attitudes. If the countertransference attitude happens to be the same as the original parental attitude, the patient will have no difficulty in repeating his original father-son conflict in the transference situation, but it will become extremely difficult for him to modify it.

Let us return to our example. Let us assume now that the analyst does not react with such indulgence to the patient's provocations. He may even unwittingly express some kind of resentment and rejection of the patient. This is a novel situation for the patient, whose old pattern does not fit. He finally succeeds in provoking the father image and therefore his own guilt for his hostility will decrease. Now he can express his hostility toward the analyst. The defense mechanism has broken down. In certain patients such an expression of hostility might be a necessary, although *only transitory*, step toward achieving a final resolution of this type of conflict.

In a difficult treatment of a neurotic young man of this type, an inadvertent expression of my resentment against the patient's provocative attitude had an unexpected therapeutic result (8). The patient was a young university student who was unable to apply himself to his studies. He idled about, spent a great part of the day in bed, masturbated excessively, read cheap detective stories, and was unable to form any meaningful social relations. He had no attachments to women, frequented poolrooms, and felt quite miserable about his purposeless way of living. His "laziness" was the symptom of a latent compulsion neurosis. During his first consultation he justified his idleness by stating that his father never loved him and never gave him anything of value; therefore, his father should support him. In his first analytic session he reported a dream: *I wanted to sell my diamond ring but the jeweler after testing the stone declared it was false.* He immediately remarked that the dream was silly because he knew that his ring was genuine. In the course of further associations it transpired that the ring was a present from his father. The dream expressed transparently the patient's defensive formula that he had never received anything of value from his father; hence, the motive for proving in his dream that his father's gift was spurious. His whole neurotic structure was founded on the belief that he owed nothing to his father.

External circumstances forced him to move from the city and he was transferred to another analyst who died after a short period. He continued with a third analyst, and a few months later asked me for an interview. He complained that as his analyst disliked him, continuation of the treatment was impossible. The analyst was always polite and kindly, but he felt that this was all calculated play-acting. In reality, he said, the therapist hated him. I talked with his analyst, who, to my surprise, substantiated the patient's story: he felt a strong aversion to the patient which he had tried his best to conceal. He urged me, and I agreed, to continue the treatment. I soon understood my predecessor's prejudice. The patient did everything to make himself disagreeable. He usually arrived unwashed, unshaven, and unkempt, bit his nails, spoke in a scarcely intelligible mumble, and criticized everything. If I kept him waiting a minute he immediately accused me of doing so because he paid less than others. He was so unpleasant in every possible way that it was difficult to tolerate him. One day I spoke to him somewhat impatiently. He jumped up from the couch and exclaimed, "You are just like your colleague. Do you deny that you dislike me and do you call it analysis being impatient with your patient?" I realized that I had better admit my dislike to him. He was extremely perturbed by this admission. I explained that his behavior was unconsciously calculated and succeeded in making him disliked. He wanted to prove that just as his father supposedly disliked him, the analyst also rejected him; this allowed him to feel hostile and continue his old neurotic pattern of life. I reminded him of the dream about the diamond ring. This session became a dramatic turning point of this analysis, which before had begun to appear as a stalemate. He became well groomed, and tried to be as pleasant as possible. He started to apply himself to his studies and to organize his daily activities.

This patient had an indulgent father for whom his son was the apple of his eye. He supported him freely without reproach, although during his schooling the boy did not apply himself to his studies. This paternal indulgence created intolerable feelings of guilt in the boy who as a defense tried, but not successfully, to persuade himself his father really disliked him.

In the dramatic interview in which he discovered my dislike for him, it suddenly became clear to him that the situation with his father could not be repeated, that it was a unique relationship, and that no one but his indulgent father would love him despite all his provocations. He realized that to be loved he must make himself worthy of love; furthermore, the guilt feelings resulting from his father's goodness diminished with the analyst's open admission of his dislike. At the end of his analysis this patient was very appreciative, presenting the analyst with a photograph of his new self. Years later he called on me. He had become successful and was happily married. Every experienced analyst has had similar experiences. The case is noteworthy because of the dynamics of the patient's remarkable improvement which was induced not by the usual understanding objective attitude of the analyst but by an involuntary display of his irritation.

The analyst's reaction was not calculated to be different from that of the patient's father. He simply lost, for a moment, the type of control which we consider so important in psychoanalytic therapy. I do not want to imply that in general this control is not necessary. My point is that the knowledge of the early interpersonal attitudes which contributed to a patient's neurosis can help the analyst to assume intentionally a kind of attitude which is conducive to provoking the kind of emotional experience in the patient which is suited to undo the pathogenic effect of the original parental attitude. Such intensive revelatory emotional experiences give us the clue for those puzzling therapeutic results which are obtained in a considerably shorter time than is usual in psychoanalysis.

The important question facing us is whether it is possible, in many cases, to manage the transference in such a way as to precipitate such intensive revelatory experiences. One thing is obvious: the corrective emotional experience is possible only after the intrapsychic conflict has been reconverted into an interpersonal relationship in the transference and the introjected parental influences are projected upon the analyst— in other words, when the original neurosis has been transformed into a transference neurosis. This often requires a prolonged meticulous period of treatment. This aim is most difficult to achieve in severe compulsion neurotics, in whom the original child-parent relationship is completely incorporated into the personality in a complex intrapsychic conflict between the different structural parts of the personality. This keeps the intensity of the transference on a relatively low level and the whole therapeutic procedure tends to become overintellectualized. In such cases, patient, prolonged preliminary work is often required before the intrapsychic neurotic system is disrupted and transformed into a neurotic interpersonal relationship.

The proposition made here is that the analyst should attempt to replace his spontaneous countertransference reactions with attitudes which are consciously planned and adopted according to the dynamic exigencies of the therapeutic situation. This requires the analyst's awareness of his spontaneous countertransference reactions, his ability to control them and substitute for them responses which are conducive to correcting the pathogenic emotional influences in the patient's past. Occasionally, as in the case of the student, the spontaneous countertransference reaction of the analyst is accidentally the desirable attitude, but this is a rare exception.[3] As a rule spontaneous countertransference reactions of the analyst resemble parental attitudes. The analyst, like the parents, is apt to react with positive feelings to the patient's flattery, with helpful attitude and sympathy to the patient's suffering, and with resentment to the patient's provocative behavior, as the parents did. Even if he does not give overt expression to his countertransference, the patient may sense it. Since the phenomenon of countertransference has been recognized, we know that a completely objective attitude on the part of the analyst exists only in theory no matter how painstakingly he may try to live up to this requirement. The main point is, however, that within the framework of the

---

[3] In one of Tower's reported cases (see page 83) the analyst's emotional involvement was also by chance beneficial for the therapeutic process.

objective atmosphere of the psychoanalytic situation, there is sufficient opportunity for replacing the spontaneous countertransference reactions with well-defined and designed attitudes which facilitate the patient's own emotional reorientation. In this connection, it should be considered that the objective detachment of the psychoanalyst is itself an adopted, studied attitude and not a spontaneous reaction to the patient. It is not difficult then for the analyst to create a definite emotional climate such as consistent permissiveness or a strong hand, greater or lesser sympathy to certain complaints, etc., as the patient's dynamic situation requires.

The intuitive analyst will often act just in the described manner. Our aim is, however, to replace or at least support intuition with conscious understanding. No matter how one feels about the use of planned therapeutic attitudes, one thing seems to be noncontroversial: namely, that the spontaneous countertransference attitude might be helpful in one case, but unfavorable in another. There is no doubt that the analyst's awareness of his actually existing spontaneous emotional reactions to the patient and a conscious control of them means a distinct and important advancement in the field of psychoanalytic therapy. It is too early to predict how much not only a conscious control but utilization of spontaneous countertransference attitudes or their replacement by planfully adopted emotional climates of treatment will increase the effectiveness of psychoanalytic therapy. One must remember, in this respect, that when Freud originally discovered the phenomenon of transference, he considered it to be a particular complication of the therapeutic process which in those days he conceived primarily as an intellectual process of self-understanding. We know today that the transference which was once regarded as an impurity has become the axis of therapy. It is not impossible that the new impurity of which we are becoming increasingly aware—the analyst's response to the transference situation—may become in the future an equally important dynamic instrument of psychoanalysis.[4] One thing is certain, namely that the lack of the analyst's insight into his own countertransference involvement may result in therapeutic failure.

I could have recognized this principle while still a student treating my first private patient. He was referred to me by Karl Abraham after I had handled a few control patients in the Berlin Institute (9). He was the son of a wealthy merchant who indulged his son financially and emotionally. He worked in his father's business, but he detested his father and was scarcely on speaking terms with him. He was severely inhibited, depressed and withdrawn to a prepsychotic degree. At the beginning of the treatment we agreed on a modest fee according to his own income, with the understanding that he would pay more after his salary was increased. It was the beginning of the inflation in Germany. A few weeks after the treatment began, the value of the German mark decreased to a fraction of its previous value. I neglected to adjust the fee to this radical change. One day he reported a dream. He went into a bakery and walked out with some bread without paying for it. His association led to the interpretation of his guilt feelings over having his analysis for practically nothing. The patient did not express rejection or acceptance of this interpretation. I still deferred changing his fee. In the next interview he declared that he could not continue the treatment with me because I reminded him too much of his father. He said he was particularly disturbed because my hair looked exactly like his father's. A torrent of loathing for his father and me followed. I dutifully interpreted his feelings both toward me and toward his father. The spoiled son could not tolerate his father's permissive and indulgent attitude because it increased his feelings of guilt toward his father, a guilt

---

[4] A similar statement was made by Balint and Tarachow in speaking of a new phase in the development of psychoanalytic technique which will give full recognition to countertransference as the analyst's contribution (16).

which was derived from an underlying vicious competitiveness. It is needless to say that giving this interpretation was like pouring water on a duck's back. The emotional tension was too far advanced to be corrected by words alone. He asked for the name of another analyst. Instinctively I thought of one experienced man who was known for being able to act quite tough and intransigent if necessary. Two days later the patient called me on the phone and said that I had sent him to a robber. The analyst had asked more than ten times my fee. I explained to the patient that this doctor was an older, more experienced man who originally would have charged him two or three times more than I, and I added that there was, as he knew, inflation which cut the value of money in half almost weekly. About a year later I met the patient on the street. He gleefully told me that he had been relieved of most of his complaints.

It is not difficult to figure out that the transference conflict had become too intensive not because my hair resembled that of his father—this was but a displacement—but because I was as indulgent as his father. He was my first private patient and I must have had a countertransference to him similar to his father's. He solved the conflict with me in the same way: he withdrew. Obviously my more experienced successor avoided such an impasse by preventing the transference conflict from reaching an intensity beyond the Freudian postulate, according to which the transference conflict is supposed to repeat the original conflict but on a less intensive and less realistic level. He avoided this unwanted intensity of the transference involvement by being intransigent and distant, quite the opposite of the doting father. My handling of the fee situation was a realistic indulgence which with some experience and better understanding of the countertransference could have been easily avoided.

A too intensive transference involvement is, however, only one of the factors retarding therapy. As mentioned before, with compulsive characters we often encounter the opposite problem: a too detached intellectual climate. This is the case so long as the intrapsychic conflict is not yet transformed into the original interpersonal conflict between child and parents or siblings. In most neuroses, at the beginning of the treatment we are not yet dealing with the original interpersonal conflict situation of childhood. In the course of the patient's development, the parental images have been incorporated and the original interpersonal conflicts have been transformed into intrapsychic conflicts. During the analysis, due to the permissive atmosphere, the analyst gradually takes over the role of the internal images. The permissive analyst becomes more acceptable than the harsh superego. In certain types of neurosis, particularly in compulsives, this process is extremely slow and frequently does not take place to a sufficient degree. The analysis becomes an impersonal, intellectual game which the patient ritualistically includes in his neurotic system. The external features of the treatment become endowed with magic significance, and the interpersonal component remains at an extremely low temperature. In such cases one can scarcely count on the spontaneous development of a workable transference neurosis, and the problem is how to induce the patient to exchange his intrapsychic conflicts with a more realistic conflict in the transference. As long as this aim is not achieved, daily contact with the patient is indicated.

The compulsive neurotic has obviously succeeded in replacing his previous interpersonal conflicts with a tight intrapsychic system which makes him independent of and impervious to the external world. The early interpersonal relations must have been completely beyond the ego's capacity to tolerate; hence the need for protecting the ego by an elaborate intrapsychic neurotic structure which often turns out to be an impenetrable fortress. At the beginning of the treatment, in such cases, we are usually very much in the dark, unable to reconstruct the early pathogenic influences. Utmost neutrality of a benign sort is the only way to avoid the repetition by the analyst of anything resembling the original parental influences. Later, however, during the course of the treatment after a workable transference neurosis has developed, the creation of an atmosphere which is in contrast to the original pathogenic one may give great impetus to the treatment.

To sum up the essence of these considerations: once the transference relationship is well established, certain countertransference reactions develop in the analyst as a response to the patient's transference. He must recognize and control these reactions. Occasionally his spontaneous countertransference reactions may by chance be helpful. In other cases—all depending on the patient's history and the analyst's own personality—he will have to replace the spontaneous responses by creating a type of interpersonal climate suitable for inducing a readjustment on the part of the patient.

The rationale of all this becomes evident when one remembers that all neurotic symptoms are attempts at adaptation to an early family situation. They arise from the awkward, unsuccessful attempts of the child to deal with a difficult situation. From this perspective we can well understand the corrective effect of the transference experience. We asked before what is the psychodynamics of the change within the personality which occurs as a result of the transference experience. Our answer is that the neurotic solution was an attempt at adaptation to parental behavior; in the transference repetition the parental response is replaced by the analyst's basically objective attitude and by *a different interpersonal climate*, which must be correctly chosen by the analyst to replace his own spontaneous reactions. Thus, the patient's old neurotic reactions become pointless, unsuited to the new situation, and *a new type of response has to be found by the ego*.

Here the objection can be raised that the objective and understanding attitude of the therapist alone is sufficient to produce such a corrective emotional experience. No doubt the most important therapeutic factor in psychoanalysis is the objective and yet helpful attitude of the therapist, something which does not exist in any other relationship. Parents, friends, relatives, may be helpful but they are always emotionally involved. Their attitude may be sympathetic but it is never objective and never primarily understanding. To experience such a novel human relationship has in itself a tremendous therapeutic significance which cannot be overrated. The old reaction patterns do not fit into this new human relationship. No doubt, therefore, the objective, understanding attitude of the analyst is in itself a most powerful therapeutic factor. This attitude, combined with correct interpretation of material which is about to emerge from repression, together with the analysis of the ego's defenses, is primarily responsible for the therapeutic effectiveness of psychoanalysis. Its effectiveness is impressive enough to make one overlook those aspects of therapy which require further evaluation.

The fact that countertransference is an unavoidable part of the therapeutic situation, just as is transference, has stimulated a great deal of ingenious thinking and led to better understanding of the therapeutic process. It is remarkable, however, how few practical conclusions have been drawn from this deepened knowledge.

It has been recognized by practically all writers on this subject that the countertransference reactions, and particularly his personality as a whole, are not obliterated by the analyst's own analysis. He can only better understand and therefore better control them.

It has also been recognized that the nature of the countertransference reactions may give valuable clues to the understanding of the patient's countertransference reaction. It has been further recognized that because every analyst remains a distinct personality in spite of his own analysis, he will retain certain reaction patterns which are typical for him and which in a significant way will enter into the therapeutic process.

The only generally accepted suggestion regarding countertransference, so far as the technique of treatment is concerned, is the admonition that the therapist should understand his countertransference reactions and learn how to control them. Originally Freud and later Glover, Balint, Fliess, Mable Cohen, Frieda Fromm-Reichmann, and others emphasized the importance of the analyst's self-awareness (60, 16, 35, 22, 53). Little makes the suggestion that the analyst occasionally admit to the patient, and discuss with him, his inappropriate reactions which result from countertransference (75). Paula Heimann questions the advisability of such a technique (64). The above-discussed example in which I reacted to a patient with impatience, then admitted it and explained it as a response to the patient's unconsciously intended provocation —which was a typical pattern of his—illustrates this procedure. In this special case it turned out to be beneficial to the treatment but I would not advocate this as a general technical principle.

When certain authors implicitly state that certain personalities are more suitable than others for treating certain types of patients, they recognize that the characteristic reaction patterns of the analyst not only may retard but favor the therapeutic process. If the therapist understands his own personality reactions and can control them, he can also consciously and planfully replace them with attitudes which are favorable in promoting what is the essence of the whole therapeutic process—the corrective emotional experience.[5] And all this is possible while retaining a basic objectivity and a helpful inter-

---

[5] This suggestion is at variance with Tower's thesis that a countertransference neurosis of the analyst is unavoidable and must be analyzed by the analyst and resolved as it occurs during treatment. It appears to me, that such a self-analysis during treatment is a somewhat belated correction of his own neuroticism. This is the function of his personal preparatory analysis, which even though it cannot protect him from having countertransference attitudes should at least prevent the development of a countertransference neurosis.

est. If we declare that this last step cannot be achieved, or that it is some kind of artificial manipulation of the therapeutic situation, it follows that the range of a psychoanalyst's effectiveness must be restricted to those patients whose problems fit his own personality and particularly his own residual neurosis.

The crucial question is what is meant by the term "control of the countertransference manifestations." It obviously means not expressing them, behaving or reacting differently from how the analyst would act if he did not know and understand his countertransference attitude. This, however, is a negative prescription. Does it mean that he should try to become completely impersonal? At the beginning of the treatment this is indicated. If, however, we agree that the personality of the analyst might be an asset rather than a detriment, we contradict ourselves in stating that the impersonal attitude is always necessarily the best in the interest of the therapeutic process. If he is as impersonal as possible in the opening phase, the analyst will interfere least with the development of the transference neurosis. Later, however, when he knows more about the patient's past history, he may well create a distinct and suitable interpersonal atmosphere. It could be argued that the personality of the analyst is something given, it is perceived by the patient, and no "play-acting" will cover it up convincingly. This is partially correct but does not exclude the possibility of assuming attitudes prescribed by the nature of the patient's conflict situation. Conscious modification of the interpersonal climate is a much less radical proposition than any role playing. This is not the same as Ferenczi's suggestion that the analyst assume the role of a significant person of the patient's past. The therapist may change the interpersonal climate of the therapeutic situation just as a teacher can handle a student in a manner best designed for his pedagogic objectives. The same is possible not for pedagogic but for therapeutic purposes, more specifically for making the corrective experience and the resulting insight more effective. The interpersonal climate in the treatment situation, particularly if it is in sharp contrast to the original interpersonal relation in which the neurotic pattern was formed, becomes a challenge for the patient's ego to find a new adjustment appropriate to the new situation.

Chapter V

TWO FORMS OF REGRESSION AND THEIR THERAPEUTIC IMPLICATIONS

ORIGINALLY Freud described regression as a trend to return from a later-acquired, more advanced form of ego and instinct organization to a more primitive phase. As a rule this occurs when the ego is confronted with a conflict situation it cannot master. It seeks its security by returning to a phase of its development which was formerly successful. In other words, it returns to a preconflictual state. These once-successful adaptive patterns Freud called fixation points. Since the ego's adjustment is never complete, these older fixation points retain some cathexis. Freud illustrated this concept with the simile of an advancing army in enemy territory leaving troops at strategic points to which it may return if it is pushed back by an overwhelming enemy force (49). According to this view there is a reciprocal relationship between fixation and regression. The greater the cathexis of a fixation point the more likely will be the regression to it if later conflicts arise. Regression serves the gratification of needs which remain unsatisfied in a new conflictful situation which the ego has not yet mastered.

Considerably later Freud described another type of regression and fixation: fixation to an unresolved traumatic conflict. The best-known examples are traumatic dreams in which the person conjures up, often in detail, a traumatic event. The recognition of this phenomenon—fixation on an unresolved trauma—was crucial for his theoretical constructions after 1921. These observations necessitated the recognition of a principle which does not follow the pleasure-pain formula. The revival of these unsettled traumatic situations does not serve any gratification. They are painful, and cannot be explained on the assumption that the organism is always motivated in the direction of avoiding the unpleasant tensions caused by the pressure of unsatisfied instinctual needs, which it tries to eliminate by seeking gratification in itself pleasurable. Freud offered an explanation for this type of phenomenon. The ego's fundamental task is to maintain a stable equilibrium within the mental apparatus. It attempts to fulfill a task which it could not achieve under traumatic conditions. Again and again the ego returns to the traumatic event in order to accomplish a subsequent mastery. The precise definition of trauma is precisely a situation in which the ego is overwhelmed by stimuli which it cannot reduce to an optimal level; since the ego is overwhelmed, it fails in its basic function. The compulsive return to such unsettled traumatic experiences of the past is another kind of regression. It is fundamentally different from the regression previously described, which accomplishes just the opposite, namely a return to a previously successful form of adaptation. In the latter type of regression the mental apparatus is seeking gratification according to an old pattern; in the former one it attempts mastery of an unresolved tension. It seeks a solution for something which has not been solved in the past.

In using the concept of regression, it is important to emphasize that we never deal with a simple photographic repetition of a former pattern. Later experiences modify the regressive behavior. These leave, like the earlier experiences (fixation points), an indelible mark upon the personality. Regression to a fixation point therefore is a complex phenomenon, not a simple return to an abandoned developmental phase.

Fenichel has pointed out that the concept of repetition compulsion should be revised in the light of these new formulations (29). He showed that the term repetition compulsion refers to quite different phenomena. He describes three of these: first, repetition compulsion, which is based on periodicity of instinct; second, repetitions due to the tendency of the repressed to find an outlet; and finally, repetitions of traumatic events for the purpose of achieving a belated mastery. The theoretical significance of this principle of mastery, in addition to the pleasure-pain principle, is sufficiently well known and I shall not discuss it further. Its application for the understanding of the therapeutic process, however, has not been investigated. I shall deal in the following pages with some of these technical consequences. They are in no sense new but to my knowledge have not yet been systematically dealt with in the psychoanalytic literature.

The transference manifestations of the patient are the best-known examples of the repetition compulsion. In the psychoanalytic situation the patient emotionally re-enacts relationships toward persons who played important roles in his past. The question immediately arises: to which category of repetition do transference manifestations belong? Do they represent a trend to return to old ego and libido positions which have been successful in the past, or do they belong to the later-discovered category of regression? Are they attempts at belated mastery? It is obvious that the evaluation as to which category they belong to should have consequences significant for therapy. Careful scrutiny of transference manifestations reveals that both types of transference reactions occur with probably the same frequency. The simplest example for the first kind, in which the patient returns to an old satisfactory gratifying fixation point, is the development of a positive dependent type of transference in which the patient attributes to the analyst the role of the good mother image. Most often this type of transference assumes the con-

notation of an oral dependent relationship. While this type
of regression is motivated by the urge to return to an old
type of gratification, it can never be realized without conflict. First of all, these regressive trends contradict the standards of the adult ego. The well-known overcompensatory defenses against, or disguises of, oral dependent gratifications
reveal the conflict between more mature standards and pregenital attitudes. This same conflict arose originally in early
childhood, when the growing child was driven out from his
pregenital positions both by the inexorable law of biological
maturation and also by the pressures exerted by the parents.
Accordingly regression to a pregenital phase during treatment
may contain both components. It may represent a return to
an old satisfactory position of instinct gratification. At the
same time, however, it may also contain an element of struggle for subsequent mastery over an unresolved conflict, which
arose as a result of maturation. Only this second component
makes this type of regression an ally of our therapeutic aims;
the regressive evasion of an unresolved conflict must be evaluated as resistance. We may formulate this insight by saying
that inasmuch as the patient regresses to a pregenital position
he is resisting the solution of another later conflict, as a rule
the Oedipus conflict; nevertheless, as a result of regressing,
he again has to face unsettled earlier conflicts of the past and
is given an opportunity during the treatment to master such
conflicts. Persistent oral dependent transferences may occur
also in persons with real emotional and sometimes nutritional
starvation in childhood.

In order to evaluate to what degree a regressive transference manifestation is evasion of a conflict and to what degree
it is an attempt of subsequent mastery, Freud's original concept of fixation appears to be helpful. As stated, he considered the relationship of regression to fixation to be determined by the amount of original cathexis retained by fixation
points. If this cathexis is relatively great, the patient most

probably has to resolve the unsettled pregenital conflict before he can progress in his treatment. If, however, the regressive return to the pregenital position is mainly an evasion of another transference problem, namely the oedipal one, it must be evaluated as the manifestation of resistance.

As a rule both components are present, the regressive evasions of a phallic or genital conflict by returning to a preconflictual phase as well as the attempt at mastery of unresolved pregenital conflicts. An estimation of the balance between these two components is often difficult or even impossible. This dilemma has long been known. It usually takes the form of this argument: Is the oral conflict the real therapeutic issue or is it the Oedipus situation? Does the patient hide his anxieties centering around the oedipal relationship with his emphasis on the oral conflict or are we dealing here with a so-called pseudo-oedipal conflict, the main issue being the still unresolved pregenital situation? It is evident that no generalizations can be made. In some cases the first, in others the second formulation is the correct one. It is equally obvious that the correct evaluation of these alternatives is of great help to the therapist in dealing with this type of material. Since we are dealing here with a continuum, extending from cases where the oedipal involvement is the central pathogenic issue to cases in which the pregenital fixations are paramount, the extreme examples on both sides of the distribution curve are most suitable to illustrate this theoretical issue in a concrete fashion.

In the treatment of a thirty-eight-year-old university teacher, who was suffering from a neurotic working inhibition, the analysis started out with aggressive and competitive material. The patient expressed his doubts about the scientific nature of psychoanalysis in general and contrasted it with the greater exactness of his own field. The undertone of his behavior was polite skepticism, which he expressed with a somewhat condescending attitude. His first dreams were of phallic nature. For example, *in an airplane flight he took over the pilot's role from the official pilot in whom he lost confidence and thus succeeded in avoiding a crash.* At the same time he began to talk about a rather recent extramarital sexual affair. He appeared punctually at the interviews and followed the instructions of the basic rules with great conscientiousness. The discrepancy between an underlying dependent gratification and the aggressive content of his material was conspicuous enough to evaluate this competitive material as a defense against the strong passive involvement. I pointed out to him that in spite of his skepticism he seemed to put great faith in the treatment, otherwise he would not co-operate so conscientiously. This remark obviously called his bluff and he left the interview with manifest embarrassment. In the next interview I called his attention to the fact that the previous day upon leaving he avoided shaking my hand, a habit I retained from my continental background. I raised the question as to whether this should not be interpreted as a retreat from personal involvement. This obviously sufficed to provoke an intensive resistance. Within a short period of interviews the whole coloring of the transference changed. The patient assumed a somewhat boyish pupil-like attitude and at the same time his dreams assumed an oral connotation. The flying dreams which occurred on almost every day of the first week gave place to pregenital material. Animals began to appear in the dreams, soft woolly animals like a llama or a shaggy dog, with which he personified an early pre-genital attitude. He regressed from a passive homosexual position to an oral receptive one which was more acceptable. There was, to be sure, a conflict about his oral demands, which had been frustrated in the past by a cold, rejecting mother. The reactive hostility to oral frustration was expressed in the form of pregenital soiling. *In a dream he represented himself as a teen-ager urinating on a wall.* In other dreams he expressed openly anal soiling trends. This type of transference of pregenital coloring lasted for over two years. Occasionally faint attempts were made to return to oedipal material, only to withdraw as fast as after the first week of the treatment.

His life history gave us the clue to this course of the analysis. He turned from a cold and somewhat rejecting mother toward his father, and in his preadolescent, and most of his adolescent, period had a close relationship with his father whom he admired and who expressed a great deal of interest in the patient, the oldest of three brothers. It was only around his fifteenth or sixteenth year that this positive relationship changed to a highly critical and rebellious attitude which was not expressed openly but manifested itself in the patient's following his own interests and putting up a passive resistance against his father's aspirations for him. This adolescent attitude was the revival of his earlier oedipal rivalry and hostility against the father, for which, however, he became completely amnestic.

The therapeutic problem obviously consisted in having the patient face the first appearance of his oedipal involvement. It could be justly questioned, however, whether or not the pregenital material which was revived in the analysis had an equal pathogenic significance. It is well known that the outcome of the Oedipus conflict depends at least partially upon the previous developments in the pregenital phases. It is difficult to make watertight divisions or to distinguish sharply between cases in which ill-resolved, pregenital conflicts are responsible for the unsuccessful outcome of the oedipal phase, and cases in which unfavorable experiences at the height of the Oedipus complex are of primary importance. Theoretically every developmental phase has an influence upon the later ones. Continuing this argument consistently, however, we should not stop at the pregenital phase. Obviously this phase is determined by constitution and possibly also by the specific events occurring during the intrauterine period. The instinct and ego developments are determined by a large number of variables and constitute continua. We have good reason to believe that in some patients the genetic factors are all-important and, no matter how favorable later developments may be, the constitutional vulnerability will always assert itself. Similarly, in other cases, unfortunate experiences during the pregenital development may be outstanding and predetermine in an almost irreversible way the outcome of the oedipal period. In a third category of patients, again, the nature of the oedipal period which is highly dependent upon parental attitudes and the whole family constellation may constitute the first serious block in development.

My first recognition of this crucial problem I can trace back to an early phase of my analytic experience. I discussed with Freud a patient whom he had referred to me. Freud interrupted my presentation by saying, "You must ask yourself when was the first time the patient rejected or was incapable of accepting a situation." [1] Once such a genetic reconstruction is made, we are in a better position to evaluate the therapeutic significance of the shifting phases in the patient's transference manifestations. If we consider this first "no" as representing the conflict situation which the patient could not successfully resolve, we can speak of *"regressions to the preconflictual phase."* These are defensive evasions of a pathogenic conflict. Here again I am hastening to qualify this statement and deprive it of its attractive simplicity. As a rule, we do not deal with one pathogenic conflict but with a series of conflicts the pathogenic nature of which is of necessity influenced by what happened in the patient's development earlier. In the majority of those cases in which the oedipal constellation is of central significance, its pregenital precursors are also important. Accordingly the analysis of pregenital material is not wasted time. On the other hand, it is obvious that if the defensive nature of pregenital regres-

[1] Quoted from memory.

sion is not recognized, the therapist may lose sight of the total picture and may expect therapeutic results before the later oedipal involvements are clarified. In other words, chronology is not always equivalent to depth from the point of view of pathogenesis.

In viewing the psychoanalytic literature from this angle one might be tempted to make the generalization that, of late, pregenital material has become popular, in contrast with earlier days when the significance of the Oedipus complex was emphasized. I hear and read repeatedly the statement that in recent decades the nature of neurosis has changed, under cultural influences: hysterias with their phallic and genital origin have become less frequent and we see, today, more organ neuroses in which the pregenital factors are outstanding. I have even heard the argument that neuroses behave like bacteria; as bacteria become adapted to antibiotics and produce strains which are no longer susceptible to them, so psychoneuroses adapt themselves to our efforts to eradicate them and withdraw from the well-advertised oedipal conflict to the depths of pregenital history. I am somewhat skeptical about this analogy. Cultural influences may very well influence the statistical distribution of different types of neuroses. This, however, does not alter the fact that in each individual case we are confronted with the task of reconstructing the pathogenetically significant experiences. In doing so, we find that so-called deep regression toward pregenital material is not always the sign of penetrating into the depths so far as pathogenesis is concerned. The emergence of such early material is as often as not the manifestation of the regressive attempt of the ego to avoid dealing with a later pathogenic conflict. In my experience the most common central conflict today, as formerly, is the Oedipus conflict. It is a barrier which, if not successfully negotiated, is apt to throw the child back to pregenital positions which otherwise would not retain their pathogenic influence to the same degree. There is no doubt about the pathogenic significance of earlier child-mother relations; they are particularly outstanding in the field in which I am most interested, the theory and treatment of organ neuroses. Perhaps my preoccupation with this type of case makes me lean over backwards and warns me to be cautious in generalization. This warning has turned out to be well justified in the study of peptic-ulcer cases. In these, frustration of oral tendencies has been constantly found to be a central issue. Sustained and frustrated oral receptive and oral regressive tendencies have a stimulating effect upon stomach secretion. In the psychoanalytic study of such cases, however, it becomes increasingly clear that the oral regression is not always due to a particularly strong oral fixation, although this may be so in a number of cases; often it is the result of regression from an unresolved oedipal conflict. So far as the organic symptom itself is concerned, the oral regression is of specific importance. The oral regression itself, however, is often induced by the oedipal barrier. In male patients I have repeatedly observed that as the analysis progresses the patients become involved more and more in transference conflict representing the oedipal phase. The oral regression serves as a defense substituting oral dependent tendencies for passive homosexual wishes. These in turn are reactions to originally competitive, hostile tendencies. On the other hand, it is true that the oedipal rivalry in orally fixated patients is a mixture of phallic competitiveness and oral envy.

We arrive then at the conclusion that we cannot expect a simple either-or answer concerning the significance of pregenital and genital conflicts. There is a complex interrelationship between them. When the analysis attacks the pregenital position, this may drive the patient to deal with his phallic oedipal problems, only to retreat back again when the battle becomes hot in the pregenital battle arena. This should not prevent us, however, from trying to form a quantitative estimate of the balance of pregenital and oedipal cathexes. In

dealing with regressive material, the most important consideration, however, is to establish whether it represents evasion
or a problem-solving return to an unsolved conflict. This
consideration applies to all phases of development and is
independent of the more specific question as to whether a
patient's neurotic problems originate in pregenital experiences or in those centering around the Oedipus complex.

A correct estimate of this balance of powers proves of
great help in conducting the treatment. In the case mentioned
above, for example, it was two years before the analysis led
us back to the crucial oedipal phase, from which the patient
retreated after the first week. Only after this had been
worked through could the treatment be terminated. The
relative ease with which the pregenital material appeared in
the second week of the analysis and the consistency with
which the patient substituted pregenital precursors of oedipal
involvements could perhaps have made me aware earlier of
the defensive nature of this pregenital material. For a long
time it has been known that the patient senses the analyst's
interest and exploits it for resistance. The material in which
the analyst shows interest and which he emphasizes in his
genetic interpretations may be employed by the patient as
a defensive weapon, such material serving as a bait. In case
discussions one often hears such statements as: "You mistake
this material for oedipal involvement; it is only a pseudo-
Oedipus complex hiding the real pathogenic material." An
argument we hear less frequently is that one overrates as
pathogenic the pregenital material which is really only a regressive evasion from the Oedipus conflict. Both arguments
may be correct in different cases. When Rank proposed his
theory of birth trauma, it was soon recognized that intrauterine dreams were as a rule regressive distortions of incestuous wishes. The same—although to a much lesser degree—
may be true for some pregenital material.

The following excerpt from the treatment of a business

executive may serve as a concrete illustration of these theoretical considerations.

The patient, a thirty-eight-year-old executive, head of a
business corporation, consulted me on account of his generally depressed state of mind, lack of interest in his job, difficulty in getting up in the morning and making the train, and
a growing irritability toward his children, his oldest daughter
in particular. His speech was retarded, his facial expression
a mixture of sadness and anxiousness. His blood pressure was
markedly elevated. He began his present job about a year and
a half before when he moved from the East to Chicago. In
the East he held a similar job with a smaller organization. The
present job gave him greater income, more prestige, and at
the same time was somewhat easier so far as the requirements
on his time were concerned. The patient had, at the time, five
children. The youngest daughter was born shortly after
they moved to Chicago. His relationship with his wife he
described as very satisfactory. He characterized his wife as
a very understanding and mature person.

During the very first interview the patient became tearful
twice, then irritable. He became tearful first when he expressed how much he loved his youngest daughter and what
a wonderful child she was. A second time he wept when he
mentioned that his youngest sister had given up a well-paid
job to become a missionary and had departed a few weeks
before for the Belgian Congo. On both occasions his voice
shook and he could scarcely finish the sentences. The third
topic about which he became disturbed was when he mentioned a seventy-year-old man, a member of the company for
over twenty years, who caused the patient a great deal of
trouble. He described this man as one who was not too competent yet made decisions without consulting the patient and
got credit for accomplishments to which the patient was entitled. He complained about the fact that he was helpless
about this man because the man was an old retainer of the

company. Although the patient was the administrative head of the company, this man had a greater influence with the board and was the real power behind the scene. In speaking about him, the patient was not sad, but irritated, even angry.

I called his attention to these three topics which had upset him. In response he reiterated how cute his daughter was, how annoying the seventy-year-old man was, and how helpless he was in the face of this situation. As for the sister, he explained his feelings about her by saying, "How pathetic it is that she is giving up a good job to take up such a hazardous assignment as that of a missionary." He added that his father was a minister, likewise his grandfather and his great-grandfather. He continued to talk about his own family background. There were seven children in the family, two older sisters, an older brother, and three younger sisters. The patient's mother died when he was six years old. He spoke of his father in terms of the highest regard and emphasized how selfless a person he was. The spirit of the family was harmonious. All the sisters and brothers liked one another and there was no dissension between them. The patient's older brother was a successful businessman; one sister became a welfare worker and was killed in the line of duty; the other sisters were married and had children.

The patient was puzzled himself as to why he became so upset about the youngest sister's becoming a missionary. He couldn't understand it and again asked me to explain to him how a person could give up a well-paying job for such a hazardous undertaking.

In the second interview the patient said that he felt very depressed and spoke mostly about the annoyances at the office. He mentioned that his term as the president of a national organization had just expired. In the interview he confessed that since his depression started, he consistently drank in the evening until he went into a torpor and finally fell asleep. When he drank he felt quiet and relaxed.

I shall not go into detail concerning the rest of the material although I have detailed notes about every interview. To illustrate the proposed theoretical considerations, I need only characterize the patient's shifting material and transference manifestations in the course of the treatment.

Soon it became evident to both of us what made him so upset about the sister's becoming a missionary. He described his intense ambition, the pride he derived from this position, how important it was for him to obtain credit for his work. He contrasted this with the altruism of his sister, who unlike him gave up material goods, a fine salary, and exposed herself to the dangers of life as a missionary in a backward, primitive colony. The sister followed the father's principles, for whom to do good was the sole purpose of life, a purpose for which he neglected everything else. He accepted a parish in a poor rural district where he felt he could do more good than in a large city. In fact the patient felt that the father neglected the welfare of the family, at least in material respects, and devoted himself to humanity. More and more bitterness came to the fore about the material deprivations the patient had suffered because of his father's overly humanitarian attitude, and gradually he expressed more and more indignation about the fact that he had had to go to school in mended clothes, and about other similar deprivations. The seven children constituted a heavy economic burden and yet the family lived in complete harmony. The prevailing attitude of the family was neighborliness and consideration for others. It was clear that the patient's wish to become a successful businessman must have been determined—partially, at least—as a reaction against economic want, as well as against the father's ideals. As soon as he left home, he spent all his energy in promoting his career and he became increasingly successful in improving his economic status. He had never relaxed, never felt any conflict about working hard, until very recently, after he was promoted to his Chicago job.

Right after this his youngest daughter was born. Obviously he belonged to the type of patient who reacts with depression to success. The problem was to explain the unconscious basis of this paradoxical reaction.

In the early part of the treatment he revealed intensive unconscious guilt feelings which were mobilized by the simultaneous occurrence of three events. (1) His competitive, hostile feelings and unconscious death wishes toward the seventy-year-old man who interfered with his ambitions revived deeply repressed oedipal rivalry with his father and death wishes directed toward him. (2) His sister's altruistic act brought into sharp relief his own self-centered ambition and impressed upon him how blatantly he betrayed the principles which his father had inculcated in the whole family, a hierarchy of values in which economic advantage is subordinated to doing good to others. (3) The birth of his youngest daughter meant added family responsibilities and at the same time deprived him of his wife's attention. As mentioned before, one of his initial complaints was a growing irritability toward his children. This conflict manifested itself in his urge to spend more time with the family and less in his office. He decorated the children's room himself and began to neglect his business obligations. The unconscious guilt connected with his business activities, in which the conflict with the senior man was central, showed itself to be another important factor which made him withdraw from business. All this, however, was only half of the picture. The other factor was the regressive return to a pregenital position.

In the first days of his treatment he was, on and off, irritable with the therapist and showed various signs of recalcitrance and hostility. In the fifth interview, however, he reported that an entirely new inclination had developed in him in the past few days. He started to reminisce in a sentimental way about the past. Before, he was always looking forward energetically and never thought of his past life. Now he was thinking about the happy days of his early adolescence spent on an uncle's farm. He remembered with tears in his eyes the creek in the pasture. Then after a pause he added, "Mother was born on this farm." This started a train of thought about his mother's death. He could not remember his mother at all, who died of an acute disease when the patient was six years old. He only remembered her death. He knew that he had cried all night after her death and that afterwards for half a year he did not go back to school. Although he could not remember how he felt about his mother and her death, he accepted my suggestion as plausible that he must have been very much disturbed about it because he had to discontinue school right after her going. The lack of emotion and of any memory about his mother was in striking contrast with his sentimental feelings about the farm. Obviously he repressed all feelings concerning his mother and his bereavement and substituted the nostalgic feelings about the farm. In this way he protected himself against the unbearable feeling of losing his mother.

A period followed in which pregenital material appeared with increasing clarity. At the same time the transference assumed an outspoken dependent connotation. *He dreamed he lost the key to his office, which prevented him from entering it. In another dream he lost his coat and again in another dream he forgot the number of his room. In another dream he saw himself teaching his little son to play the drum.* Music was always one of his greatest relaxations. *Then he dreamed he was in a hotel in Atlantic City at a convention but had to take care of his little daughter who was with him.* Actually he had spent a few days in this hotel at the convention in great luxury, all expenses paid. He immediately understood, himself, that the dream expressed a self-indulgent trend. He got vicarious gratification from taking care of his daughter, with whom he obviously identified himself. During this period he began to stay away more and more from his office and played with the children, participating in their games as if he were a child himself. He felt more relaxed and after a few weeks actually resigned from his job. I reminded him of his agreement not to make irreversible decisions during the treatment. He excused himself by pointing out that he would have been fired anyhow because he was neglecting his duties and there was an inquiry pending which had been initiated by his enemy, the old man. He decided not to look for another job for at least half a year. He was assured of his salary for this period. His depression left, he felt relaxed and content; his blood pressure, which was seriously elevated when he started his treatment, went back to normal.

This material, particularly the self-castrative dreams of losing his key and his coat, indicated that the patient retreated from his competitive ambitions to a pregenital position. He played the role of a mother toward his children, vicariously enjoying their role. At the same time he re-erected in himself the lost object by identification with the mother. Regressive dreams continued to appear. *In one he was climbing down from a high office building.* He interpreted it as the expression of his urge to give up his business career and his ambition for a high position. *In another dream he was driving in a communist country. Someone tried to impress upon him how well off the country was. They all had a sumptuous dinner. The patient was skeptical and thought he should warn his staff that they were closely watched.* In this dream, he expressed his discomfort that I was watching his regressive evasion. He was disturbed by my constant interpretation showing that he was evading facing his problem, particularly his future and the conflict which introduced his illness, the conflict with the old man. Whenever this topic came up he refused to recognize his own rivalrous tendencies and tried to explain the conflict as his reaction to the old man's nefarious strategy.

A second dream of the same night when he dreamed of

the communist country clearly expresses his concern about his economic future. *In this dream he came out of a restaurant; before giving him back his hat and coat the hat-check girl gave him a manicure and a massage which cost him only three dollars.* In his associations he tried to reassure himself that he could safely take a half year's vacation without getting into financial trouble. Without my help he recognized the self-indulgent, passive trend expressed in this dream in which he gave me the role of the girl who took care of him. The three dollars was a fraction of the fee he paid me. A passive homosexual trend can be assumed as a further factor producing this dream.

About ten days after this dream the patient discontinued his treatment with the excuse that soon the analyst would leave for summer vacation anyhow, and he felt well, was no longer depressed, his blood pressure was down, and he had stopped drinking. In the fall he would look for a job and then would return to his treatment. The fall came but the patient did not return. He phoned that he would not start work before January 1st and that he was continuing to feel relaxed and contented. By January 1st I had left Chicago and my follow-up note says that the patient phoned again saying that he had several good job offers, felt well, and would start working soon. He thought that he would not need any treatment immediately and would wait for my return. My impression is that even if I had stayed in Chicago, he would not have returned at this time for further treatment.

The treatment came to an end before the patient became conscious of the central pathogenic conflict, centering around his death wishes directed against the father substitute. As mentioned before, in the transference his negative feelings appeared at the very beginning of the treatment and gradually yielded to a dependent positive attitude which lasted until the interruption.

The question arises as to how to evaluate the relation of

the two outstanding dynamic factors which were operative in this case: the withdrawal from the father conflict and the fixation to a dependent oral position. A definite solution of this question is not possible because of the incompleteness of the analysis. The fact that I have extensive notes about every session, allowing a careful re-examination of the material, can hardly make up for this incompleteness. The patient interrupted his treatment in the phase of pregenital withdrawal from both the positive and negative aspects of his father conflict and before we had an opportunity to attack this central conflict. There are strong indications that the pregenital regression did not represent a return to an unsettled pregenital conflict but was a regressive evasion from oedipal involvement. The patient's depression, which was the first he had ever had, began shortly after the tension between him and the senior member of the corporation had developed. It is true the material indicates that the patient had a strong oral attachment to his mother. He reacted to his mother's death with a severe disturbance which kept him from school for half a year. He succeeded in repressing his reactions to his bereavement by becoming amnestic to the whole happy period of his first six years in order to save himself from frustration. This early period before his mother's death constituted a fixation point to which he regressed when in his business career he had to face the unresolved father conflict precipitated by his unconscious death wishes toward the senior man. This was not a regression to an unresolved conflict as we see in traumatic neuroses but a regression to a once successful and gratifying period of adjustment. In addition to the conflict with the senior man, this regressive retreat was favored by increased responsibilities, as well as by deprivation of his dependent needs after the birth of his fifth child. An additional depriving factor was his moving into a new environment. These increased responsibilities and his guilt about his destructive ambitions *pushed him back* toward the dependent pregenital attitude; at the same time he was *pulled back* by his fixation to the oral dependent gratification which had been successful in the first six years of his life.

It is not possible to evaluate precisely the relative weight of the pull-back exerted by the oral fixation point and the push-back resulting from oedipal guilt feelings. The fact that until his recent breakdown he had consistently, vigorously, and successfully pursued a steadily rising business career would incline me to believe that the unresolved Oedipus conflict should be considered as the primary pathogenic factor in this case. If this assumption is correct, we may predict that his improvement will be only of a temporary nature and he will relapse as soon as he becomes involved in some other competitive struggle with a father image in his new job. Moreover, it would also follow that should he resume treatment, the primary therapeutic goal will be the resolution of the father conflict and not of an unsettled early pregenital involvement. This does not mean that this patient did not retain a great amount of cathexis on the oral level. It can be assumed, however, that this pregenital regression would never have been activated if he had not encountered the oedipal barrier when his ambitions were thwarted by the senior member of the company.[2]

Only further treatment could decide with certainty whether or not this evaluation of his conflict pattern is valid. I submit this case not because I can answer this question with certainty but because I wish to illustrate in the next chapter the technical consequences of differentiating between two types of regression during treatment: one to an unresolved conflict for the sake of its subsequent mastery, and one which represents a return to a once satisfactory phase of development.

[2] Since this was written, in a later interview the patient reported that he had a new job. In his new work situation he has to deal again with a senior member of the firm, but this time he handles this situation satisfactorily.

Moreover I want to call attention to the fact that chronological depth is not always equivalent to pathogenetic depth, and to show the fallacy of attempting to find one general formula valid for all cases.

Chapter VI

TECHNICAL PROBLEMS
CONCERNING THE REGRESSIVE
EVASION OF PATHOGENIC
CONFLICTS

THE DISTINCTION between two types of regression (see Chapter V) raises the technical question as to ways and means by which the patient can be induced to face those conflicts from which he retreats into a phase relatively free of conflict. It has been pointed out that the analyst's interest as well as his interpretations may be exploited by the patient in the service of resistance. The patient continues to furnish pre-conflictual material and deludes himself as well as his therapist that he is cooperating in an effort to achieve the therapeutic goal. The principle of laissez faire which is an important element in the technique of free association may become here a double-edged sword. One accepted rule is to follow the trend chosen by the patient and not to interfere. It is to be expected that this natural course will follow the line of least resistance: the anxiety which is aroused by approaching a major conflict drives the patient away from this material and, as demonstrated in the previous section, it often drives him back regressively toward preconflictual, still happy, periods of adjustment. Since evasive regression is in the service of resistance, the technical problem arises: How can one counter-act such regressive evasion and bring the patient back to the conflict which he evades?

There is no disagreement that our first recourse is correct interpretation of the total dynamic situation. Correct inter-pretation in such a case consists of making the patient aware of this regression as a form of resistance by interpreting the regressive preconflictual material primarily as an evasion and not as something of primary pathogenic significance. With such interpretations the analyst may force the patient back to the conflict which he regressively evaded. As has been demonstrated in the previous section, the original trans-ference situation is often a repetition of the central patho-genic conflict. If it does not clearly repeat the central con-flict, it repeats a close derivative of the conflict. The two cases reported in the previous chapter represent a frequent pattern. The analysis began in both cases with the central pathogenic conflict, or at least with a close derivative of it, which is reflected in the initial transference situation. This may be covered up with superficial defenses. A familiar ex-ample is the peptic-ulcer patient who in the first interview assumes a superior attitude, emphasizing that he does not really need any help, that he came on the advice of his friends and is quite skeptical that this type of treatment can benefit him. His attitude is: "Well, what can I do for you, Doctor?" It seldom takes more than a few interviews, some-times only one, for the patient to reveal the underlying de-pendent tendency which hurts his pride and which he there-fore hides under a casual detached attitude.[1] It has been pointed out that this oral regressive trend is of central signif-icance so far as the patient's organic symptoms are con-cerned. Yet, the denial of this attitude indicates the aggres-sive, competitive component which is derived from the Oedipus constellation. This conflict will have to be dealt with

[1] See Chapter V.

before the patient can give up his oral dependent needs. During the later course of the treatment the analyst should never lose sight of the fact that the oral regression has two dynamic components: one, the attractive force of the fixation point and two, the repelling force of anxiety derived from the oedipal conflict which initiated the return to the fixation point.

Since two such dynamic nodal points are present in all cases, it would be erroneous to draw the conclusion that the regressive material is of no therapeutic significance. It has been emphasized before that in such regressions to previous fixation points both factors are active, the struggle for subsequent mastery and the evasion of a later conflict. In other words, the "limiting case," in which the patient returns to a still conflict-free fixation point, is seldom seen; maybe it never exists, in reality. The patient regresses to a *relatively conflict-free phase,* choosing the lesser evil. He returns from a more intensive, more anxiety-laden conflict to a relatively lesser conflict. This regression gives an opportunity to deal with earlier unresolved conflicts. To disregard such preconflictual regressions in our interpretative work would be equivalent to trying to solve later conflicts without cleaning out those earlier phases of development which contributed to these later difficulties. My point is not to disregard these earlier conflicts but to evaluate correctly the degree of defensive regression as compared with the struggle for subsequent mastery. It is important that the therapist never lose sight of those later conflicts which initiated the regression. Eventually they have to be solved and their solution can be considered to be the final goal of every treatment.

This leads us to the consideration of the actual life situation which introduced the onset of the neurosis. There was, and I believe still is, an inclination to underestimate the significance of the actual conflict situation.

In our joint publication, *Psychoanalytic Therapy,* both

French and I stressed the significance of giving continued attention to the actual life situation which initiated the patient's neurosis. I expressed this by saying:

It is important to keep in mind that the patient will finally have to solve his problems in actual life, in his relationships to his wife and his children, his superiors and his competitors, his friends and his enemies. The experiences in the transference relationship are only preparations, a training for the real battle (14).

French in a similar sense states:

The more we keep our attention focused upon the patient's immediate problem in life, the more clearly do we come to realize that the patient's neurosis is an unsuccessful attempt to solve a problem in the present by means of behavior patterns that failed to solve it in the past. We are interested in the past as the source of these stereotyped behavior patterns, but our primary interest is in helping the patient find a solution for his present problems by correcting these unsuccessful patterns, helping him take account of the differences between present and past, and giving him repeated opportunity for actual efforts at readjustment within the transference situation (14).

Rado also emphasized that understanding of the past is subordinated to the goal of facing the actual life situation:

To overcome repressions and thus be able to recall the past is one thing; to learn from it and be able to act on the new knowledge is another. . . . The patient must learn to view life, himself, and others in terms of opportunities and responsibilities, successes and failures. He must learn to understand his doings in terms of motivation and control, to evaluate his doings in terms of the cultural context, and to understand his development in terms of his background and life history (82).

While these views are fundamentally correct, they require a qualification which I have omitted in my previous publication.

The pathogenic significance of the actual life situation varies following a distribution curve in which one extreme end is represented by cases who would develop a neurosis almost in any novel situation on account of a chronic, never-resolved, latent neurotic potentiality. On the other extreme end of the distribution curve lie those cases who had a relatively well-adjusted early history and who broke down with a neurotic disturbance under the influence of extremely traumatic life conditions (52). In the first group of cases, the past, in a sense, is still alive in the present and the old conflicts are of primary significance. In this group the schizophrenic represents the most extreme example. In the second type of case, the regression is initiated by the traumatic effect of the actual life situation which the patient evades by regressing. It is obvious that the therapeutic task is different in these two extremes. In the first type of case very early conflicts have never been settled and the analyst's task consists in utilizing the regression in the transference for their resolution. In the second type of case, which offers the best therapeutic chances, the main issue is to induce the patient to face the actual conflict. The attraction of the fixation points is only effective because of the intensive anxiety aroused by the traumatic onset situation. It is, of course, not arbitrary to what phase the patient will regress. Obviously in these cases, too, the regression will take place either to the relatively strongest fixation point or to those old unresolved conflicts which resemble the onset trauma. In other words, the pathogenic nature of the onset trauma never depends solely upon its objective nature. Even a particularly difficult traumatic event may be more upsetting to one person than to another according to their previous history. Everyone is sensitized through his past experiences to certain conflict situations occurring in adult life. We come again to the conclusion that no generalizations can be made and even in the two extreme groups the same general principles apply: in both types of cases one has to deal with the regressive push-back of the later traumatic situation as well as with the attractive pull-back of the fixation points. The correct evaluation of the relative significance of these two factors, however, can serve as a guide in our interpretative work.

In the first of the cases discussed in the previous chapter, two years were spent in dealing with pregenital material before the patient returned to his oedipal involvement. Could this period have been shortened if the therapist had recognized the primarily evasive nature of this material? Since an experiment with the same patient is no longer possible, no definite answer can be given. Just because such experiments are not possible, it is necessary to vary our technique experimentally in cases which show a similar structure.

One can divide the course of analyses, roughly, into three phases: the opening phase, the middle period, and the terminal phase. It is perhaps no accident that a similar pattern obtains in chess. Both analytic treatment and chess are procedures of strategy in which two minds oppose each other. In chess each party tries to win the game. In analysis the two opposing forces are: the analyst and the patient's conscious ego cooperating in the effort to resolve a neurotic pattern, opposed by the total effect of those forces which we call resistance. Our technical problem may then be stated: Can the most prolonged part of the treatment, the tedious middle game, be shortened by improved strategy? The function of interpretation is to evaluate correctly the two components in every regression, the one which is in the service of the therapeutic effort, namely the struggle for subsequent mastery, the other, which is regressive evasion.

In addition to, and not as a substitute for, interpretation a technical device has been suggested as a result of our therapeutic experimentation in the Chicago Institute for Psychoanalysis: the reduction of the frequency of interviews and tentative interruptions of the treatment. This technical device aims to control one of the significant variables, the intensity of the dependent component of transference involvement.

The patient's regression manifests itself in two ways: (1) in the content of his associative material (genital, phallic, or pregenital) and (2) in the nature of the transference. By its very nature the transference is a regressive phenomenon, no matter whether it represents primarily a struggle for subsequent mastery of traumatic conflicts or regressive evasion. As the treatment progresses the latter component increasingly prevails. This explains why many patients who come to the analyst in a disturbed state gradually achieve an emotional equilibrium; this is due to the increasing prevalence of the dependent gratifications which the transference affords.[1]

This dependent component of the transference often becomes the greatest obstacle to the treatment. According to the law of diminishing returns, as the treatment progresses, the gain obtained from the revival of earlier conflicts becomes less while the gratification and security which the patient obtains from his regression become greater. This is the phase in which reduction of frequency of contact with the analyst may serve as a powerful device to push the therapy forward toward its goal.

I. FREQUENCY OF INTERVIEWS

We arrive at an important quantitative problem of the technique: the handling of the ever-present dependent component of the transference relationship. I believe this is the least understood problem of analytic therapy and constitutes the weakest link in our standard approach. In one of his papers Freud recognized this technical problem in a terse statement: "This transference . . . to give it its shortened name . . . soon replaces in the patient's mind the desire to be cured" (53). In his early writings on technique he dealt extensively with this central problem of psychoanalysis— how to overcome the patient's resistance to the resolution of the transference. This resistance, of course, is not surprising

[1] See also Franz Alexander, "The Quantitative Aspects of Technique" (9).

since the transference neurosis is the substitute for the original neurosis, and the same dynamic factor which makes the patient hold on to his neurotic gratifications is operative in his resistance against renouncing a new edition of his neurotic gratifications in the transference.

To this traditional explanation another consideration must be added. In the transference situation the intrapsychic conflict is translated back again into the original interpersonal relation between the child and his parents and/or siblings. Through this transformation the component of gratification increases. At the same time the component of suffering inherent in the original neurosis markedly decreases. After the resistance against the emotions in relation to the analyst has been analyzed and the emotions are understood and justified as a necessary, unavoidable aspect of the therapy, the transference neurosis frequently loses much of its painful connotation. For the patient it becomes a legitimate phase of the treatment which will lead eventually to his recovery in the distant future. The patient's shame because of his dependence, and guilt because of his hostile feelings, which are now understood in the light of past experiences, diminish. The original neurosis was a combination of conflictful gratifications and suffering; the transference neurosis retains both these features, but in the course of the treatment the conflictful elements diminish and the gratifications increase. Soon a stationary equilibrium sets in. Many patients come to the analyst when they are at the end of their rope, when their subjective state has become well-nigh intolerable. After the transference neurosis has replaced the original one, they may go on in a fairly comfortable subjective state for years, provided they can see their analyst regularly. This is the explanation of Freud's early observation that in his earlier practice he had difficulty persuading his patients to continue their treatment and later he had difficulty in inducing them to give it up.

A scrutiny of the nature of transference gratifications

reveals that they consist primarily in the satisfaction of the patient's dependent needs. In repeating past experiences, the transference is always regressive. The trend of regression is to return to a libido and ego position which predates the unresolved or poorly resolved conflicts. Such regressive evasion of a conflict goes back to the last still relatively satisfactory phase in development; it is in the direction of increased dependency. We saw in the previous chapter that this original formulation is valid, but we must remember that there is also a universal tendency to regress to unresolved conflicts.

Previously a brief reference was made to the pathogenesis of peptic ulcers. In the treatment of such cases, as soon as the patient's guilt reactions and narcissistic sensitivity against his oral dependent needs are relieved, he develops a comfortable, dependent transference relationship and experiences rapid symptomatic relief. In the first interviews this type of patient often patronizes the analyst, declares that he does not need any help—in fact, he offers his help to the analyst. Soon, sometimes after a few interviews, his false pride diminishes and he becomes what George Wilson appropriately called a "couch diver." As soon as he can accept a help-seeking relation by justifying it to himself as a necessary part of the treatment, he can freely indulge his dependent needs. The deeper analysis of such cases—I refer to male patients—shows, however, that the oral regression is primarily a retreat from oedipal rivalry. At first these patients overcompensate their rivalry with a passive homosexual attitude toward the father, and then they attempt to evade this threatening solution of the original conflict by substituting oral receptiveness toward the mother for passive homosexuality, as a less dangerous and narcissistically less injurious solution. This shows my point clearly—that the pathogenic material is not always the earliest material chronologically. In these cases it is more difficult to mobilize oedipal than oral material, because it is more repressed. This does not mean that in peptic ulcers oral fixation and oral conflicts are not important genetically; it shows only that the coincidence of oral conflicts with an unresolved Oedipus complex is decisive. In other words, not one set of factors, but the coincidence of two sets of factors is required to explain this disease. In such cases the oedipal material will be mobilized only if one succeeds in thwarting the relatively comfortable oral regression, that is to say the dependent transference, and thus drive the patient against the oedipal barrier which he evades by regressive evasion in returning to oral dependence. By no means is this always an easy task. I have found it most advantageous to use the technique of thwarting the dependent gratification by reducing the frequency of contact. Interpretation of the transference situation, of course, is imperative, but the effect of interpretation is greatly enhanced if at the same time the dependent gratifications of the transference are actually curtailed. In other words, facts are stronger than words alone.

This technique is in principle nothing more than the application of the abstinence rule in the extended sense of Ferenczi. Freud's original abstinence rule is based on one of the fundamental principles of mental functioning. Only such needs become conscious as cannot be satisfied by reflex or automatic performances. The function of the conscious ego is to take care of the gratification of needs which require reality testing and integrative, cognitive performances. A person fed automatically every half hour would never become conscious of hunger. If one prevents the automatic gratification of unconscious tendencies, one forces them to become conscious.[2] This is the rationale of Freud's abstinence rule and Ferenczi's technique of preventing the automatic gratification of unconscious impulses. These measures may be as simple as forbidding a patient to scratch the wall beside the couch. This

[2] See previous discussion, Chapter I.

forces hostile impulses against the analyst to be consciously expressed in words instead of being discharged without the patient's awareness, by automatic activities of the fingers.

Reduction of frequency of interviews is one of the most powerful means of bringing dependent needs vividly into consciousness. Well-timed reduction of the frequency of interviews is, of course, not restricted to the treatment of peptic ulcers. I select this example only because of my extensive experience with such cases.

The powerful influence of changing frequency of interviews upon making the patient aware of his dependency needs is well illustrated by Edith Weigert. She states (94):

A change of frequency sometimes brings frustration and infantile conflicts into focus, which the patient covered by petulance or pacified with daily interviews. A patient of this kind told me after a reduction of hours: "For the first time I have understood my dependency needs on you not with my head, but with my heart." Simultaneously a dream brought a lost memory of a terrifying desertion experience in the third year of her childhood, a tonsillectomy in which the parents failed her. The anxiety was re-lived in full force.

The regressive evasion of an unresolved conflict by assuming an earlier dependent attitude is one of the most common occurrences in psychoanalytic treatment. This regressive defense is ubiquitous and is the most powerful and intractable form of resistance. I have come to the conviction that the extreme prolongation of some treatments is due primarily to the fact that this regressive evasion is often misinterpreted as a sign of penetration into depth, instead of as a retreat from unresolved conflicts. I believe that our research interest in the pregenital material which emerges during this phase of the analysis is at least partially responsible for many therapeutic impasses in the so-called interminable cases. The analyst's interest in this scientifically so significant early material only encourages the patient in his regressive evasion. I am afraid that we analysts must reserve our scientific curiosity to explore this early phase of life primarily for the treatment of schizophrenias, perversions, and other disturbances in which the pathogenesis actually lies in these early pre-oedipal periods. With our advancing knowledge of the specific etiology of different cases, the thesis that the aims of therapy and research run parallel is no longer fully tenable. The time has come when our technique must be adjusted to the therapeutic exigencies of each type of patient. The reduction of frequency is indicated whenever we have to drive the patient out of regressive evasion of his crucial pathogenic conflicts. Since such a regressive evasion is a universal phenomenon, this technique has application in most cases.

2. PLANNED INTERRUPTIONS OF TREATMENT

Prolonged psychoanalytic treatment, often extended over several years, is of necessity interrupted from time to time for shorter or longer durations. The therapist's vacations are taken for granted and are traditionally respected because of the limits of human endurance. Intervening sicknesses both of the patient and therapist also necessitate unplanned interruptions. The effects of such interruptions are varied and to my knowledge have never been subjected to systematic study.

It is often stated that uninterrupted treatment is necessary to assure continuity in the appearance of unconscious material. Some patients, however, even after an interruption of several weeks' duration, take up the therapeutic process just at the point where the treatment was interrupted. An extreme example is a patient suffering from a severe compulsion neurosis, who began his first interview after two months' interruption with a sentence which started, "And then I told him . . ." This referred to an episode which he did not finish in the last interview before the interruption.

Many patients react to the interruption with material which shows clearly that they felt deprived during the vacation. They may express resentment and sometimes have a vivid insight into how dependent they have become on the analytical procedure and upon the analyst himself. Others report changes in daily behavior and in relationships to other significant persons in their lives. These changes in a number of cases can be evaluated as definite improvement. The scrutiny of the patient's material shows that this improvement is based, as a rule, on what might be called an increased self-confidence. It is as if the patient discovered that he no longer needs the analyst to the same degree as he thought and that he can function satisfactorily without the analyst's aid. In such cases an interruption may activate the patient's desire to finish treatment. Of course in a large number of cases this desire may be nothing but a manifestation of resistance. It is not always easy to evaluate the total change in the emotional equilibrium which such an interruption has produced. Certainly in prolonged treatment the analytical experience becomes an essential part of the total mental equilibrium of the patient. In some cases, in which the patient's condition improves as a result of the treatment, this improvement is conditional, dependent upon the gratification of regressive dependent needs which the transference situation affords. As soon as this gratification is withdrawn the patient may regress and react with his previous symptoms or neurotic behavior patterns. It is obvious that the interruptions must be correctly timed. In general this problem can be compared with the simpler one of a person who is learning how to swim. After he is taught the correct movements he tries them out, while attached to a rope which the swimming teacher holds. Following a period of practice, the rope is no longer necessary except for increasing the patient's confidence. This is the time when the rope can be dispensed with. Continuation of its use would only prolong the learning period.

In the complex field of psychoanalytic therapy it is more difficult to determine the optimal point of the withdrawal of the emotional support which the dependent component of the transference affords. Moreover, the therapeutic process represents a continuous learning process in which different aspects of the problem of integration are taken up in a sequence. I do not know of any generally reliable criteria either for the termination of the treatment as a whole or for correct timing of temporary interruptions. All the indications we have lack quantifiable data. The improvement of the patient's behavior, as has been stated before, might be conditional upon the fact that the patient is still in treatment. Increased insight, removal of memory gaps, change in transference manifestations are all useful indications and yet they do not permit a precise prediction as to how the patient will react either to an interruption or to a termination of the treatment. The patient's own inclination to terminate or interrupt the treatment is not a reliable sign. It may as often as not be a sign of resistance, as if the patient would say, "So far so good; I am satisfied with what has been achieved and there is no need to stir up further problems." The complexity of the whole psychoanalytic procedure and our inability to estimate precisely the quantities of the emotional involvements make it well-nigh unavoidable to use the technique of experimental interruptions. This gives us an opportunity to study the patient's reaction to interruption and to decide whether the patient exploits the interruption for resistance or whether the interruption increases the patient's confidence in making use of the achieved results of his treatment without the emotional prop of further interviews. The traditional way of dealing with this problem was the tapering off procedure at the end of the treatment. While this may suffice in many cases, I have found experimental interruptions of great value. When the patient returns to his treatment after an interruption, his material often gives us a definite clue as to what has been accomplished and what problems remain unsolved.

It appears to me that temporary interruptions give us a

solution for one of the most tantalizing technical problems of psychoanalytic treatment, namely, the problem of termination. Ferenczi and Rank in their brochure, which has been discussed earlier, recommend an enforced termination which should be imposed when the analyst feels satisfied that the recapitulation of the significant pathogenic conflicts in the transference has been accomplished (34). Freud in his paper on "Analysis Terminable and Interminable" deals with this problem extensively (50).

The technique of experimental interruptions seems to offer the most satisfactory solution of this problem. Because of our inability to account quantitatively for all the factors involved, interruptions, the duration of which is tentatively agreed upon by both therapist and patient, offer an opportunity to evaluate the patient's readiness for the termination of the treatment. The greatest advantage of such temporary interruptions is that the patient's material after interruption brings to the fore in a concentrated fashion both the nature of the patient's resistance and the conflicts still unresolved. At the same time the patient becomes more conscious of his dependent needs, which have been frustrated during the interruption, and, if the interruption was correctly timed, he will be more willing to renounce further dependence upon his therapist.

Chapter VII

SOME CONTROVERSIAL ISSUES

SOME OF the technical suggestions proposed in *Psychoanalytic Therapy* (14) occasioned more or less heated arguments. In spite of the fact that these polemics were often based on misinterpretations and contained many reiterations of preconceived notions, the book achieved a great deal of the authors' hope

"that our book is only a beginning, that it will encourage a free, experimental spirit which will make use of all that detailed knowledge which has been accumulated in the last fifty years in this vital branch of science, the study of the human personality, to develop modes of psychotherapy ever more saving of time and effort and ever more closely adapted to the great variety of human needs."

It brought dynamic psychotherapy into the focus of interest. We must admit that the misunderstandings and misinterpretations which this book occasioned were not solely the fault of the critics. It was not sufficiently emphasized in this publication that no revolutionary changes were proposed either in basic theory or in practice. This was taken for granted and, therefore, not explicitly underlined. In fact no fundamentally new technique was proposed; what was advocated was simply the flexible application of the known therapeutic factors. Some critics, however, looked for basic deviations from the theory of psychoanalytic treatment and found them even if they were not present in the text. The main purpose of the book was to try to make explicit certain technical devices which are being used by many, if not all, analysts in their daily practice, devices which were seldom discussed explicitly and were often not recognized by those who used them. In other words, it was an attempt to show that the actual conduct of analysis is different from the theoretical model which is found in the textbooks.

The issues which aroused most controversy may be listed as follows:

1. Technically indicated changes in the frequency of interviews.
2. Some technical measures to enhance the effectiveness of that particular type of emotional experience which is the central feature of the psychoanalytic process. For this I used the term corrective emotional experience. The term is new, but the phenomenon was long recognized implicitly as an integral part of psychoanalysis. This concept was misunderstood by some authors; however, it was not challenged by most of them.
3. Finally, a great deal of heated argument arose in connection with the question whether psychoanalysis and dynamic or uncovering types of therapies should be considered as two extremes of a continuum in which the same therapeutic factors are used in different quantities, or as two radically different procedures.

1. The changing of the frequency of interviews for technical and not merely practical reasons has been used ever since I have been a psychoanalyst (by now thirty-three years), but its rationale and the effects upon the course of treatment have never been systematically studied.

The technical device of changing the frequency of interviews has been criticized by some because it is not an "analytical" device but a "manipulation" and therefore psychotherapeutic in nature. This is the argument of Rangell, who comparing psychoanalysis with psychotherapy states:

As an example of the contrasting formulae in the two therapies, one can consider the patient who is "becoming too dependent" upon the therapist. Alexander "does something", e.g., cuts the frequency in order to show the patient that he is wrong, that he need not be dependent, in order to educate him to something different (85).

The reduction of frequency, however, as has been repeatedly explained, is not an educational measure but serves the purpose of making conscious the patient's dependent feelings by thwarting them—a principle which has been used first by Freud in his abstinence rule and later by Ferenczi in counteracting symbolic acting out in order to create frustration which favors insight. It is the application of the general principle of not allowing unconscious tendencies to be satisfied automatically or inadvertently because only if they are frustrated is there a need of becoming aware of them. This becomes particularly important in dealing with the dependent component of the transference when the patient utilizes regression toward a dependent pregenital attitude as an evasion of later pathogenic conflicts.

Gill, of course, is right when he stresses the regressive nature of the transference and states that this emotional regression is an indispensable and most powerful therapeutic factor. What he ignored, however, was the difference between two kinds of regression—regression to an unsettled conflict as distinct from the regression from a later conflict by returning to a preconflictual, or less conflictual, phase of development.[1]

2. The other controversial issue concerns technical suggestions to deepen the corrective effect of the patient's transference experience. The Chicago Institute's publication reemphasized the therapeutic significance of the transference experience as the prerequisite of effective insight, particularly that the interpretations of the analyst have an effect because the patient at the same time experiences the difference between the analyst-patient and his own parent-child or child-sibling relationship. Experiencing this difference was called "corrective emotional experience" and an attempt was made to describe and define it in concrete terms.

I agree with E. Bibring's (19) appraisal of my position when he states:

[1] See Chapters V and VI.

There seems to develop a general trend to shift the emphasis from insight through interpretation toward "experiential" manipulation, that is, learning from experience seems to become the supreme agent rather than insight through interpretation. One could add the minor tendency to consider the therapist as a catalyst and to leave to the patient most of the "working through" and "working out" of his problems. Some therapists go even farther by relying heavily on the patient's unconscious understanding.

I would merely add that these two factors—conscious insight and emotional experience—are not mutually exclusive, a view which Bibring seems to share. I do not follow him, however, in his statement that

In psychoanalysis proper, all therapeutic principles are employed to a varying degree, in a technical, as well as in a curative sense, but they form a hierarchical structure in that insight through interpretation is the principal agent and all others are—theoretically and practically—subordinate to it.

Since the discovery of the transference as the dynamic axis of treatment, this hierarchy of the therapeutic factors is no longer tenable. Insight imparted to the patient by interpretation if it is not accompanied by emotionally experiencing what is interpreted has no great therapeutic value. Such interpretations give only what Fenichel called "dynamically ineffective knowledge" (28).[2] In Chapter III I tried to show that most technical controversies of the past have been centered around this very question.

This controversy is, however, older than psychoanalysis. It is the same issue which divided Plato and Aristotle, Plato believing that the rules of good life can be deduced and learned by reason alone just as are the laws of geometry and Aristotle maintaining that they must be learned by practicing them.

No reader of the case reports published in *Psychoanalytic Therapy* can justly maintain that the significance and role of interpretations were overlooked, or minimized by the authors.

[2] Translated by the author: *dynamisch unwirksames Wissen.*

That insight has an incomparably greater effect when the interpreted material is at the same time experienced, certainly is not a revolutionary or even novel statement. Our aim was to establish more explicitly what is meant by saying that the patient is "experiencing" that which is interpreted. We were particularly concerned with the quantitative aspects of the therapeutic process: the ways and means by which optimal— or less pretentiously stated—a workable intensity of the emotional experience can be achieved. In his latest technical publication Freud's own interest centered on these quantitative aspects of the treatment. This may justify the Chicago authors' claim that—whether successfully or not—they tried to develop further the basic theoretical concept of psychoanalytic treatment in varied practical applications.

The great concern of some critics of *Psychoanalytic Therapy* that the suggested quantitative variations of some of the therapeutically significant variables such as changing of frequency of interviews or planned alteration of interpersonal climate means the abandoning and replacing by manipulations the fundamentals of psychoanalysis (imparting insight by interpretation) is only understandable if one realizes that these critics overlooked that the sole aim of these measures is to deepen the emotional experience and simultaneous insight. By reduction of frequency the dependent needs are activated and forced into consciousness.[3] By lending the interpersonal climate a quality which brings into sharp relief the irrationality of the transference reactions its corrective effect is enhanced. One may question the effectiveness of such measures but there is no reason to consider them as contradictory to the basic principle of psychoanalysis, namely, to impart insight based on emotional experience.

The concept of corrective emotional experience has not been understood by a number of critics. Eissler (25), for example, had no reason to ask:

[3] See example quoted by Weigert, Chapter VI.

Alexander introduces a term which it is difficult to determine whether it is just a new name for a well known fact or whether it describes a new therapeutic principle.

In describing the nature of the corrective emotional experience I clearly stated that:

It is important to realize that the mastery of an unresolved conflict in this relationship becomes possible, not only because the transference conflict is less intense than the original one, but also because the analyst assumes an attitude different from that which the parent had assumed toward the child in the original conflict situation.

. . . . . the analyst's objective, understanding attitude allows the patient to deal differently with his emotional reactions and thus to make a new settlement of the old problem. The old pattern was an attempt at adaptation on the part of the child to parental behavior. When one link (the parental response) in this interpersonal relationship is changed through the medium of the therapist, the patient's reaction becomes pointless.

In the formulation of the dynamics of treatment, the usual tendency is to stress the repetition of the old conflict in the transference relationship and to emphasize the similarity of the old conflict situation to the transference situation. The therapeutic significance of the *differences* between the original conflict situation and the present therapeutic situation is often overlooked. And in just this difference lies the secret of the therapeutic value of the analytic procedure. Because the therapist's attitude is different from that of the authoritative person of the past, he gives the patient an opportunity to face again and again, under more favorable circumstances, those emotional situations which were formerly unbearable and to deal with them in a manner different from the old.

This can be accomplished only through actual experience in the patient's relationship to the therapist; intellectual insight alone is not sufficient (14).

Only after I had pointed out that the objective understanding attitude of the analyst *in itself* brings about a corrective experience did I make the further suggestion that the effect of this experience can be augmented if the analyst succeeds in creating an interpersonal climate which brings into sharp relief the difference between the patient's past attitudes in the family situation and the patient-therapist situation. The rationale of this suggestion is based on the growing recognition that the analyst is not, as originally believed, a blank screen but remains a person in his own right. Consequently there is a specific interpersonal climate existing in each analysis which depends upon the analyst's own personality features. I made the suggestion that this spontaneous interpersonal climate can be consciously modified, and at the same time the fundamental objective helpful attitude still retained. Right or wrong this is not a revolutionary technical device. It attempts to spell out explicitly what is meant by intuition or the "art of psychoanalysis." Handling of the interpersonal climate in an intuitive fashion is a component of every analysis as practiced by experienced therapists. To aid intuition by conscious deliberation based on understanding the patient's original conflict situation is not a radical deviation from accepted theory. It is an attempt to incorporate into theory an unrecognized part of the therapeutic process.

3. The most heated argument arose concerning the question of how to differentiate psychoanalysis from psychoanalytically oriented psychotherapy. Gill criticizes the point of view presented by the author—that psychoanalysis and uncovering psychotherapies constitute a continuum. Yet at the end of his article "Psychoanalysis and Exploratory Psychotherapy" he comes to a similar conclusion (56).

I wish not to be misunderstood. I am not suggesting that psychotherapy can do what psychoanalysis can do; but I am suggesting that a description of the results of intensive psychotherapy may be not merely in terms of shifts of defense but also in terms of other intra-ego alterations. The problem of the derivative conflict is a case in point. Both Gitelson and Reider speak of the fate of these in psychotherapy, though Gitelson emphasizes that they are partly solved, and Reider that they are partly unsolved. The implication is that there exists a basic conflict and that without resolution of the basic conflict no real solution of a derivative conflict can be made. This may be true, but I would still like to hold open the question that even though the basic conflict is unsolved and under sufficient stress can once again reactivate the derivative conflict, the derivative conflicts develop a relative degree of autonomy and exist in a form which allows a relatively firm resolution even under psychotherapeutic techniques, of the more intensive and less directive form I have described. This may result in a quantitative shift which may not be so completely different from what often happens in psychoanalysis, going back to our previous discussion of Freud's later emphasis on quantitative factors in therapy.

In the same article he also states:

I feel that if I have not been clear or if I have been misunderstood, it will be said that I first demonstrated that psychotherapy cannot possibly do what psychoanalysis can and then said that it does in fact do so. Rather than that, I have tried to say that techniques and results in psychoanalysis and intensive, relatively non-directive psychotherapy are not the polar opposites which they are often declared to be, and that a more positive and detailed description of changes both in psychoanalysis and in psychotherapy, which will take account of our newer formulations in ego psychology and include descriptions in terms of intrasystemic alterations and techniques of adaptation, will help to make this clear.

It is obvious here that Gill, while still somewhat uncertain about where he stands, takes a tentative step in the same direction, the same step as that which has been taken by this author.

Concern over the trend to bring psychoanalysis and psychotherapy closer to each other by basing both on the same theoretical foundations cannot be easily understood if one considers that this trend—as Kris recently reminded us—was foreseen by Freud himself.

. . . . . many current problems concerning the variation of technical precepts in certain types of cases, as well as the whole trend of the development that at present tries to link psychoanalytic therapy to psychotherapy in the broader sense, were accurately predicted by Freud (70).

In the next Chapter (pages 153ff.) I attempt to show that the opposition to viewing dynamic psychotherapy and psychoanalysis as the two ends of a continuum has motivations that are primarily emotional and practical, and is not based on logically valid arguments.

Both Gill and Bibring show a trend to evaluate psychoanalysis and psychoanalytically oriented psychotherapy not in terms of Aristotelian dichotomy but as a continuum in which the same therapeutic factors are utilized in different quantities.

Bibring in discussing the different therapeutic factors no longer shows the emotional bias which characterized earlier reactions to the various therapeutic applications of psychoanalytic knowledge.

He ends his judicious article with the admonition:

Be this as it may, the increasing tendency among certain groups of psychotherapists to rely on manipulative principles in combination with or in place of insight makes a theory of experiential manipulation for its proponents a very urgent task (19).

It is hoped that the present book may at least partially answer this need. It must be admitted that it is easier to propose a consistent theory of "experiential manipulations" than to demonstrate precisely their therapeutic effect. This difficulty, however, pertains equally to the standard procedure.

Chapter VIII

PSYCHOANALYSIS AND

PSYCHOTHERAPY

PSYCHOTHERAPY as a systematic method of treatment based on a knowledge of mental illness is one of the latest developments in medicine; psychotherapy as an emotional support offered to a suffering patient is as old as medicine itself. In fact, emotional support is a universal component of human relationships. Everyone who tries to encourage a despondent friend or to reassure a panicky child practices psychotherapy. These common measures employed in daily life are not merely empirical—as are the home remedies for bodily ailments, which are used without any understanding of the symptoms they are intended to cure. Psychotherapeutic home remedies are based on a common-sense understanding of human nature.

People have always known intuitively that they could calm down a worrying person by listening patiently to his story. It is only recently that the relief obtained from such an unloading has been known in scientific jargon as abreaction. People have long known that a reassuring, friendly, and somewhat authoritative attitude toward a confused, frightened person was helpful; they have known, as a matter of common sense, that such a person needs to lean on someone. Today psychiatrists formulate this knowledge by saying that the ego's integrative capacity is lowered under the influence of fear. In the same way, it has long been recognized that an enraged person may be more reasonable after he has given vent to his feelings. Today the psychiatrist would say that rage, like fear, narrows the integrative capacity of the ego, that it can be mitigated by allowing the person to express his feelings. Prescientific knowledge of human nature is a well-developed faculty which every healthy person possesses without systematic learning. In fact, without it one could not survive in social life.

Every science consists in the improvement of common-sense reasoning. But improvement in the natural sciences has been so fundamental that the knowledge resulting is often directly contradictory to the prescientific reasoning about nature, as is best exemplified by modern cosmology. Similarly in psychology the conclusions resulting from systematic observations and reasoning are steadily widening the gap between common sense and scientific knowledge. It is often overlooked, however, that psychology, while it still has many real methodological shortcomings, started from a more advanced level of common-sense knowledge than did the physical sciences, since in psychology the observer and the observed are of the same kind. In physics and chemistry, when the observer deals with the behavior of material objects in time and space, he must rely entirely on his observations, because he does not know from first-hand experience how the objects will behave. If he throws an object into the water, he cannot predict by means of common sense whether it will sink or float. He must know its specific weight, and the establishing of this knowledge requires a long series of systematic measurements plus a hydrodynamic theory.

When we observe another person's behavior, however, we can put ourselves in his place because the object of our observation is another human being. We can "identify" ourselves with him; and thus we can predict with fair accuracy what he will do next because we know how we would act in

a similar situation. This is one of the reasons why psychotherapy can be practiced with a fair degree of success by a
person who does not know much about the theory of personality and psychoneurosis so long as he has what is called
a "good common-sense knowledge of human nature." This is
why the field of psychotherapy, until recently, has been a
free-for-all. A definite transition has come about from
common-sense psychotherapy, practiced by anyone who
thinks he can do it, to so-called scientific psychotherapy as a
medical specialty. Even today, the claim that medical psychotherapy is superior to the emotional help given in everyday life is still questioned by many people, whether well
educated or ignorant. The claim is based, however, on the
fact that there exists today a systematic knowledge of human
personality and its disturbances—a knowledge which is derived from systematic and refined methods of psychological
observation and reasoning.

I refer here to a new and fundamental trend—namely, the
use of psychotherapy as an etiologically oriented method of
treatment which requires specific knowledge and training.
The fact that this knowledge is, to a large degree, derived
from psychoanalysis has occasioned heated disagreement
among psychoanalysts regarding the relationship of psychoanalytic therapy to other forms of psychotherapy. The fact
that psychoanalysis has developed outside academic medicine
and psychiatry and away from academic psychiatrists and
physicians is only partially responsible for the high emotional temperature characteristic of these controversies. Another element in these controversies is the fact that many
psychoanalysts grew up in an era in which psychoanalysis
was regarded with mistrust and emotional bias by academic
psychiatry, so that they came to feel a mistrust of academic
psychiatry and have preferred to practice and develop their
science apart from the medical fraternity. They have felt that
psychoanalysis could not be accepted in an undiluted form by

those outsiders who were not psychoanalyzed themselves, because of emotional resistance to the workings of psychoanalysis. These psychoanalysts have felt that they must keep the teaching and practice of psychoanalysis under their own control. They have lost sight of the fact that psychotherapy is older than psychoanalysis and is the traditional domain of the psychiatrist. It has been difficult, therefore, for many psychoanalysts to recognize the radical changes which have gradually transformed the whole scene around us, to the extent that psychoanalysis is no longer regarded with the same mistrust. In fact, Freud, who is said to have disturbed the sleep of humanity, has in our time succeeded thoroughly in awakening a great part of it.

Psychiatrists have come to recognize more and more the fundamental nature of Freud's discoveries; and psychiatric practice is at present highly influenced, both directly and indirectly, by psychoanalysis. Many of us feel that this change in the cultural climate has changed our role and responsibility. Now, when psychiatry is not only ready but eager to assimilate in an undiluted form the teachings of Freud and the work of his followers, we feel that it becomes our responsibility to guide and facilitate this process of incorporation. For this process is steadily going on in this country and, aside from sporadic resistance, the emotional barriers on both sides —analysts and other psychiatrists—are rapidly disappearing.

This is well expressed in a statement of Fenichel (29).

There is no doubt that the psychoanalytic understanding of the ways in which nonanalytic psychotherapies work can be utilized for a planned systematization of the procedure to be chosen. As long as any psychotherapeutic school had its own "theory," the results were unpredictable and dependent on change, or rather entirely on the therapist's intuitive skill. The methods of psychotherapy, therefore, have remained the same since the times of the earliest witch doctors; the results were perhaps not bad, but they were not understood and thus were unreliable. You never could tell whether or not they would be achieved at all.

A short psychotherapy, based on psychoanalytic knowledge, can change this state of affairs. An analyst is able to use the patient's symptoms, history, behavior and utterances for the purpose of establishing a "dynamic diagnosis" about the patient's leading conflicts, the relative strength of the repressing and repressed forces respectively, of the defense system and its weak spots, of the patient's rigidity or elasticity, of his general accessibility. This dynamic diagnosis will enable him to predict with a certain degree of probability what the patient's reaction to certain measures will be. Combinations of limited interpretations, provocation of certain types of transference, provision of well-chosen substitute outlets, alterations of the environment, suggestions or prohibitions of unconsciously tempting or reassuring situations or activities, the verbalizing of actual conflicts, and advice about mental hygiene can very well be systematized. This has not been done yet on a large scale, but there are promising beginnings, from Aichhorn and Zulliger to the Chicago Psychoanalytic Institute and many American psychiatrists and psychiatric institutions.

It is now rather generally accepted, both by analysts and by nonanalytic psychiatrists, that psychoanalytic concepts—the theoretical knowledge of psychodynamics and neurosis formation—are necessary for every psychiatrist and that they make up one of the basic sciences of psychiatry.[1] Since psychoanalytic theory has become the common property of the whole of psychiatry, the identity of psychoanalysis as an isolated discipline now rests almost exclusively on the ability to distinguish the specific nature of psychoanalytic therapy.

There can be little doubt that the absorption of psychoanalytic theory and techniques into the field of psychiatry in particular, and medicine in general, will become complete in the not-too-distant future, for this course of events is dictated by the immanent logic of the field. Yet there are great practical problems to be solved before this unification can be consummated. First, the preparation for psychoanalytic practice requires more than theoretical instruction and experience; it requires a personal analysis of the student as a preparatory

[1] See statements by leading psychiatrists, Chapter X.

step in order that he may master the technique intellectually and be free from disturbing emotional involvements of his own in handling patients. The inclusion of the personal analysis in the academic curriculum of all psychiatrists would present many practical complications which are well known and needs no further discussion here.[2]

A related difficulty arises from the practical dictates of policy on the part of the psychoanalyst. Because of his different training background, the psychoanalyst feels it important to preserve his identity and for practical reasons justly insists on doing so. But it becomes more and more difficult to make a sharp distinction between psychoanalytic treatment and other methods of psychotherapy used by so-called traditional psychiatrists which are based on the utilization of psychoanalytic observations and theory. The practice of psychiatrists is becoming more and more similar even though some may practice pure psychoanalysis and others may practice psychoanalytically oriented psychotherapy, or to use another popular term, dynamic psychiatry. This in itself should not be disturbing; on the contrary, the basing of all psychological approaches to psychiatric patients on solid foundations—on the theoretical knowledge of the disturbance—is a healthy sign. But no matter how desirable may be the trend toward uniform basic principles in all psychotherapy, the psychoanalyst who wishes to retain his identity as such is faced with a practical problem.

Let us consider the difficulties of such unification both from the point of view of logic and that of practical policy.

It is not difficult to show the logical cogency of the position that since we possess today a basic understanding of human behavior, all treatment of personality disturbances should rest on the same scientific principles no matter who undertakes the treatment or what particular technique he

---

[2] Some suggestions concerning practical measures to deal with these difficulties will be discussed in Chapter XI.

employs. There is no particular kind of anatomy of physiology, no particular theory of antisepsis, which is considered applicable to abdominal surgery as opposed to brain surgery, for example. The basic principles are the same and must be taught to every surgeon. While it is customary to divide psychotherapeutic procedures into two categories—the supportive and the uncovering—it must be borne in mind that supportive measures are knowingly or inadvertently used in all forms of psychotherapy; and conversely, some degree of insight is rarely absent from any sound psychotherapeutic approach. Thus, in this complex field, pedantic distinctions do not reflect what actually takes place.

In general, all uncovering procedures, whether they are standard psychoanalysis or psychotherapy based on psychoanalytic principles, aim to enhance the ego's ability to handle emotional conflict situations which are entirely or partially repressed and therefore unconscious. Such conflicts usually originate in infancy and childhood, but are precipitated in later life by actual life situations. In the uncovering procedures, the therapist tries to re-expose the ego, in the treatment situation, to the original conflict which the child's ego could not handle and therefore had to repress. Repression interrupts the natural learning process and does not allow a corrective adjustment of the repressed tendencies. The aim is a new solution to the old, unresolved or neurotically solved conflicts. The principal therapeutic tool is the transference, in which the patient relives in relation to the therapist his early interpersonal conflicts. Regression to the dependent attitudes of infancy and childhood is a constant feature of the transference, and, in the majority of cases, the central one. This regression in itself has a supportive effect. It allows the patient to postpone his own decisions and to reduce the responsibilities of adult existence by retiring into a dependent attitude toward the therapist which resembles the child's attitude in the child-parent relationship. In many instances the greatest therapeutic effect of psychoanalysis is found precisely in this kind of support. The fact that the patient is then unwilling to give up such treatment indicates that, no matter what the therapist originally aimed at, the treatment is supportive in nature. As soon as the treatment is interrupted, the patient relapses. On the other hand, many so-called "rapid transference" cures persist, even though in the therapist's judgment they are not based on any real change in the personality. Such favorable transference results occur frequently when the ego's integrative capacity has been only temporarily impaired by acute emotional stress. Once the emotional support provided by the therapeutic situation reduces this stress, the ego is able to regain its functional capacity without any further activity on the part of the therapist. The ego's natural function is to master internal tensions by its integrative function. Emotional support relieves emotional tension and thus increases the natural integrative capacity of the ego and accounts for improvements which are not due to particular therapeutic measures.

In spite of this overlapping of uncovering and supportive effects in all forms of psychotherapy, it is not difficult to differentiate between the two main categories of treatment—primarily supportive and primarily uncovering methods. Primarily supportive measures are indicated whenever the functional impairment of the ego is of a temporary nature caused by acute emotional stress. In such cases the therapeutic task consists, first of all, in *gratifying dependent needs* during the stress situation, thus reducing anxiety. Another important therapeutic device consists in reducing emotional stress by giving the patient an opportunity for emotional *abreaction*. A more intellectual type of support consists in *objectively reviewing* the patient's acute stress situation and assisting his judgment, which is temporarily impaired under the influence of severe emotional tensions; the patient thus becomes able to view his total situation from a proper perspective. In addition to these three forms of support, the therapist will occasionally have to *aid the ego's own neurotic defenses*. This is indicated whenever there are definite reasons to mistrust the ego's capacity to deal with unconscious material which threatens to break into consciousness through the weakened defenses. Finally, whenever the neurotic condition results from the patient's chronic involvement in particularly difficult external life situations which are beyond his ability to cope with, the manipulation of the life situation may be the only hopeful approach. This is, of course, indicated only in cases when, for external or internal reasons, there is no hope of increasing the ego's functional capacity by prolonged treatment.

These five procedures—gratification of dependency needs, abreaction, intellectual guidance, support of neurotic defenses, and manipulation of life situations—constitute the essence of supportive measures. Their use may require a shorter or longer series of sessions; occasionally results may be accomplished in only one or two interviews. There is no way to predict precisely the duration of such treatment; the therapist must proceed empirically, basing his judgment upon the therapeutic progress.

It is widely but erroneously held that supportive psychotherapeutic methods require less technical and theoretical preparation than psychoanalysis. I believe that every psychotherapist should be able to understand the underlying psychopathology and to apply the different therapeutic tools according to the specific needs of each patient. Supportive measures, if undertaken without such understanding, not only may be ineffective in certain cases, but they may jeopardize the chances of recovery by undermining the patient's confidence in the efficacy of any psychiatric treatment. Not infrequently even such common-sense procedures as giving consolation to a depressed patient or urging the phobic patient to overcome his fears may, if improperly applied, result in aggravation of the condition. Similarly, ill-timed provocation of emotional abreaction in an acting-out neurotic may have serious consequences; and the strengthening of existing neurotic defenses in certain cases may not only be superfluous, but may unduly prolong recovery. All forms of psychotherapy must, therefore, be based on a knowledge of personality development and psychodynamics.

Chronic conditions in which the ego's functional impairment is caused by unresolved emotional conflicts of childhood require a systematic and rather prolonged type of treatment in which the ego is re-exposed to earlier pathogenic experiences. No hard and fast rules exist for predicting the length of such treatment, but it may vary from a few months to several years.

Because of the recent concern lest the identity of psychoanalysis be lost, there is a strong tendency to try to differentiate sharply between psychoanalytic therapy proper and other uncovering procedures utilizing the principles of psychoanalysis. For a while this controversy appeared to center around such spurious issues as the frequency of interviews, the duration of the treatment, and whether the patient should lie on a couch or sit face to face with the analyst; these were considered as the crucial criteria.

Some of us maintained an opposing view. We felt that the frequency of interviews and the whole duration of treatment depend upon several factors which cannot be precisely appraised quantitatively in our present state of knowledge. In each case the therapist must feel his way and find the optimal intensity of treatment. Anticipation of duration at the beginning of treatment is seldom possible; certainly no accurate estimates can be made in advance.

From all this it should be clear that neither the length of treatment nor any other external criteria are the most suitable bases for differentiating various forms of uncovering procedures. As long as the psychological processes in the patient are the same, and the changes achieved by these processes are of a similar nature, it is not possible to draw a sharp dividing line between psychoanalysis proper and psychoanalytically oriented psychotherapy.

A sharp dividing line requires differences in the psychological processes which take place in the patients treated by psychoanalysis and by psychotherapy.[3]

Obviously a great variety of patients makes variations in approach necessary. Since this is the case in all fields of medicine one might expect that such a flexibility would prevail also in the field of psychoanalysis. The fact that most psychoanalysts have used precisely the same so-called classical procedure for all their patients has been due to various circumstances. For many years the general procedure among psychoanalytic therapists was to accept those cases for therapy which appeared suitable for the classical procedure and to advise the others not to undergo psychoanalytic treatment. In other words, the patients were selected to fit the tool.

Psychoanalytic treatment is the primary source of psychoanalytic knowledge, and the original procedure is best suited for research. Since in the early phases of psychoanalysis the primary concern was that of increasing basic knowledge, the classical procedure was rather universally used. Some of us have come to the conviction, however, that the time is now ripe to utilize the accumulated theoretical knowledge in different ways, so that not only those patients who appear suitable for the original technique but the whole psychoneurotic population as well may benefit from our present knowledge. This extension of psychoanalytic help to a great variety of patients is an important new trend in our field.

Why this distinction between analysis proper and analytically oriented therapy has been such an important issue can only be understood if one considers its practical implications. First of all, the identity of the psychoanalyst, particularly in the eyes of the public, is threatened by the flexible use of

[3] See the discussion of these differences on pages 160 ff.

analytic principles. It would appear that now anyone may claim recognition as a psychoanalyst who uses analytically founded psychotherapeutic methods, since the psychoanalyst can no longer be easily identified by some external criteria of his technique.[4]

In the heat of a recent discussion of this problem, one psychoanalyst exclaimed that insistence on daily interviews in every case is important because this clearly distinguishes the psychoanalyst from other psychiatrists! "Other psychiatrists see their patients once a month, once in two weeks, or maybe once a week. Some of them," he continued, "might see their patients twice a week—but the psychoanalyst sees them five or six times!" While this may sound thoroughly nonsensical, it has a kernel of sense. A product which cannot be easily identified by external criteria can be easily confused with other products which appear similar though essentially different.

At the present moment when psychotherapy is such a comprehensive term for all psychological methods—some of them based on common sense, others on various theoretical concepts—the feeling of psychoanalysts that their procedure should be identified by its name is quite justified. This practical consideration should not be an impediment to the natural evolution of the field. Psychoanalytic principles today are being applied in various forms. The only logical solution is to identify as similar all those related procedures which are based essentially on the same scientific concepts, observations, and technical principles and to differentiate them from intuitive psychotherapies and from those treatments which are

[4] It may appear that the author in this statement disregards his own previous warning (Introduction) that by interpreting the unconscious motivations of an argument one cannot prove its fallacy. I do not offer, however, this interpretation of the concern about the rapprochement between dynamic psychotherapy and psychoanalysis as an argument against the validity of this concern. Only after I tried to show its intrinsic fallacy on the basis of logical analysis of the two positions do I offer the above interpretation of motives in order to explain the reason for the heat of this controversy.

based on different theoretical concepts and basically different therapeutic procedures.

In this connection, it should again be emphasized that the use of psychoanalytic principles in a more flexible way requires not less, but more, knowledge. A student who follows the classical procedure in every detail does not have to face the problem of evaluating what kind of deviations should be used, when and how. Routine protects him from making independent decisions, which have to be based not only on a general understanding of the case but also on a precise appreciation of the momentary psychodynamic situation. For example, the analyst who is not protected by routine may, at a given time, have to consider whether he should try to reduce the intensity of the patient's emotional involvement; he may decide that the patient's dependency can be counteracted by making it more conscious, and therefore he may reduce the frequency of the interviews or interrupt the treatment temporarily so that the patient will be on his own for a while and will be made to feel that he need not rely continually on his therapist. Such considerations require evaluations which are not necessary if the psychoanalyst proceeds according to a standardized procedure.

The boundary between psychoanalysis proper and uncovering types of psychotherapy becomes less sharply defined the more all psychotherapeutic practices operate with the same conceptual tools and in the same theoretical framework. Disregarding the practical considerations discussed above which make it desirable to separate clearly the two types of therapy, the question then becomes whether there are essential differences which justify such a sharp division.

There are a great many practitioners who do not consider it difficult to separate psychoanalysis and psychoanalytically oriented therapy on the basis of the essential nature of the two procedures. One of the common propositions is that while psychotherapy may uncover unconscious factors, it never revives the genetically important neurotic conflicts in their totality and therefore, it can never thoroughly reconstruct the personality structure. In other words, the absence of a full-fledged transference neurosis in psychotherapy is the differential criterion which sharply separates psychoanalysis from all other therapeutic procedures.

This distinction appears at first to be merely of a quantitative nature because transference develops in all psychotherapeutic situations. In psychoanalytic treatment, however, as the treatment advances the originally presenting transference undergoes a gradual transformation. The presenting form of transference is often a defense against other conflict situations which in turn are defensive reactions of an even deeper layer of conflict. I refer the reader to Chapters V and VI, in which this stratification of conflicts has been discussed in detail.

For example, a male patient may soon develop toward the analyst a competitive father transference which is a defensive reaction against his passive dependent longings. Further penetration into the depths may lead to a third layer, the original oedipal situation, which the patient evaded by regression to a dependent or passive homosexual attitude. Without working through these different types of transference reactions, the original conflict cannot be brought into the patient's consciousness. A psychotherapy which does not systematically uncover all these secondary and tertiary defenses, and deals only with the patient's initial spontaneous transference reactions, can be well differentiated from the systematic psychoanalytic procedure which proceeds from layer to layer, reconstructing the whole genetic picture. There seems to be general agreement that this systematic procedure requires specialized skill and experience of a kind which can be acquired at present only in psychoanalytic institutes. Accordingly only those psychiatrists who have acquired such experience and skill are entitled to be recognized as psychoanalysts.

Although this position is consistent it does not entirely resolve our problem, the relation of psychotherapy to psychoanalysis. In treatment our aim is not to reconstruct the history of the patient's conflicts for the sake of theoretical knowledge but for therapeutic purposes. The most important question is to consider the criteria which determine the necessary depths of our penetration. Here we come to one of the least explored areas of our field.

Because in the past research and therapy were so closely interrelated, this practical question has not been considered of great importance. The tacit assumption was that in order to achieve thorough therapeutic results a complete reconstruction of the ego development was always necessary. If the treatment had to stop short of this goal, it was primarily because of external circumstances such as lack of time and opportunity. Occasionally the limited strength of the patient's ego makes a further penetration inadvisable. This, however, cannot be decided at the beginning of the treatment. Moreover, the general opinion was that by gradual working through the resistances, a slow, step-by-step penetration into the depths is both possible and desirable in most chronic cases. The fact that a considerable number of schizophrenics have been successfully treated strongly supports this assumption.

Equally impressive observations, however, challenge the validity of the general thesis that reliable therapeutic results can be based only on a thorough reconstruction of the whole pathogenetic history. One of the confusing and sometimes even discouraging facts in our field is the unpredictability of the results. Patients who according to the textbook should recover, stubbornly refuse to improve, and others with an initially bad prognosis unexpectedly recover. The most baffling fact is the "rapid transference cure" which often persists even if no further treatment is administered. During the last ten years I observed a large number of persisting transference cures as I began to experiment with different therapeutic applications of psychoanalytic principles. As mentioned before, such transference cures require no special explanation in cases in which the ego's functional capacity has been impaired only temporarily under the influence of excessive emotions, mostly of anxiety.[5] Yet there are cases in which not only do transference cures persist but marked personality changes take place in the following years. It appears as if the transference experience changed something in the parallelogram of conflicting forces which allows further ego maturation through permitting further continuation of the learning process that had been interrupted by infantile conflicts and repressions.

This brings us to a consideration which appears to be of importance for the further development of all forms of psychotherapy, including psychoanalysis. It pertains to the regenerative faculties of the living organism which are considered a basic property of life. In our young field we have not yet emancipated ourselves from the magical traditions of medicine. Modern medicine recognizes that healing is possible only because of the regenerative powers of the organism. It recognizes that a physician's function is by removing obstacles to create conditions in which the regenerative powers can best exert their influence. Active immunization is one of the best examples. Our intervention stimulates and frees the defensive powers of the organism. Primarily, nature and not the physician heals; the physician only helps the healing process. Even in the most active therapy, as in surgery, the surfaces of the wound grow together because of the regenerative process. The surgeon can favor this healing process; he cannot initiate it. The same is true for psychotherapy and psychoanalysis. We are still inclined to believe that a patient must be cured on the couch. The couch, however, is only the beginning of a natural healing process. In the field of personality disturbances, the ego's integrative function is the

[5] See page 155.

basis of the regenerative process. Without any therapeutic aid the ego is occasionally able to accomplish this task, as demonstrated by spontaneous cures. In psychoanalysis we re-expose the adult ego in the transference situation to the same, though less intensive, conflicts as those the infantile ego could not cope with. The infantile ego defended itself against them by repression, and thus interrupted the natural learning process. This re-exposure is essential in all chronic cases where the learning process—or, as it is commonly expressed—the ego-development, has been interrupted in early life. The therapeutic problem is to determine when this task has been accomplished. The crucial question is how far our therapeutic intervention is needed. The continuation of therapy beyond this point may lead not to further consolidation of the results but to further regression and increased dependence upon the therapist. In a large number of patients who today consult the psychoanalyst, the unresolved conflict which interferes with further development is highly circumscribed. In these cases the reawakening of the central conflict, in the transference, may suffice to stimulate the regenerative powers of the ego and may result in unexpected and lasting therapeutic results without extensive reconstruction of the past.

In psychoanalysis, too, we rely on the regenerative faculties of the ego. We refer to them rather vaguely as the patient's will for recovery, or even more vaguely as his ability for co-operation. No matter how vaguely this basic motivation of the patient is defined and no matter how difficult it is to express it in quantitative terms, it is our most important consideration when we undertake a treatment or continue it over a long period of time. Our prognosis is determined largely by this indispensable factor which lies in the patient, in his own tendency toward recovery. We re-expose the patient's ego, in the transference, to an unsettled conflict of the past. Ultimately it is the patient's ego which will have to attempt a new solution. The therapist's task is to give the ego a new opportunity. Our interpretative work can facilitate his finding a new solution but cannot supply the motivational cathexis.[6]

The ego's biological function is an integrative one; once the unconscious material is brought into the scope of the integrative faculties of the ego, in the case of many adult neurotic patients, the rest of the therapeutic task can be entrusted largely to the ego. War experiences have shown that in many traumatic neuroses simple sedation may suffice. This allays the anxiety that temporarily interfered with the ego's integrative faculty. One is inclined to assume that in procedures like narcosynthesis the major therapeutic effect is the relief by sedation of anxiety which temporarily hampered the ego's integrative capacity.

I expect that one of the major advances in psychotherapy, including psychoanalysis, will result from developing criteria indicating at what point active therapeutic interference is no longer needed and the patient's ego can be entrusted to take over. From such criteria we may expect two major gains. First, we shall reduce the number of cases which are overtreated, that is to say, cases in which continued therapy is not only unnecessary but may retard recovery. Transference, like x-ray, can be given in overdoses. Second, a larger, maybe substantially larger, number of cases can benefit from our therapeutic skills. Freud considered it a fortunate circumstance that the aims of research (that is, the exploration of the genetic background of neurosis) and the aims of therapy run parallel. We can study and cure our patients at the same time. However, as early as 1910, he stated that the aims of research and therapy do not run completely parallel (48).

We may expect that in increasing our understanding of the therapeutic process, particularly of its quantitative aspects, this divergence between the goals of therapy and research will widen. In other words, the more we know about the

[6] See discussion in Chapter IV.

quantitative aspects of the therapeutic process, the more precisely we shall be able to administer to each individual patient
the type and amount of therapy he needs for his recovery.

This amount can seldom be determined at the onset of the
treatment. The most difficult task of the therapist is first to
adjust the therapy to the nature of the patient and his problem, and second, to know where to stop. The end phase of
the treatment is the most deceptive, particularly in cases in
which the patient has regressed to a preconflictual phase of
development and brings in chronologically deep but pathogenetically irrelevant material, retreating to the "good old
days" with their relatively minor conflicts. We have to face
the problem of how to deal with this type of regressive evasion in practically every treatment, whether we call it psychoanalysis or uncovering psychotherapy. This presents the
greatest challenge to therapeutic experience and knowledge.
It is the basis of the contention which several psychoanalysts
have expressed that the psychotherapeutic applications of
psychoanalysis require more expert skill and more training
than does the practicing of standard psychoanalysis. In the
latter, one relies on a course of events which develops spontaneously if the proper technique is applied and which finds
its natural end. It has never been examined whether this spontaneous course is always the most desirable one from the point
of view of therapy. Persistent transference cures on the one
hand and unterminable cases on the other cast a great doubt
upon the belief that the therapeutic process, left to take its
own course without any particularly quantitative modifications of the different significant variables, is always the best
procedure. The unpredictability of therapeutic results—unexpectedly rapid or prolonged treatments—adds to these
doubts. Every case requires a thorough psychodynamic evaluation not only at the beginning but throughout the course of
treatment.

In the light of these considerations it does not appear realistic to train psychotherapists on two different levels; to produce psychoanalysts who have both the theoretical knowledge and treatment experience which enables them to make such evaluations, and psychotherapists who have to rely on some general theoretical knowledge of psychodynamics but mainly on their intuitive feeling in deciding how to deal with a patient. Neither is it realistic to declare that the latter type of psychotherapist should handle only patients whose treatment can remain on the supportive level and in whose treatment complex psychodynamic appraisal is not likely to be needed. Such a policy overlooks the fact that it is not entirely in the therapist's power to regulate the patient's transference involvements. The therapist bound to a predetermined course of treatment, for example to give only emotional support or an opportunity for ventilation of feelings, may soon discover that in spite of his best intentions the patient gets involved in a transference neurosis which will require uncovering measures. For him to refer each of such patients to a psychoanalyst is neither practical nor conducive to increasing his confidence and his self-respect as a psychiatrist.

Fortunately what actually happens in practice is that good, experienced psychiatrists who are well acquainted with the basic concepts of psychodynamics, even though they did not have formal psychoanalytic training, will handle such situations with techniques similar to those of a trained psychoanalyst (see Chapter XII). They will recognize and interpret transference conflicts and resistances. We might add that often they do this as well as or better than many formally recognized psychoanalysts. This was expressed at the Conference on Psychiatric Education held at Cornell University, June 19 to 25, 1952. "It is not necessary to be psychoanalyzed in order to develop competent psychiatrists, including competence in psychotherapy and psychodynamics" (68). The validity of this pronouncement few psychiatrists or psychoanalysts would challenge. In fact it reflects the present state

of affairs. It should not, however, be concluded that psychoanalytic training would not enhance the technical skill and
judgment of psychiatrists who do well without it. This
qualification is stated in the second pronouncement of the
same conference: "It is highly desirable that some persons
should receive a personal psychoanalysis and psychoanalytic
training because of the contributions which psychoanalysis
may make in varying degrees to the personal adjustment of
the psychiatrist, to his skills as a therapist, and to his understanding of the basic science of psychodynamics. For those
who are to practice the specialty of psychoanalytic therapy,
such psychoanalytic training is considered a necessity."

This statement does not further qualify the expression
"some persons." It may imply that not all residents are suitable for such further training in psychoanalysis, but it may
also imply that it is not possible for all residents to obtain
such training because of limited training facilities. In the
following chapter this particular issue will be further discussed.

At this point it appears worth while to reflect further on
the fact that effectiveness in psychotherapy is not necessarily
related to the fact that a therapist has or has not undergone
psychoanalytic training including a personal analysis.

Even today when we do possess a reasonable and well-
established theory of personality and of treatment, psychotherapy, in all its forms, including psychoanalysis, is more an
art than a science. Aptitudes—intuition and empathy—although not always reliable, are possibly more important for
competence in therapy than is theoretical knowledge. The
therapist's personality, his intangible suitability to certain
types of patients and refractoriness to others cannot be disregarded. Moreover, specialization in psychoanalysis, with
its strict adherence to a standard procedure, does not prepare
the therapist to deal most effectively with the great variety of
patients, the majority of whom are either not suited to being

treated by psychoanalysis or do not require it. This disadvantage, of course, would disappear if psychoanalytic institutes would undertake as one of their major responsibilities to give their candidates a broader instruction and experience not only in psychoanalysis proper but in the modifications of the standard procedure. There is a gradual trend in many institutes toward assuming this responsibility and toward expanding their curricula accordingly.[7] In spite of all this, the significance of the intangible personality factors which are not basically modified by the training analysis will remain of pre-eminent importance for a long time to come.

The selection of candidates for psychoanalytic training, therefore, is of great significance. I believe that those candidates who prove unfitted for psychoanalytic training will likewise not constitute the best material for training in any form of psychotherapy. Intractable personality difficulties, extensive blind spots, tendencies to project emotional instabilities —to mention only a few of the disqualifying factors—will hamper a resident in all his psychotherapeutic activities.

Such a sharp division of the profession probably will not persist very long because it is both artificial and unrealistic. One cannot draw barriers against knowledge. A practitioner who may at first restrict his practice to incipient and acute cases will gradually learn more and more about psychodynamics from his own experience and will then undertake treatment of cases which require further penetration. Moreover, it is scarcely possible, even for the experienced man, to decide in advance what course a treatment will take. Every psychotherapist who knows the significance of unconscious factors, who utilizes the patient's transference reactions for therapeutic purposes, who understands the nature of resistances— briefly, whose therapeutic procedure is based on the fundamental concepts of psychoanalysis—engages in a procedure

---

[7] In the revised curriculum of the Chicago Psychoanalytic Institute the fifth year is largely devoted to this type of teaching.

which is modeled after the traditional psychoanalytical technique, although he may use the various therapeutic agents in different degrees.

I do not believe that anyone using an uncovering type of therapy can always stop arbitrarily and say to himself, "So far I go and no further." The transference involvements may necessitate dealing with earlier conflict situations which at the beginning was not expected. Since all uncovering techniques of necessity are based on psychoanalytic principles, the only logical distinction would be between psychiatrists who restrict themselves entirely to supportive treatment and those who use uncovering methods. Many treatments begin, however, as psychotherapy and end as standard psychoanalysis, and vice versa. As has been stated above, even pedantic differentiation between the supportive and nonsupportive approaches is not always possible in reality because supportive and uncovering elements are present in all treatments (see pages 154–155).

There can be little doubt that a well-trained psychiatrist who does any psychotherapy at all should know psychoanalytic theory, particularly because at present even if we teach him all that we know, we can offer him relatively little knowledge considering the magnitude of the problem which every patient offers.

The practical consequences of these considerations are in many respects discouraging. They seem to imply that psychoanalytic training, including a personal analysis, is desirable for every psychiatrist who intends to deal primarily with the psychological aspects of this field. It is a discouraging conclusion because the length of such a training alone presents an almost insoluble practical problem. Instead of proposing a solution, I shall offer (in Chapter X) a review of current opinions prevailing in this field.

A more realistic subspecialization in psychiatry is seen in the steadily increasing interest in biological research and somatic therapies. This gradually leads to a natural division within psychiatry between those who specialize in the psychological and those who follow the newer somatic approaches. Even this division, however, is not complete. All present indications are that the pharmacological and other somatic approaches will have to be coordinated and complemented by psychotherapeutic measures. It is not to be expected that pharmacological treatment, or shock treatment, should bring about such miraculous changes in the total structure of the personality that those conditions which produced a neurosis or psychosis will be eliminated. The indications are that these measures have only a temporary effect; that they change the dynamic equilibrium so that the patient becomes more amenable for psychotherapy.[8]

All this shows that subspecialization in the field of psychiatry is an extremely complex problem. Even though certain psychiatrists may specialize in certain techniques, there can be little doubt that all of them have to possess an up-to-date knowledge of the functioning of human personality and be thoroughly acquainted with the current theories and practices of psychotherapy.

It would appear that the thorough training given to students by the psychoanalytic institutes today may serve as a model for the future training of all psychiatrists who are interested chiefly in the psychological approaches in therapy. Selection of suitable persons to be admitted to the study of psychiatry will become more and more important. A portion may be selected for specialization in psychotherapy. Once we are able to select persons suitable for training in all forms of psychotherapy, the only questions will be those of facilities, time, and economic factors. At the present time the training of a psychiatrist is more costly than that of most other

---

[8] Pyschosurgery alone would be an exception as the only procedure which brings about irreversible changes. Its evaluation does not belong in this writing.

specialists. Nor can it be predicted with any certainty that if the responsibility for the training of all psychiatrists were to rest with the medical faculties, the cost, or even the time of the training, would be substantially reduced.

I am well aware that these conclusions at the present moment may appear Utopian. "Utopian" should not be used in a derogatory sense. If Utopia means an ideal state of affairs, our task consists in modifying and improving current procedures, thus gradually approaching, even though never reaching, the ideal goal. The opposite attitude, often qualified as "practical" or "realistic," is neither realistic nor practical.

If with our present methods of screening we select those students who appear suitable to become good psychotherapists, we will also have to develop means and methods to give all of them a thorough and up-to-date knowledge of what we know today about the human personality and its disturbances. We shall have to offer them thorough training in the principles of all therapeutic procedures. Personal analysis is a necessary preparation for such training. Specialization in certain techniques—psychotherapeutic or standard psychoanalytic—is then a secondary question and should be left largely to the initiative of the student.

Chapter IX

TEACHING OF PSYCHOANALYSIS

In this chapter I shall discuss two distinct topics: the teaching of psychoanalysis to residents in psychiatry, and training in psychoanalysis for those residents who want to specialize in psychoanalytic therapy. The latter topic I shall discuss first.

1. TRAINING OF PSYCHOANALYSTS [1]

Organized teaching of psychoanalysis in institutes has been carried on for thirty-five years. The first psychoanalytic institute was established in Berlin in 1920. Before this psychoanalysis was taught only in a highly individual teacher-apprentice relationship. Very few authentic reports of that period exist. The spirit of this phase is well reflected in Hanns Sachs's book *Freud, Master and Friend* (88). These early days of the heroic past of psychoanalysis are shrouded in the mists and mirages of mythology.

The first institute was founded in Berlin by Max Eitingon with Ernest Simmel as his associate. The Institute had from the beginning an autonomous status administratively separated from the Berlin Psychoanalytic Society. It had no well-defined constitution. The staff was invited by the director in consultation with the local members of the Society. Its structure was informal but there was a clear distinction between the Society, consisting of the recognized, practicing psycho-

[1] Based on an address given to the Association of the Candidates of the Institute for Psychoanalysis, Chicago, 1951 (11).

analysts, and the Institute as an autonomous school to supply members to the Society. Candidates could apply for membership in the Society after they finished their training.

The first formal curriculum was worked out by a committee of which Sandor Rado was chairman; Mueller-Braunschweig and I were members. The training was divided into three major phases: first, the training analysis of the candidate; second, theoretical instruction; and third, practical, clinical training consisting of supervised analyses and case seminars. This structure of psychoanalytic training has been retained in principle by most institutes to the present date.

In the Berlin Institute the theoretical training consisted of introductory lectures covering the fundamental concepts of psychoanalysis, specific neuroses, instinct theory, dream analysis, and metapsychology, and a course on the theory and practice of psychoanalytic treatment. Gradually, with the growth of the student body, the case seminars became divided into several parallel groups, each group having not more than ten members.

The most important feature of the Berlin Institute was the outpatient clinic which supplied the material for the supervised analyses. The patients were admitted by the director and treated by a growing number of students. The patients were seen as a rule three times a week. Eitingon experimented at the beginning with half-hour interviews. These were found unsatisfactory, and extended fifty-minute interviews were introduced. The three-hour-a-week schedule, however, was found in general to be satisfactory and was retained. Eitingon also experimented with interruptions of the treatment, for which he used the expression, "fractioned analysis."

The supervised sessions of the students were held according to need. Some of the candidates were seen quite frequently, others at much longer intervals. The student body was small and a highly individual plan for teaching each candidate was both possible and natural.

Soon the case seminars were recognized as the most valuable instrument of training. The weakest spot in the program, the narrow margin of clinical experience, was discovered early. The students studied a few cases intensively in their controlled analysis, but because of the prolonged nature of each treatment it took years for a candidate to see even one case of each nosological group. The only way to expose every student to a larger number of cases was through case seminars.

With the growth of the student body the need of the students to have their own organization appeared. This took the form of the so-called "children's seminar," [2] a weekly meeting of the students among themselves in which they freely discussed everything they wished. No staff member was admitted. Two students conducted these meetings jointly, Fenichel and Schultz-Henke. The discussion centered around Fenichel's exposing the officially accepted, theoretical concepts and Schultz-Henke in the role of the critic challenging the official doctrine.

When the faculty first heard about these meetings, they became alarmed about possible demoralizing effects. It was felt that the existence of the "children's seminar" was a tacit complaint on the part of the students, both at not receiving enough attention from the staff and also possibly against the prevailing trend toward indoctrination. In the seminar they could express their doubts freely and pose questions which officially they did not dare to ask.

This "children's seminar," by its very constitution of having two leaders, one defending the official view and the other a critic, was the first manifestation of the trend which

[2] They referred to themselves as children in contrast to experienced psychoanalysts.

has since led to the formation of two factions in a great many centers of psychoanalysis all over the world, one conservative and one critical of the status quo in theory and practice.

Under the political upheavals starting in the early 1930s in Europe, both the Berlin and Vienna Institutes disintegrated. Most members of both institutes emigrated to England and to the United States.

The development of organized training in the United States followed in principle the patterns established originally in Berlin and Vienna.[3]

To understand the American development and the controversial issues which evolved in the course of time, it is necessary to realize the extent of the isolation from the rest of academic life in which European psychoanalysis existed. The Institutes had no official or even semi-official connection with any of the psychiatric departments in the universities; teaching of analytic principles in the medical schools was almost completely absent; the psychoanalysts had their own organizations, societies, training institutes, and publishing company. They developed their own standards. Psychoanalysis thus became a specialty of its own on the borderline of medicine, retaining its extraterritorial status. At the same time Freud's teachings profoundly influenced the perspective of most educated Europeans and made a deep imprint upon contemporary philosophy, literature, and the arts. The isolation of psychoanalysis existed mainly in regard to the official academic institutions such as universities, professional journals, and medical societies. For example, when Karl Abraham on one occasion was invited by the Berlin Gynecological Society to discuss his observations regarding psychogenic irregularities of menstruation, it was considered an almost unprecedented occurrence. Psychoanalytic books were seldom reviewed seriously in psychiatric journals and as a whole the medical

[3] About the developments in England I have no first-hand information.

profession kept aloof from this new and strange brand of therapeutic specialty. Psychoanalysis aroused deep emotional resistances, which were primarily responsible for the lack of appreciation and understanding by everyone who had not undergone a personal analysis. In the early period of psychoanalysis when Freud and a handful of his followers developed this new field in complete cultural isolation, they had to defend their new discoveries against a hostile world. In the present day, when every issue of *The New Yorker* has a cartoon on psychoanalysis, when most psychological novels and dramas freely utilize analytic insight, when many parents are eagerly attempting to save their children from repression of their infantile sexuality, emotional resistance against psychoanalysis has become less and less evident.

It is true that in the early 1930s, when the first attempts to organize psychoanalytic training in this country were undertaken, all these changes in the outlook of the public had not yet fully taken place. Yet to most of us who undertook the task of organizing psychoanalytic institutes and who knew the European situation, it appeared that the emotional climate in the United States was about ready to accept psychoanalysis as a medical specialty. We felt that the policy of isolationism was no longer justified; on the contrary, it was apt to retard development. I could not formulate this conviction more precisely today than I expressed it in my presidential address to the American Psychoanalytic Association in 1937 (12):

Much of the traditional attitude of psychoanalysts still bears the earmarks of our romantic and heroic past. One still encounters especially among older analysts the stubborn-martyr attitude of the fanatic, the insistence upon the specific nature of the psychoanalyst as distinct from all other scientists, an antagonistic attitude toward medicine which is a historical remnant of the initial feud between Freud and the Viennese medical group. . . . It is most important that psychoanalysts adjust their emotional attitudes to the changes which time has wrought in their environment. They should lose the defensive attitude of a minority group, the militant soldiers of a *Weltanschauung* attacked by and therefore antagonistic to the world. Rather than disseminators of a gospel they must become self-critical scientists. For psychoanalysis as a whole, this leads to the simple but unavoidable conclusion that the sooner psychoanalysis as a "movement" disappears, the better. . . . Insofar as psychoanalysis consists of the study of the functioning of the mind, it is part of and a method in general psychology: insofar as it is a therapy it is an integral part of the larger body of medicine.

For all of these developments the American soil proves to be much more suitable than was the European. Not only geographically but psychologically as well, we are far from the emotional attitudes which led to the feud between psychoanalysis and medicine. The issues in the early development of psychoanalysis which have created these traditional attitudes continued to exist in Europe but have had much less significance in this country; moreover the development of psychoanalysis in America took place after the older emotional controversies had subsided and the fundamental discoveries of psychoanalysis had become a common possession of clinical psychiatry. Finally the tolerant and critical intellectual atmosphere in this country, its political and social traditions, are conducive to the development of every investigative science. The upswing of psychoanalytic research is only one manifestation of the intensive general scientific life in America which is rapidly taking the lead in this field as well as in others.

This was written in 1937 and expressed my convictions, and those of my collaborators in the Chicago Institute for Psychoanalysis, which governed our policies in the first eight years of the Institute's existence. They remained our guiding principles in our teaching activities and outside policies. We felt that the traditional attitudes of the psychoanalyst must be brought into conformity with the changed ideological scene. First of all the traditional insistence on uniformity of opinion had to be modified.

In the past, under concentric attack by critics, the psychoanalyst quite naturally had to stress internal unity. Internal dissension was thought to play into the hands of intellectual enemies. Yet the insistence upon uniformity is a lethal enemy of all scientific progress, which lives on differences in ideas and conceptions. Only a religion based on belief can insist on uniform tenets—science must not only tolerate but encourage criticism and diversity of ideas. Research is an eternal groping toward the unknown. Formulations are only approximations which require constant revisions. This in itself requires constant disagreements of greater or lesser degree. Insistence upon complete uniformity of views is incompatible with science.

Related to this intolerance of diversity of opinion was the lack of perspective concerning the validity of theoretical formulations and the lack of that self-critical humility which is characteristic for all natural sciences and which, paradoxically, increases with the advancement of knowledge.

The staff of the Chicago Institute not only proposed this view in theory but tried to translate it into practice. First of all, we taught the principle of presenting psychoanalytic theory to our students, even to the beginners, in a critical rather than dogmatic fashion. At the same time teachers were encouraged to expose without hesitation their own deviations from traditional formulations, stating their reasons for their divergent views. Our emphasis was on teaching the student to think in dynamic-motivational terms above everything else. This type of teaching does not produce students who are particularly good in examinations, but does make for students who will learn how to learn from their own experience. This form of learning, in my opinion, is the only valuable approach in those fields which cannot rely on a routine repetition of well-established techniques.

Furthermore we tried to counteract the trend toward "isolationism," a kind of scientific nationalism or provincialism, by insisting that psychoanalysis not be considered a separate discipline and a profession strictly distinct from the rest of psychiatry. Undoubtedly the view that psychoanalysis is distinct from the rest of psychiatry had a strong validity in the past; it was the only position that could be adopted by the psychoanalysts. Originally it was not the psychoanalysts who drew the line between themselves and the rest of the medical profession, in particular psychiatry, but the physicians who were responsible. Freud, himself a neurologist, developed his own views in further elaboration of Charcot's experiments in hypnosis. Freud's first collaborator, Breuer, was also a practitioner of medicine. It was the medical profession which turned its back on Freud and this necessitated the growth of psychoanalysis in splendid isolation. Yet there cannot be any doubt that as a method of treating psychiatric conditions, psychoanalysis belongs to the field of psychiatry. As a biologically oriented theory of personality, psychoanalysis constitutes one of the basic sciences in the study of man and belongs both to medicine and the social sciences. Its place is obviously in the universities and it is only for specific historical reasons that psychoanalysis developed outside academic institutions.

The founders and staff of the Chicago Institute maintained the firm conviction that the universities were in the process of becoming ready to incorporate this new branch of science and therapy, and they therefore considered it their task to eliminate those obstacles which were attributable to our own outdated traditions. We decided to build a small model institution—a kind of small university which would operate according to the accepted standards of scientific research and teaching—as a first step toward the unification of psychoanalysis with medicine.

While our student body in the first years consisted primarily of practicing psychiatrists who took advantage of the opportunity the Institute offered in psychoanalytic training, from 1942 on the character of our student body changed. It recruited itself primarily from the residents in the psychiatric divisions of universities and hospitals in Chicago and the Middle West. Psychoanalytic training became the most

sought-after part of their psychiatric curriculum. The penetration of psychoanalysis into psychiatric training began with
a considerable impetus and increased so rapidly that by 1949
the Institute had a population of about 150 candidates in different phases of training.

The reason I present the developments in Chicago is not
that they were unique but that I know them from first-hand
experience. Parallel developments took place in other parts
of the country.

A year before the Chicago Institute was founded, Sandor
Rado, upon the invitation of A. A. Brill and with the help
of Bertram Lewin, Lawrence Kubie, and others, developed
the New York Psychoanalytic Institute, adopting the Berlin
model as Chicago did. Within a few years the psychoanalytic
societies in Boston, Topeka, Detroit, Philadelphia, Baltimore,
Washington, Los Angeles, and San Francisco established
similar schools. Although the orientation of the different
institutes was not the same, in general the trend toward the
integration of psychoanalytic and psychiatric training pre-
vailed.

With this increased demand for training, two major problems arose. One was the bottleneck caused by the training
analysis and the other the problem of how to integrate the
psychoanalytic curriculum with the rest of psychiatric training of which it had become a vital part. Residents of psychiatry
insisted upon psychoanalytic instruction and this problem
could no longer be disregarded by the heads of psychiatric
departments.

Concerning the first problem, the Chicago Institute from
the beginning took the position that the training analysis is
an indispensable prerequisite of psychoanalytic training rather
than a part of it. Its aim is to prepare the student for the training. Later this conception of training was adopted by the
American Psychoanalytic Association and the expression, "preparatory analysis," was used as a synonym for training analysis.

The Chicago Institute has always regarded the preparatory analysis as a highly individual process, a matter between analyst and analysand, and we have tried to combat the growing trend to standardize the process of analysis by quantitative regulations concerning the total number and frequency of interviews. We maintained that any such quantitative regulation, aimed at the raising of standards, would lead to a deterioration of standards. Each analysis is judged as successfully accomplished not by external and formalized considerations such as duration but by an evaluation of the students' actual achievements. This can be done by having the students begin to work with patients under supervision during the last phase of their own analysis. Thus the supervisors have a real opportunity to observe the student in actual therapeutic work and can determine whether or not the analysis accomplished its purpose—whether it *did* free the student from those emotional blind spots which interfere with his therapeutic work. The question of evaluating the effectiveness of a training analysis is still an open one. It has preoccupied analytic societies and institutes for many years. This question will be discussed in connection with newer developments in training practices (see pages 189ff.).

The fact that the training analysis has two distinctive aims, the one of training and the other of reconstructing the candidate's personality, makes the therapeutic task greater than that of analyses of patients. Perhaps the greatest difficulty consists in the fact that the training analysis as a standard requirement is the first hurdle which the student has to take. This adds a nontherapeutic motivational force which complicates the problem of the training analysis.

The even larger problem of the integration of psychoanalytic instruction with the entirety of psychiatric training in psychiatric departments of universities is another current and urgent issue. It belongs not so much to the past as to the future of psychoanalytic training.

The first systematic undertaking in this direction was the establishment in 1944 of the Psychoanalytic Clinic within the framework of the Psychiatric Department of Columbia University by the concerted efforts of Drs. N. Lewis, Rado, Daniels, Kardiner, Millet, Levy, and others. A great emphasis was laid on giving the students a well-rounded clinical experience, and the learning was centered on the students' own experience with a great variety of cases. More recently similar developments have taken place in the Long Island College of Medicine under the direction of Sandor Lorand.

In Chicago we met the problem of the coordination of the psychoanalytic training of residents with their psychiatric curriculum in a somewhat different manner. Instead of affiliating with one university, the Institute entered into a functional relationship with three different centers of psychiatric residency training: the University of Illinois, the University of Chicago, and the Post Graduate Medical School of Michael Reese Hospital—and more recently with Northwestern University—by forming the Associated Psychiatric Faculties. These four institutions together with the Chicago Institute for Psychoanalysis are in the process of working out a coordinated program in which the Psychoanalytic Institute undertakes the major part of the psychoanalytic instruction of the residents in a close and systematic coordination of all phases of the psychiatric curriculum.

As in the Columbia Institute, and in our Institute, the original Berlin model of training has been modified by an increasing emphasis upon teaching both practice and theory through first-hand experience of the students with clinical material. This principle was implemented by a carefully planned curriculum which has been worked out in detail by a committee under the chairmanship of Thomas French and further elaborated more recently by a committee under the chairmanship of Joan Fleming. This revised curriculum retains the same principles as the previous curriculum but succeeds in making a better integration of the theoretical courses with the clinical work of the students.

The strict sequence according to which theoretical indoctrination should be followed by practical application has in a sense been reversed by exposing our students from the very beginning—in clinical demonstrations, case seminars, and diagnostic seminars—to a large number of patients and by presenting to them both the traditional and the more recent theoretical views on the basis of their own first-hand observations. The previous system of early theoretical indoctrination, however, is so deeply rooted that this new trend will only gradually be accepted as a general principle.

Another modification of the curriculum in the Chicago Psychoanalytic Institute consists in dividing the personal analysis of the candidate into two phases. The second part of his training analysis takes place after the candidate has successfully conducted one or two supervised cases. This means a period in which the candidate's training analysis is interrupted. The interruption takes place when the training analyst feels the candidate is ready to undertake his first supervised case. This interruption has been introduced on account of the frequent observation that the candidate's personal analysis often interferes with his supervised work. Under the influence of his own analysis he is apt to project his own problems into the patient's material. This system is not rigidly enforced but is conceived as the general design of the training to be applied individually, allowing for exceptions.[4]

Another kind of recent development is, in my opinion, most promising from the long-term point of view. It consists in the organization of analytically oriented university departments of psychiatry or the reorganization of existing ones to include this orientation. These developments have validated the belief we have maintained for over twenty years that in

[4] See the remarks of Appel about the temporary disturbing significance of the personal analysis upon candidates' therapeutic work. See Chapter X.

the United States the medical schools are in the process of becoming ripe for the full acceptance of psychoanalysis. It can be expected that in these new university departments of psychiatry complete assimilation of the teachings of psychoanalysis, both in the psychiatric curriculum and undergraduate teaching, will gradually be accomplished. Psychoanalysis as a medical discipline will find its way back to its birthplace and natural homeland, the university, from which it has been separated for the last sixty years only because of the inertia of the human mind.

However, even after psychoanalytic training has become the responsibility of the psychiatric departments of medical schools, the fact will remain that not all residents of psychiatry will specialize in psychoanalytic therapy. This brings us to the next and most pressing issue—the teaching of psychoanalytic theory to residents who will not practice psychoanalysis in its traditional form.

2. RESIDENCY TRAINING OF PSYCHIATRISTS

Traditional attitudes and institutions have a tendency to survive even if the conditions which originally created them no longer exist. I have repeatedly pointed out that logically there is little reason for having the training of residents in psychoanalysis separated from the rest of their psychiatric training, to be carried out in two different institutions, one in the department of psychiatry and the other in an independent psychoanalytic institute. As long as psychoanalysis had to guard itself against the corrosive influence of emotional resistances, such an isolation was not only necessary but most desirable. Today the emotional atmosphere has changed. The prestige of psychoanalytic training has risen in the eyes of the student as well as with the university administration. The general trend in this direction is unmistakable although it may be argued that most universities are not yet ready for a complete assimilation of psychoanalysis. Only a careful survey of the present situation could give a satisfactory answer to this question. There can be no doubt, however, that in a large number of leading universities psychiatric residents are more or less systematically exposed to psychoanalytic principles taught by trained psychoanalysts. Some of the residents are also encouraged to become candidates of psychoanalytic institutes in the vicinity.

The question today is no longer whether or not psychoanalytic training is an essential and basic part of psychiatry. It is recognized that the understanding of personality development, unconscious processes, functions and dysfunctions of the ego, and the general theory of neuroses are as basic for psychiatry as are neuroanatomy, neuropathology, and neurophysiology. The problem which we are facing today is the nature and amount of psychoanalytic instruction to be offered to residents.

While psychoanalytic knowledge is a fundamental requirement, the application of this knowledge in the form of traditional psychoanalytic treatment is only one of its therapeutic applications. Moreover, psychiatry today offers a great many other methods of treatment. Not every resident of psychiatry is going to become a psychoanalyst. Psychoanalytic institutions in the past as well as in the present have been concerned exclusively with the training of future psychoanalysts. It is obvious that psychiatric residency training has to be broader and less specialized. At present a great part, probably the majority, of psychiatric residents are inclined to undergo complete psychoanalytic training and to be recognized as psychoanalysts.

This, of course, is only an impressionistic evaluation of the present state of affairs, since no polls have been taken. The number of applications to psychoanalytic institutes from residents of psychiatry, applying to be accepted as candidates, however, unmistakably shows the trend.[5]

[5] According to a recently published statement in *Trends and Issues in Psychiatric Residency Programs*, formulated by the Committee on Medical Edu-

Psychoanalysis today is a subspecialty in the field of psychiatry. All candidates for psychoanalysis are required to have completed psychiatric training or to begin the course of training when they apply to psychoanalytic institutes.

As has been stated, a large portion of candidates plan to get further training in psychoanalytic institutes. Not all of them achieve this goal, principally for three reasons.

1. The most important factor is the scarcity of training facilities: only a fraction of applicants to institutes can be accepted.

2. Yet even if all residents could receive training, it is generally recognized that personal suitability would make a careful selection necessary.

3. Psychiatry is in the process of offering many other new methods of treatment and some residents are more interested in the nonpsychological approaches.

Each of these factors deserves further discussion.

1. *Restricted training facilities.* The prolonged nature of the psychoanalytic curriculum in itself poses a serious problem. The preparatory analysis, however, is the main source of the bottleneck. The length of the training analysis is unpredictable. As a rule it tends to be even longer than a patient analysis because of the more complex motivational background of the training analysis.

A further difficulty has arisen out of the need for an increasing standardization of the training requirements. With a large number of candidates, individual considerations became less and less possible. Some candidates needed shorter, others much longer preparatory analyses. The American Psychoanalytic Association, in order to avoid substandard training, developed a policy of setting a minimum number of interviews. The wisdom of this policy has been questioned by

---

cation of the Group for the Advancement of Psychiatry, all of 165 residents to whom a questionnaire was sent "indicate their desire for personal psychoanalysis and psychoanalytic training. Twenty per cent are actually having personal analysis, and another twenty-six per cent are having analytic training, concurrently with their residency."

many (see page 182). Trying in this way to combat the evil
of insufficient preparatory analysis of candidates is introducing undesirable effects. The highly individual nature of
psychoanalytic treatment is not compatible with applying
the law of averages. If a certain time is set as a compulsory
minimum requirement, many candidates may have only
formal reasons for continuing their personal analysis beyond
the point of necessity; others again may feel when they reach
the minimum that they are ready for further training, although this may be far from the case. Psychoanalytic treatment is a highly personal and individual matter and every
attempt at standardization by means of averages is incompatible with its basic nature. An analysis can be successful
only with the full unreserved cooperation of the analysand.
The desire to finish it for extraneous reasons is complicating
and retarding. Of course a great number of candidates, those
who were correctly selected, will not be greatly influenced by
these factors. This is another reason why selection is so
fundamentally important. Those who are not suited per-
sonality-wise will not become successful analysts with or
without the retarding effect of bureaucratic regulations. In
other words, the unfavorable effect of a standardization of
training would become less important if we succeeded in
developing adequate selection procedures. But even if it were
possible to handle each training analysis individually, adjusting it to the candidate's specific needs, the bottleneck resulting from the relatively small number of training analysts and
the prolonged nature of the personal analysis would still
persist.

2. *Suitability*. Despite the fact that the principles of
psychodynamics and its application in therapy are becoming
more and more precisely formulated, and thus more teachable,
experience shows that not every person is equally suited to
becoming a successful psychoanalytic therapist. The problem
of selection of candidates according to their personality make-

up has been for years one of the main concerns of psychoanalytic institutes. In almost all centers (particularly the
Menninger Clinic (24, 65, 66) and the Chicago Institute) constant experimentation has been carried out to find selection
procedures which fulfill the expectations of the admission
board. In national conventions round-table discussions deal
repeatedly with this problem of determining the suitability of
a candidate for becoming a psychoanalyst.

The treatment situation gives ample opportunity for a
subtle expression of the analyst's own emotional needs. For
example, the patient's dependence upon the therapist may
help the therapist to build up his own feeling of importance.
Even more serious problems arise from the fact that the
analyst may project his own unresolved conflicts onto the
patient by the mechanism: "I am not the one who is insecure
or destructive, but he is." He will discover his own sins in
the patient. The tendency to dominate, to direct, the urge to
re-create the patient after his own image, all these have an
ample opportunity to be expressed in the therapeutic situation.
Though gratifying to the analyst's own unconscious needs,
they are interferences in the therapeutic process.

One of the most important functions of the candidate's
preparatory analysis is to resolve emotional conflicts of this
kind and thus increase the candidate's suitability for becoming a therapist. Experience shows, however, that there is
a much greater chance that this goal will be achieved if the
candidate is a mature person who has no extreme neurotic
conflicts. The training analysis can by no means completely re-
mold a person. It can only reduce his neurotic problems and
free his personality assets.

What are these assets, the native talents, and how can we
improve them? A good soldier should be basically courageous,
yet he must learn not only such technical details as how to
handle a gun but he must be hardened against strain and
dangers and educated to accept discipline. This is a kind of

psychological training in contrast to technical training. From the psychoanalyst too we require such a psychological preparation. Just as some persons make good soldiers, so certain personality types are better suited to becoming psychoanalysts than others. What types of personalities, then, are most qualified for becoming psychoanalysts? Obviously the faculty of understanding other persons' motivations is essential. Although every mentally healthy person of normal intelligence possesses a certain amount of the natural faculty of understanding other people, this faculty varies tremendously from man to man. Some people have a fine grasp of space and time relationships, often seen in those mathematically inclined. Such people will obviously make good engineers; they will not necessarily make good psychologists. Mechanical and psychological aptitudes are not always found together in the same person. Obviously, we shall have to choose psychologically gifted persons. Not all of these, however, would make good therapists. Many salesmen, hotel managers, and head waiters have a good practical ability to size up a customer. This faculty is mainly the result of vast experience in dealing with people. Quite different is the fine, sensitive understanding of poets, novelists, and dramatists. It is a truism that people who themselves have suffered mental anguish develop a fine psychological grasp. Mental suffering makes people introspective. It is like pain, a permanent irritation which focuses the person's attention on himself. This explains why so many neurotics are interested in psychology and gifted in it. Some neurotics develop a keen sense for other people's weaknesses because they find consolation for their own difficulties in discovering the same weaknesses in others. Another group of neurotics becomes sensitive to other persons' psychological problems out of empathy: they readily identify themselves with their fellow sufferers.

The common denominator of the types who have a good

intuitive grasp of other people's mentality is that they all have a well-developed introspective faculty which is often the result of mental suffering experienced in the past. Some of these sufferers have succeeded in overcoming their difficulties without developing pronounced neurotic trends. Unfortunately, this healthy group of psychologically gifted persons forms the minority. The psychoneurotic group therefore constitutes a large portion of the human material from which we will have to choose. Many of them can be helped by psychoanalysis and become good psychoanalysts.

According to my experience, they can be roughly subdivided into two classes. The first is the *sympathetic* type who because of his own suffering easily identifies himself with the neurotic sufferer and by helping him tries to solve his own problems. The other is the *aggressive* type who finds consolation from discovering and emphasizing the same weaknesses in others that he senses in himself. The preparatory analysis of these two types offers distinct problems. The aggressive type is by far the more difficult and will need an extremely thorough emotional reorientation before he can become a good psychoanalyst; the oversympathetic type, too, will have difficulties in his practice. These latter are those overtactful analysts who never dare to make a painful interpretation, who never dare to touch an open wound. On the other hand, their great advantage is that they have a strong therapeutic inclination. The aggressive type often unconsciously begrudges the patient who improves, especially if he himself could not solve his own neurotic problems. Among them are the analysts who can never finish an analysis: they often have extremely perfectionistic attitudes as to when a patient should be considered cured. Their natural inclination is to declare the other person neurotic and not to grant him mental health. They are apt to find everybody neurotic and to request that everybody be analyzed.

We must face the fact that we deal with these neurotic types among our students. A large number of them can benefit from their personal analysis and should be considered suitable material for training. If we exclude them, we will reduce the training material to a relatively small group of mentally healthy and yet psychologically gifted persons. These are the people who have been exposed to mental suffering, which made them introspective and aware of their own internal problems, and yet who have succeeded in overcoming this suffering without developing distinct neurotic trends. This is by far the most promising group. We have no general rules as to how to recognize them, either by cursory examination or psychological tests or both. The study of their life history and previous adjustment gives us the most valuable clues.

We see then that a certain amount of introspective inclination is a necessary quality for the would-be psychoanalyst. Since this is often the result of neurotic conflicts, an optimal amount of neuroticism seems to be a desirable quality. As has been mentioned before, severe neurotic conflicts may offer great therapeutic difficulties, particularly in the training analysis. A great amount of freedom from conflict, on the other hand, often goes with a lack of sensitivity for others and a lack of curiosity about psychological matters.

We have no general rules or yardsticks, I repeat, to find this optimal amount of neuroticism, and past experience shows that two kinds of errors have been frequently committed: candidates have been admitted with neurotic conflicts which did not sufficiently yield to the preparatory analysis, as well as candidates who were handicapped by their lack of native perspicacity for the understanding of motivation, their own or another's.

The chief requirement, however, is what might be called emotional integrity or maturity. We must admit that there are few professions which give more opportunity for the exploitation of other people's weaknesses than psychoanalysis. The patient developing a transference regresses to the helpless attitude that the child has toward his parents. The patient's confidence in the physician is the sine qua non of every psychoanalytic treatment. No matter how important the manifestations of the negative transference may be, they must always be overshadowed by the basic confidence of the patient in the physician. A man who is not strong enough to withstand every possible temptation to use the transference of the patient for other than therapeutic purposes is not qualified to be a psychoanalyst. This temptation can take the most variegated forms. Freud pointed out the sexual temptation. Only in extremely neurotic analysts is this a real danger. Apart from this primitive form of temptation, there are the more subtle emotional exploitations of the analytic situation which have been discussed above only in the most general terms. The analyst who exploits the psychoanalytic situation for his own emotional needs can never be a good therapist.[6]

The question is how to recognize emotional integrity in our applicants. Experience and intuition are our most effective means. It has been recently found, however, that individual experience and intuition can be checked by group interviews and the comparison of individual findings of several interviewers. Even when we use the greatest precautions, we nevertheless often discover an irreversible lack of emotional integrity in our candidates only when they begin to treat patients during their supervised clinical work. The training staff must be willing to refuse further training at this late point to those whose lack of emotional integrity appears to be refractory to treatment. All these circumstances readily explain why leaders in this field have come to recognize the significance of improving selection procedures.

3. *Broader aspects of psychiatry.* From the time that hos-

[6] The question of emotional integrity was discussed by me in a Roundtable discussion of the American Psychoanalytic Association annual meeting, Richmond, Virginia, May 6, 1941.

pitalization of the mentally disturbed was introduced at the end of the eighteenth century until the advent of psychoanalysis, psychiatric treatment consisted chiefly in custodial care, to protect the psychotic and his environment from his destructive and self-destructive behavior. The first effective etiologically oriented organic therapy (chemotherapy) appeared at the beginning of the twentieth century and was restricted to postsyphilitic conditions. Ambulatory treatment of the milder forms of emotional disturbances (psychoneurosis) was the concern of neurologists largely as a side issue. An etiological approach to psychoneurotic disturbances developed only under Freud's influence. Office practice of psychiatry on the present scale is a novel phenomenon, one of the characteristic features of our present era, and psychoanalysis has more and more influenced the ambulatory treatment of personality disturbances.

In recent years, with the development of shock therapies and more lately of new effective pharmacological agents, interest in the organic approach to mental disturbances has revived. At present a resident of psychiatry, preparing himself for his practice, can choose between different approaches of treatment. It appears, however, that both the shock therapies and pharmacological treatments are more effective when used in conjunction with psychotherapy. The prevailing experience is definitely that these other procedures, if properly used, are only auxiliaries of psychotherapy. Their main function is to render a patient suitable for psychological forms of treatment. A basic orientation in personality theory as well as in the principles of psychotherapy, therefore, must remain a central part of the training of every resident (see Chapters X, XI and XII).

The extraterritorial status of psychoanalytic institutes and the fact that they still—and justly—consider it their responsibility to develop the standards and curricula of psychoanalytic training present us with probably the most pressing issue in the whole training situation.

As stated above, organized training in psychoanalysis can look back over an experience of thirty-five years. Its principles have been developed in psychoanalytic institutes, which operate outside of universities. It is only natural that psychoanalytic organizations should feel that they cannot and should not relinquish their responsibility on the instant and transfer it to universities which, in the past, have not given a place to psychoanalysis. Training institutes have developed traditions and high standards which stand up well in comparison with the best-developed branches of medicine.

However, the separation of psychoanalytic training from the residency training is becoming less marked as time goes on.[7] Most of the teachers in psychoanalytic institutes also hold teaching positions in psychiatric departments of medical schools and hospitals. Moreover, most university departments are not only willing but eager to give thorough instruction in psychoanalytic concepts to their residents. With this trend prevailing, it can be expected that the present policy of the Psychoanalytic Association to preserve the autonomic status in teaching will gradually yield to the necessity to integrate the complete training under one unified curriculum. Such a program, in fact, is being approached by some of the university departments of psychiatry. The prevailing policy, however, is to encourage candidates who wish to specialize further in psychoanalysis to apply to psychoanalytic institutes which function as centers for this type of postgraduate training.

Whether or not it is desirable for these institutes to remain autonomous outside of university departments has been recently discussed by Kubie (73), who summarizes the ad-

---

[7] This is borne out also by the report of the Committee on Medical Education of the Group for the Advancement of Psychiatry: ". . . the historical dichotomy of psychiatric and psychoanalytic training is slowly being modified, and certain trends toward integration are discernible."

vantages and disadvantages of the independent institutes. The advantages, according to him, are mainly of a practical nature. The individual nature of psychoanalytic training requires large staffs, and few medical schools have been willing, or able, to add a psychoanalytic unit of appropriate size. A further practical advantage is that an independent institute can give training to residents in several medical school departments of psychiatry in their neighborhood. This is well exemplified by the Associated Psychiatric Faculties in Chicago, in which four psychiatric departments of medical schools and hospitals in that city and the Illinois State Hospital System are affiliated with the Chicago Institute for Psychoanalysis. The residents of these institutions receive their training in psychoanalysis from the Chicago Institute in a program which is integrated with the rest of their psychiatric training.

A disadvantage, according to Kubie, is that the independent schools are forced to operate largely as night schools with the "energies of tired men." Moreover, on account of their varied responsibilities, the students' work cannot be as easily controlled or supervised as it would be if "all of their activities were concentrated in one single organization which had the authority and prestige which universities and medical schools command."

Kubie further mentions the difficulties of independent institutes in providing the students with suitable outpatient material. This difficulty has never been felt at the Chicago Institute, which from the beginning has sustained an outpatient clinic as the axis of the whole Institute.

And finally, the difficulty of financing independent institutes is also considered by Kubie.

I may add a more basic disadvantage of the independent institute which is not of a practical nature but pertains to the whole plan of postgraduate training in psychiatry. Psychoanalytic theory and practice, as has been emphasized several times in this discussion, is in the process of becoming an inttegral part of the whole of psychiatry. Consequently, much of the theoretical training in psychoanalytic institutes is being duplicated in the departments of psychiatry. Psychiatry deals with the cure of all disturbances of personality and as such constitutes a unity. Basic psychiatric training, training in psychoanalysis and psychotherapy will eventually have to be organized according to a unified plan, even though advanced training in psychoanalysis will have to be reserved for residents particularly fitted for and interested in this further specialization.[8]

There is no logical reason why this further specialized training could not be carried on within the framework of the same department provided the latter can build up an appropriate teaching staff, including training analysts who can participate in the theoretical instruction and can undertake both the preparatory analysis and the supervision of the candidates' clinical work. The separation of psychoanalytic training from medical schools has historical but not logical reasons. As soon as those cultural factors which necessitated this separation disappear—and they are in rapid process of disappearing—it will be only a question of time when this unification of training in psychiatry and psychoanalysis will be carried out within the existing medical schools.

The only meaningful question today is how fast this unification should take place. Should it be encouraged as something which is long overdue; retarded because it is premature; or should a laissez-faire attitude let natural growth take its own course? I do not think that there is a positive answer. Much depends upon local conditions such as the orientation of the heads of the departments, the attitude of the rest of the medical faculty, availability of training analysts, and a number of other local factors.

[8] See Appel's statement in the next chapter in which he points out further advantages of incorporation of psychoanalytic training into university departments of psychiatry.

It is important to realize that we are dealing here with two separate questions. The one is whether or not both the generally required basic training for all residents of psychiatry and the further specialization in either the somatic approaches or in psychotherapy and in psychoanalysis can, and should, take place in the framework of the psychiatric departments of medical schools. The other question is how to integrate the general training for psychotherapy with psychoanalytic training, no matter whether it takes place in the university departments or partially in universities and partially in autonomous psychoanalytic institutes.

In regard to the first question I have repeatedly expressed my expectation that the unification of general psychiatric and specialized psychoanalytic training within university departments is inevitable and will take place in the future, in some universities sooner than in others.[9] If psychoanalysis continues to be gradually incorporated into medicine and psychiatry as an integral part of it, the ultimate outcome can be predicted with certainty. The prevailing trend among residents is to seek full training in psychoanalysis. One can predict that the future teachers of psychiatry, recruited from the present-day residents, will feel competent to organize psychoanalytic training within their departments.

It is a source of satisfaction to reread a plea I wrote in 1932 for the incorporation of psychoanalysis into both undergraduate and postgraduate curricula in medical schools (13).

[9] The Committee on Medical Education of the GAP came to similar conclusions: "The current trend toward integration of psychoanalytic and psychiatric training seems not only inevitable but constructive. . . . *There is a definite trend toward the assimilation of psychoanalytic training into psychiatric residency programs. This trend has created new problems for both the resident and the psychiatric educator. The Committee notes with concern that the value of alternative possibilities of independent, concurrent, or integrated psychiatric and psychoanalytic training still rests on inadequately supported personal opinion. Because of this there is a need for objective, critical examination of what different teachers teach in their various settings, the basic assumptions underlying their teaching and the effect of their teaching on the learner. Regardless of institutional setting, a dispassionate, investigative attitude is urgently needed.*"

It is not necessary to repeat the reasons why the young psychiatrist has to learn modern psychopathology outside the universities in private institutions and frequently at a financial sacrifice. Denied support, education in psychoanalysis is at present a private undertaking. This circumstance alone is responsible for the unusual expense which training in psychoanalysis involves. . . .

The importance of psychoanalysis for psychiatry should be sufficient to warn the medical authorities that it must not be left to the private initiative of the students to learn the basic concepts of psychopathology which in the last two decades have proved therapeutically more useful and productive than the morphological investigation of the central nervous system. There is no justification for assuming that this condition will last. Progress in science has always followed advance in methodology and although the prevailing methods of brain research seem to be approaching their limit, no one can tell when new inventions will enlarge the possibilities of somatic research.

Teaching, however, cannot be based upon future possibilities. . . . In training the psychiatrist, the acquaintance with psychoanalysis has proved to be at least as important as somatic studies. There is no objective justification for the one-sided and primarily somatic training of the psychiatrist. . . .

The special training of the psychiatrist should be divided in two equal parts: training in the morphology and physiology of the central nervous system and its disturbances and in psychoanalytic normal psychology and psychopathology. . . .

To sum up my proposition: the teaching of psychoanalysis in medical schools should take place in three different required courses, the first two for undergraduates and the last one for graduates:

1. Elementary introduction in Psychoanalytical Normal Psychology, (a) Manifestations of the Unconscious, (b) Development of the Personality given at the beginning of the medical curriculum parallel with the courses in anatomy and physiology.

2. Theoretical course in general psychiatry, one part of which should be devoted to psychoanalytic psychopathology.

3. Training in psychoanalysis during or following the internship in a psychiatric hospital consisting of (a) didactic analysis, (b) theoretical training and (c) practical training.

The third part of this scheme is well established through many years' experience at the Psychoanalytic Institutes and has actually been followed by many young psychiatrists of both continents. Its introduction into the official postgraduate training of psychiatrists does not involve any innovation or experimentation and would mean merely the official and formal sanction on the part of the medical faculties of a procedure which is followed more and more by the younger psychiatric generation. . . .

If I have succeeded in convincing the medical profession that the present state of affairs, in which a fundamental, practical and theoretical contribution to medicine is excluded from the medical schools, is unjustified and undesirable, this book will have served its purpose.

To a great extent these proposals have now been realized, twenty-two years after these sentences were written.

The answer to the second question concerning the integration of psychoanalytic teaching within residency training depends upon both practical and theoretical considerations. There is no generally accepted solution. It has been stated before that psychoanalytic training in the last thirty years has developed its own traditions, while psychotherapy and therefore the teaching of psychotherapy are much less uniform and standardized. On the other hand, psychotherapy is in rapid process of transformation from intuitive, free-for-all procedures into rational approaches based mostly on the same theoretical concepts and techniques that are used in standard psychoanalysis.

The all-pervasive impact of psychoanalysis upon the whole of psychiatry in the United States, on both psychiatric practice and training, is of comparatively recent origin. It is perhaps somewhat arbitrary to set the date at the Second World War and the years immediately following. Oberndorf traces back the influence of psychoanalysis to the twenties (80). With the formation of organized psychoanalytic institutes in the thirties this influence was greatly enhanced. The Second World War, through the pressing psychiatric needs of the Armed Forces, accelerated the penetration of psychoanalytic thought. It is not astonishing that the full impact of psychoanalysis upon psychiatry, particularly on psychiatric training, has not yet been organized and formalized. There is no more urgently pressing task in the field of psychiatric training than to channel this influence in a desirable direction.

We are in the midst of a rapid development which cannot be changed fundamentally by any organizational measures. Organization can only retard or hasten an inevitable course of events. In order to predict the direction, the speed, and the exact nature of this natural development, one should first know the actual training practices and opinions of leaders in psychiatry. To this end I asked a number of teachers in psychiatry to answer the following questions:

1. Do you consider it necessary for every psychiatrist to get theoretical instruction in the basic concepts of psychoanalysis, particularly in a) psychodynamics, b) ego development, c) instinctual development, d) utilization of psychoanalytic principles in making a diagnosis and prognosis, e) theory of psychoanalytic treatment, f) the utilization of psychoanalytic concepts in psychotherapy?

2. Where do you draw the line between teaching psychoanalytic theory to psychiatrists and to candidates for psychoanalysis? How sharp is this line? How much individual consideration do you make according to the student? Do you have any idea whether those psychiatrists who do not become candidates of a psychoanalytic institute do use in their practice psychoanalytic principles which they learned in their residency training and do they keep within the limits of their instruction? What is your experience? Do many of them engage in psychoanalytic therapy considering themselves something like dynamic psychiatrists although they do not get formal recognition from the American Psychoanalytic Association? Particularly I should like your opinion of the actual situation.

The following chapter deals with the answers to my questions.

Chapter X

OPINIONS OF CONTEMPORARY
TEACHERS IN PSYCHIATRY

I RECEIVED twenty answers to my questions; fifteen of the answers are quoted here verbatim and five, which were not comprehensive statements, are partially quoted or summarized.

Kenneth E. Appel, M.D., Professor and Head of the Department of Psychiatry, University of Pennsylvania:

General remarks:

The constructive contributions of psychoanalysis to understanding human behavior and to clarification in psychiatry have been inestimable. My concern is that psychoanalysis maintain its positive contributions and potentials by subjecting its formulations and procedures to continuous scrutiny and re-evaluation, which is the method of progress in the basic sciences and medicine. It is in this spirit that the following comments are submitted.

The teaching of psychoanalysis in my experience is best done around actual case material—psychiatric patients—whether psychotic, psychoneurotic, psychosomatic, character neuroses, social psychopaths, drug addicts or alcoholics, marital problems, educational and vocational difficulties, or organic conditions (such as arteriosclerosis or heart disease) if psychological factors are involved.

Case conferences can be held in which a group of residents and the staff participate, led by an analyst of experience or a training analyst, with comments contributed by residents in psychoanalysis, by former residents in psychoanalysis, and by residents with no psychoanalytic training. Observations, criticisms and contrasts, suggestions and even phantasies or extrapolations are helpful, enlightening and stimulating. The case conference method offers the opportunity for growth and learning in action, and practice, rather than in vacuo, or largely through lectures and theory. It affords vital communication and clarification in connection with living, challenging problems—episodic vividness instead of only the outlines and theories which come from lectures. The latter may afford verbal mnemonics rather than usable tools for understanding and therapy. In the exigencies of meeting problems in actual practice, theoretical refinements are minimized and the basic contributions of psychoanalysis stand out. The liveliness of emphases of different students, drawing on their varied backgrounds and reading, makes psychoanalysis a growing experience rather than the recall of paradigms and theory.

The same applies to seminars giving continued study to a single case, to the supervision of intake interviews, to supervising conferences of residents on cases, and to correlation courses before a medical class, with members of other departments or disciplines of the medical faculty actually participating. In a case of obesity, for example, psychiatry and psychoanalysis can be correlated with medicine, endocrinology, biochemistry and physiology.

Straight lectures on psychoanalysis can become formal, dry, nonvital. There is a tendency to overrefinement, overemphasis on details and theoretical differences. The lecturer is apt to stick too closely to the particular school or persuasion in which he happened to have been trained. Lectures, therefore, tend to be far less stimulating than discussions which come from the challenge of problems and serious emergencies where decisions have reality and importance for patient and doctor alike. Students can be referred to articles and books in the psychoanalytic literature to clarify certain points on aspects of theory and therapy. The difficulty of the patient stimulates the resident to search in the literature for the experience of others. All this is stimulating and means something vital to the resident. It is a usable lever rather than an intellectual excursion, however fascinating. Study in practice helps the resident see what the patients' processes present in actuality, rather than in the simplified stereotypes so often presented in lectures and textbooks.

In our institute and medical school ninety percent of the residents are ultimately analyzed. They go to the Institute or the Association to receive their formal courses in psychoanalysis. If I were in an area where such facilities did not exist, I would have a psychoanalyst on the staff to give the instruction and conduct discussions as suggested above. Or I would import an analyst for case conferences and seminars once a week or twice a month. For third-year graduate students more systematic seminars, discussions, and lectures could be held. For some especially sophisticated or gifted residents, this might be afforded in the second year of training, but in my experience preferably in the third year.

Answers to specific questions:

While personal analysis is most desirable for most psychiatrists, it is not necessary for all. However, theoretical and practical instruction in (a) psychodynamics, (b) ego development, (c) instinctual development, and (d) the theory of psychoanalytic treatment is necessary for all psychiatrists for comprehensive thinking in psychiatry today. Instruction, however, should not be limited to psychoanalytic thinking. There is neurophysiologic, endocrine, chemical, and medical knowledge that is quite as necessary—for example, the recent discovery of the neuroanatomic center for stimulation which is selected by animals in preference to food, resulting in starvation. Psychodynamics (a) has become such a part of standard psychiatry that it has almost lost its psychoanalytic origin. Instruction in (b), (c), and (d) should be given stressing the divergent emphases of different reliable investigators. An adequate and fair presentation of differing observation and emphases is lacking, so far as I am aware, in most institutes of psychoanalysis.

As was indicated above, psychoanalytic instruction, in my opinion, should first consist of case discussions as a sort of "vital staining," always with assigned reading relevant to the case material and doctor-inpatient problems, both texts, journals and theoretical articles. Theoretical lectures should come in later years of residency or years of experience (i.e., the third, fourth, or fifth years).

The utilization of psychoanalytic concepts in psychotherapy is important but more difficult for both resident and teacher. It is important for the student to learn when not to use some kinds of psychoanalytic therapy. There are many times when there is an attempt to use psychoanalytic concepts of therapy in the practice of psychiatry when it is a waste of time and even harmful. This applies to prolonged exploration in prepsychotics by inexperienced doctors, with the danger of precipitating a psychosis, or attempts at free association and interpretation in the case of mild psychotics, misdiagnosed as neurotics or character neuroses, or the use of uncovering techniques when ego-support is needed, or attempts at prolonged intensive therapy when brief therapy is indicated. Many people do well on a half hour a week when fifty minutes twice a week may be advised, which would overstimulate dependency or serious anxiety.

The use of psychoanalytic principles in making a diagnosis and prognosis is the least solid ground of psychoanalysis. The drive for psychoanalytic practice or the use of psychoanalytic principles in practice for self-reassurance or status and prestige often leads to premature use of psychoanalytic principles or the unjustified, unwise, or harmful use of them by inexperienced people. This drive for status and sophistication has led to overemphasis on the psychoneuroses; difficulty in the diagnosis of mild psychoses because of inexperience with severe ones; and insufficient familiarity with the natural history of many psychiatric reaction types. It has led to mistaken diagnoses of the severe reaction types, misevaluation of the depth of the processes involved, or disregard of the value of pharmacological or physical methods of treatment. Fascination with psychological problems has often led to long and expensive psychotherapy when drugs and other methods would have brought amelioration or relief.

It is difficult to draw a line between teaching *psychoanalytic therapy* to psychiatrists and candidates for psychoanalysis. At the University we do not make any distinction because the analytic student will be going into the psychoanalytic institute. Ideally students headed for the practice of psychoanalysis should receive more training in practical work with the psychoses and chronic conditions so that they can become familiar with the natural history of diseases, in order to be able to make more accurate diagnoses, to prescribe the appropriate treatment and not rely on one type indiscriminately, and to be able better to evaluate the results of therapy. Rigid uniformity of training seems to me stultifying. It is illogical to expect that one standard routine of treatment will be appropriate to a variety of different conditions, such as conversion hysteria, anxiety states, reactive depressions, endogenous depressions, obsessive phobic conditions, and preschizophrenias. In graduate education, the same type of education to all without discrimination seems unwise. I believe there has been too much rigidity and uniformity both in therapy and in the training of analysts. Some day I would hope that curricula would be variously developed so that different courses, different requirements, and different types of supervision would be available for (1) those planning to practice psychoanalysis alone, (2) those planning to practice general psychiatry, (3) those planning to teach, and (4) those planning a life of research.

My answer to the question as to whether psychiatrists who do not become candidates of the psychoanalytic institutes use, in their practice, the psychoanalytic principles which they have learned in their residency training and keep within the limits of their instruction is in the affirmative. I believe there is surprisingly good ethics among residents who have not had psychoanalytic institute training and yet who have learned psychoanalytically oriented thinking and therapy in their residency training. There is surprisingly little misrepresentation. I believe they are better therapists for their training. Nonanalyzed psychiatrists are better therapists if they have rubbed shoulders with residents or psychiatrists in psychoanalytic training and under instructors who have been psychoanalyzed especially in the more liberal centers.

Many students or residents lose confidence in themselves when they go into psychoanalysis. They lose their security and mistrust even their own observations and their capacity to draw conclusions. As a result of their anxieties they often withdraw into ultra-passivity, hesitating to make positive statements or decisions. Patients feel this intuitively and frequently want to change doctors. Or they withdraw behind dogmatism and devotion to ritualized paradigms, adopting without discrimination an inflexible non-giving attitude (when it is appropriate to afford security) even to the extent of sadistic, defensive aloofness. This also applies to relationships with families, relatives, and family doctors. They are left hanging in ignorance with no attempt on the therapist's part to explain that contact with the family and others may be detrimental to therapy. Unreserved deference and submission to the judgments of the young sophisticate are often expected. I do not see psychoanalysts of experience developing these difficulties or exhibiting such poor public relations. The anxiety of the resident or young doctor in psychoanalytic treatment or training not infrequently limits his effectiveness up to forty or sixty percent of his previous capacity.

This situation may last from one and a half to two and a half years. It does not happen with the older, more mature, more stable psychiatrists or those who have had a number of years in psychiatry before they have been analyzed.

Dynamic psychiatrists inevitably use psychoanalytic principles and concepts of psychoanalytic therapy. *Much of psychoanalysis has become standard psychiatry today:* the influence of childhood experience, especially familial experience with dependence on the mother or father, the limitations and prohibitions of authority from the parents; overprotection, domination, rejection, indifference; the importance of sibling relationships; acculturation; repression; resistance; disassociation; transference; symbolization; the importance of the unconscious and its indirect, compromised, or substitutive manifestations, and its tapping through free association, dreams, and phantasies. There is less use of free association, more anxiety about regressive and sado-masochistic phantasies, less use of interpretation and little use of the couch on the part of the dynamic psychiatrist in contrast to the pure psychoanalyst. Many dynamically practicing or psychoanalytically oriented psychiatrists are doing excellent jobs, treating types of patients that analysts do not work with and are not interested in, and doing excellent teaching. I have seen excellent senior psychiatrists—men with years of experience—do better jobs of psychotherapy than many analysts of the same age group. I have seen younger men, alert, keen, warm, perceptive, empathic, with a lot of common sense, do better jobs with therapy than their psychoanalytically trained colleagues. The man, I believe, is so much more important than the method or the school to which he belongs. I have seen effective practical work done by men analyzed in the classical school and poor or mediocre work done by those with liberal psychoanalytic training, although by experience I favor the latter in spite of my own classical training.

I have many apprehensions about psychoanalysis in spite of the fact that *it has been of the greatest significance to psychiatry* and to the behavioral sciences. Rigidity, dogmatism, assertion, conviction, authority, indoctrination, so prevalent in many psychoanalytic institutes, are not education. They are like the apprenticeship of the guild system. Preoccupation with rituals, details, and money are frequent. They are indicative of obsessive-anal tendencies. The same applies to the hostilities, rancor, uncompromising spirit, and emphasis on authority. Much of this is not mature or realistic and is often paranoid. This is not to say that there are not men—idealistic, mature, and sincere—who are convinced that the best training is prolonged psychoanalysis in the classical orthodox manner. I would say there always ought to be such but there ought to be provision made for those of more than average curiosity, resourcefulness, and ability to try the new. All the answers are not in. Freud himself spoke of the need of the pure gold of psychoanalysis being alloyed with the copper of practical modifications. And he did not hesitate to use brief psychotherapy when it was indicated. Changes and developments in psychoanalysis bespeak not rigidity, but flexibility, vitality, and progress.

Remarks were made above about the ineffectiveness that often appears in residents during analysis as a result of their anxiety. It was indicated that this was not inevitable and inherent in psychoanalysis. Another related point is the delay in productivity and maturity. Creativity or efforts at creativity are often crushed. Curiosity is not encouraged, often stultified. Curiosity and questioning should be encouraged in graduate education. This I do not find in much of psychoanalytic training today. Somehow the training is too long. By the time a man is through the institute and has had his control cases he is past his middle thirties and often pushing his forties. Then it will take eight to twelve years before he practically and personally sees the results of his analytic methods and the natural history of many conditions. At this time of life, with a profitable practice having developed, there is little likelihood that he will be critical, open-minded, objective, curious, and productive. The important problems, as I see it, that psychoanalysis must solve are the following: not to educate students too young so that they have blind spots to everything except psychology and psychoanalysis and not to prolong psychoanalytic training so long that ossification and crystallization occur, so that activity can only take place in limited and profitable directions.

Personally I believe that the greatest and most permanent contribution of psychoanalysis is its method of investigating human personality. Next would come personality development, but knowledge of this will be greatly modified as new observations pile up. Least effective is psychoanalysis as we know it today as therapy. Evaluative statistics of the results of psychoanalytic treatment ran into great difficulties (1947). It was difficult or impossible to find a definition of psychoanalysis which satisfied a large group of members of the American Psychoanalytic Association.

Conclusions:

More collaboration with medical confreres and members of the basic science faculties in medical schools is desirable. Full-time professors of psychoanalysis are needed on medical faculties to teach, for consultation on patients, to participate in conferences with medical colleagues as do members of other departments. Fellowships should be available for residents, who should be selected on the bases of ability and promise and psychoanalyzed for a minimum fee—selected as are residents in other departments, on the basis of capacity.

Psychoanalysis has been set apart (for historically understandable reasons) in that the teachers have not joined university or medical faculties as full-time men. They have not, therefore, participated around hospitals and medical schools in consultations, in caring for emergencies or seriously ill patients. They have not shared in the medical responsibilities of a hospital. They have not collaborated regularly in joint conferences with other members of the faculty. They have not shared the responsibilities of administration and committee work. They do not rub shoulders in the discussions of critical problems, diagnoses, and treatment or in the discussion of medical, physiological, and chemical problems, in connection with patients or research, in a mutual give and take of suggestions and criticisms, as do our other members of medical faculties. This is of importance to psychoanalysis both as stimulation and criticism, for as soon as candidates of psychoanalytic institutes are finished with their training, often they withdraw from the universities to their private practices where they are immune from the questions of their medical colleagues, and where they teach their students in ways entirely different from their medical colleagues. This separation, geographical, economic, educational, and traditional, makes for isolation and arouses suspicion. This does not make for good public relations for psychoanalysis in medical schools. These handicaps are not necessary; they are not all essential parts of psychoanalysis. Research analysts and teachers could and should join medical and university faculties like other medical faculty members. The organization of facilities for residents should be similar to that for residents in other medical disciplines. They should be relieved of the great financial burden involved, which is unwholesome in itself, which sets them apart from residents in other medical specialties, and early focuses the young trainee inordinately upon the financial aspects of medical practice. A new arrangement could also remove the financial interest of the instructor in his student. Foundations, deans, educators, and prominent analysts should tackle this problem seriously. It would raise psychoanalysis to a new level of education and morale, make for its greater integration with medicine, and I believe increase greatly its possibilities for advancement and research.

More attention should be paid to the personality of the student, his breadth of interest and acquaintance with the humanities as well as science. Capacity to interpret one's self and one's science is especially important in psychiatry and psychoanalysis and we have fallen down here egregiously with our medical colleagues except in a few centers.

Psychiatrists and psychoanalysts have a professional handicap because of their small numbers, compared with the great demand for their services. They are immune from professional competition and almost from criticism. A straw is better than nothing. Personal qualities of integrity and dedication, as well as intellectual capacity, are especially important for psychoanalysts and psychiatrists. Unfortunately some who know the characteristics of maturity and urge their patients to be mature and realistic have not been distinguished for these qualities themselves. They are often very wishful and defensive. Apropos of maturity, it is sometimes observed that, after analysis, formerly friendly, warm, responsive, genial, cooperative persons become hard, defensive, hostile, distant, more self-considering, even suspicious at times, less contributing, more self-seeking financially. When this happens, they are more difficult to work with around hospitals and less collaborating in medical schools. Sometimes this is spoken of as becoming more realistic and more mature. There is often a lack of a sense of humor and of objectivity along with an increase in one-sidedness, due to indoctrination and a sense of loyalty and devotion. Obviously, these are not necessary consequences of psychoanalysis and do not always follow by any means, but they happen frequently enough to be a matter of observation and concern.

It is to be hoped that some day certification by a board will be worked out in some arrangement with the American Board of Psychiatry and Neurology, so that some imprimatur of basic training in psychoanalysis will be effectively recognized.

Also it seems desirable for institutes of psychoanalysis to become associated with departments of psychiatry in medical schools, where graduate training and the idea of a "university" will supersede the craft apprenticeship and guild associations which were perhaps inevitable and necessary in the early days of psychoanalytic development.

Experiment, trying the new, re-evaluation, change, new developments, hypothesis and validation, prediction and prevention are the life of science. Deficiencies in many of these areas are indications of the youth of psychoanalysis. If it is to live up to its tradition and fulfill its promise, it must be experimental and develop new methods and postulates. Psychoanalysis should not and cannot be held static.

Karl Bowman, M.D., Professor of Psychiatry, University of California School of Medicine, and Medical Superintendent of the Langley Porter Clinic, San Francisco:

I agree that it is necessary for every psychiatrist to get theoretical instruction in the basic concepts of psychoanalysis, particularly in the six topics you specify. However, I would raise several questions. To my mind there is considerable divergence of opinion among the different psychoanalytic groups regarding these so-called basic concepts. I understand it is because of this that in many cities there are two or more psychoanalytic groups professing the Freudian orthodox theories. Personally, I would not limit it to this. I feel that the Jungian and Adlerian theories should also be taught to all of our residents. As you know now, we have a fairly strong group of Jungians here in San Francisco, and they have teaching positions in the Department of Psychiatry. I would emphasize at this time that my idea is that all residents should be taught the varying theories of basic psychiatry and psychoanalysis, and that they should be exposed to teachers with different viewpoints. I feel very strongly that at the present time we have a group who have a religious fervor in trying to force the belief in what they consider to be the truth. I do not believe science should be taught in this fashion. We should try to teach our residents to think for themselves and not try to indoctrinate them with a particular point of view.

Since I am not a psychoanalyst and do not participate in the teaching of psychoanalysis in any of the institutes, I probably cannot answer the second question. I would have all of our residents taught the various psychoanalytic theories and if some of these residents are going on to didactic or therapeutic analyses I would still have that a part of our training course. I cannot answer about whether the residents who are taught something of psychoanalytic principles but who are not analyzed "keep within the limits of their instruction." I am sure all of them are influenced by what they have heard about the Freudian doctrines—some of them swallow these teachings uncritically; some reject them rather strongly; some accept part and reject part. This latter method seems to me evidence of a better balanced personality. Since I do not know completely and do not agree with the limits which a nonanalyzed person must observe in giving psychotherapy, I can hardly answer this question. So many things in psychoanalysis have been completely incorporated into modern psychiatry and so many things from outside have been incorporated by psychoanalysis, as if they were the sole property of psychoanalysis, that I find myself in many semantic difficulties. I believe that many of our residents who have not been analyzed are doing psychotherapy which, if you like, can be called "psychoanalytically oriented," and that they would certainly regard themselves as dynamic psychiatrists. I do not see orthodox Freudianism as the sole possessor of dynamic psychiatric concepts.

Henry Brosin, M.D., Director, Western Psychiatric Institute and Clinic, Pittsburgh:

As a teacher of residents in psychiatry and medical students, I believe it essential for every psychiatrist and physician to have some instruction in the basic concepts of psychoanalysis. As a matter of fact, most colleges are offering such courses so that a very large percentage of our residents already come to their training with more or less information. In a few schools interested students form clubs which meet occasionally to review the Freudian literature. Some of these may have the advantage of tutoring under the auspices of a nonmedical teacher or a psychoanalyst. Because psychoanalysis has been a prominent component in the current stream of thought in periodicals, books, and the drama, very few students escape some knowledge of Freudian theory. The very brief review of the influence of psychoanalysis on current thought in *Dynamic Psychiatry* by Alexander and Ross (University of Chicago Press, 1952) illustrates how pervasive Freudian theories are in current literature as well as in the social and biological sciences. The single volume by F. J. Hoffman, *Freudianism and the Literary Mind* (Louisiana State University Press, 1945) describes how deeply Freudian roots have affected the mainsprings of first-rate American writing. These are only a few examples illustrating the fallacy of acting as if psychoanalytic theory were a private commodity. It is all too true that many lay and professional writers misunderstand and misuse this theory but it is a vain effort to shield the student from it.

I need not discuss in detail each of the six categories which you have outlined since it seems to me they are all part of the total matrix of teaching diagnosis and treatment. More emphasis will be given to one or another of these categories according to the bias of the teacher and the needs of the student. I doubt if curriculum planning with weighing of each of these six subspecialties will meet the needs of students since they come to us as highly differentiated adults with widely disparate abilities and education. A core curriculum with small group discussions and tutorial assistance in advanced reading seems to me the best way to introduce the resident to a serious study of Freud. Beyond that his learning will be the function of his own abilities to assimilate experiences under the supervision of men who are well-trained, competent therapists.

The question of where to draw the line of teaching psychoanalytic theory to psychiatrists and to candidates for psychoanalysis seems to me a nebulous one. Current practice in most university training centers does not devote as much time to the study of basic psychoanalytic theories in the residencies as we find scheduled in the psychoanalytic institutes. The residency must of necessity concern itself with a huge amount of theoretical and practical learning in many diverse fields so that it is not feasible to devote as much time to Freudian theory during these thirty-six months as is possible in the psychoanalytic institutes. Obviously the distinction based upon the amount of time spent is not a satisfactory one. Some residents are not as able or interested in the first year in studying Freud as they are in their second or third years so that individual tutorial and supervisory assistance is highly desirable in order to accelerate the student's learning when he is ready for it.

I would like to raise the question, which is well known to you, whether any validated theoretical distinction can be made between teaching psychoanalytic theory to one or another group of interested students. Granted, there will be tremendous differences in their ability to assimilate the various component parts of the Freudian structure, but on the whole it seems to me that a theory about human development and behavior is of a global nature and in a sense can only be taught as a unitary system. It may be true that parts of this system are defective in logic, based upon inaccurate information, deficient in coherence and internal consistency, or may even contain part systems which are fallacious. There may well be irreconcilable experiments or paradoxical effects which are not thoroughly understood or congruent with the overall unitary systems. Perhaps examples from other sciences would be of help to your exposition. The Newtonian description of the attraction between masses is not negated by the flight of airplanes nor was the Ptolemaic system validated by the democratic experience that the earth is flat or that the sun revolves around it. Similarly the apparently irreconcilable debate with "experimental proof" in favor of both the Newtonian corpuscular and the Huygens' wave theory needed an entirely new and quite improbable solution in the form of the quantum theory. I am told that we now have expectations that a similar solution to the Hering-Ladd controversy about color vision may be found in the construction of new *principles*. All of this is all too familiar to you, but I will repeat it for the sake of the development of the argument.

It follows that in other sciences we expect to teach large principles such as gravitation or color vision as unitary theories even though we search them carefully for factual or theoretical inaccuracies and fallacies. One may devote a few hours to such considerations to one student and several hundred hours to another due to the differences of the local setting. All of this has nothing to do with the experimental practice of validating experiments or gaining technical skills in order to accomplish some desired purpose. The proper amalgamation of theory and practice is a special problem in education. For example, I do not know how much more theoretical or experimental physics in engineering the pilot of a large jet bomber needs as compared to the pilot of a B-36. Presumably teachers will draw upon their own experience and that of their colleagues through free communication in order to arrive at an optimal schedule.

You ask whether psychiatrists who do not become candidates of a psychoanalytic institute use psychoanalytic principles in their practice and keep within the limits of their instruction. My experience is that well-trained residents do not exceed the limits of their competence. It is true that a number of the more ambitious wish to act as if they are well-trained psychoanalysts during the early periods of the residency, but this can, in the overwhelming majority, be handled by trained supervisors. If a resident persists in the practice of "wild analysis," we terminate his contract and advise him to seek a therapeutic analysis. It is surprising how modest and well controlled most residents are in relation to this question. In fact, I can recall that in past years, young psychiatrists who had no training at all in psychoanalytic psychotherapy were much more apt to attempt to do psychoanalysis than the well-trained resident who understands his limitations through first-hand experience and insight through supervision. Since this point is of major interest to you I will attempt to say it in another way. From my experience at Chicago and at Pittsburgh it seems to me that the better the training and supervision during the psychiatric residency, the less likely a man will be to attempt to emulate a formal psychoanalysis. There will always be exceptions, but I have been gratified to find that this seems to be true in a large number of young men with whom I have had some experience. It is my impression that men who come from relatively unsupervised residencies with poor faculty control are those who fall victim to the lure of attempting to do psychoanalytic therapy as from a cookbook. Unless a man is relatively isolated, both socially and professionally, from his colleagues, he is not likely to do "wild analysis" because of the criticism to which he is liable. In communities where there is a relatively high standard of moral and medical ethics, therapists are not apt to risk their reputation by practicing methods outside of their competence because these facts become known rather quickly.

I have always had theoretical and practical difficulty in understanding or accepting the propositions by Thomas M. French that partial training in therapeutic methods can be theoretically or practically delimited in a series of logical propositions. Dr. Levine has an excellent statement in support of the position that "limited training" is possible in *Twenty Years of Psychoanalysis*, edited by Alexander and Ross, W. W. Norton and Company, New York, 1953. Grinker, in the same book, points out the paradox [74]:

"Curiously enough, Dr. Levine's expression, by means of a series of comparative phrases, of his concept of the level of the resident's understanding and therapy points out not so much what the non-psychoanalytically trained resident should know more about, but what the psychoanalyst who is doing psychiatry should know in addition to his highly specialized knowledge of unconscious processes (p. 83)."

There is no doubt that there are many differences between residency training and training in psychoanalysis. The time factor, the experience factor, the age factor, the curriculum, and the personal analysis of the candidate in psychoanalytic training are the more obvious identifiable differences. More intangible factors such as loyalties to the institute, unresolved transference phenomena, deep personal experience with the interpretations of resistances, direct experiencing of manifestation of the infantile neurosis, intensive acquaintance with dream interpretation, and the advantages of free association in a special setting are other experiences which are possible criteria for differentiating between the resident in psychiatry and the candidate in psychoanalysis. However, it seems to me to wrong our theories of the unconscious to try to determine mastery of these concepts by a system which limits itself to using time spent, number of cases seen in analysis, or the successful completion of a curriculum as criteria because men vary widely in their abilities to learn in this field. There are a very few men with unusual aptitudes who can learn easily and quickly. Others may never be qualified in the best sense because of their own ego structure. In between we have a wide variety of men with aptitudes in one or another of the various functions with which psychoanalytic training is concerned. The rate of development is often uneven and this in various fields. I would suggest that at some future time when circumstances are propitious the actual management of patients in treatment be closely examined by well-trained psychoanalysts in a group of third-year residents and a group of third- or fourth-year candidates. It may be found that a few gifted residents early in their careers are already exhibiting skills which compare favorably with the more advanced group in spite of the differences in age and experience. This is not to say that psychoanalytic training is not distinctive training and valuable. I believe it is and recommend it to all residents who might benefit from such training. It does suggest that much better criteria must be found in the future. This can be done by hard work and careful attention. It also suggests that selection of both residents and candidates may be the single most vital means by which we can improve the future of experimental psychoanalysis and the practice of psychoanalysis in therapy.

Joan Fleming, M.D., Staff Member, Chicago Institute for Psychoanalysis, and Member Attending Staff of Michael Reese Hospital:

I believe that today it is necessary for every psychiatrist to have some theoretical instruction in the basic concepts of psychoanalytic psychology. The principles of personality structure, dynamic interaction in the mental processes, and the concepts of development of the adult personality form a basis for understanding mental illness which cannot be omitted from any program where individuals who want to understand mental illness are taught. A cornerstone is the psychoanalytic concept of conflict and anxiety as the source of the interference with normal growth and function which results in mental illness.

I believe that many of these fundamental concepts can be taught to medical students so that it is possible for a psychiatric resident to possess a basic understanding of normal processes which may be distorted by various factors and result in maladjustment. The idea of malfunctioning as a cause of illness is taught to every medical student, but the idea that psychological malfunctioning can produce changes in the functioning of the biological organism and that all of these factors can interfere with social adjustments is something that has been neglected in the undergraduate medical school. It should be part of every medical curriculum but must be emphasized again for those who are specializing in the field of psychiatry.

Paralleling these basic concepts in importance for the training of psychiatrists is the idea that for the understanding and the treatment of illness the relationship between the doctor and the patient is paramount. If the resident has learned to recognize that the interpersonal experiences in childhood and in the course of the individual's life span have influenced his personality structure and functioning, then the idea that the relationship between the patient and the doctor is basic for their working together in treatment will not be such a new or difficult one. I believe that the psychoanalytic explanation of the significance of this relationship as described in the concept of transference is of the utmost importance for the resident to understand.

The concept of transference, however, is a very difficult one to teach beginning psychiatrists. It is often defined in a way that covers everything that goes on in the relationship between the doctor and the patient. Every transaction between the doctor and the patient probably contains elements of transference. But not every transaction is of equal significance, quantitatively or qualitatively, in its transference implications. The blanket definition of transference does not allow for the various levels in depth and in intensity which a psychoanalyst knows are a part of the total phenomena of transference reactions.

The confusion that results from the failure to recognize variations in depth and intensity, in positive or negative feeling, in defensive or growth-producing function of the behavior of the patient in relation to the physician results in mistakes in diagnosis and in therapeutic procedure which may actually endanger the patient. The various levels of transference phenomena have different meanings in the picture of the total personality and for the course of the therapeutic process. These differences call for different techniques because they require different experiences for the successful therapy of the patient.

In spite of the difficulties, I believe that it is important to try to teach to psychiatric residents something of the concept of transference and to differentiate the transference elements from other phenomena that are manifested in the interpersonal relationship with the doctor. Many of the latter can be handled and used constructively by individuals untrained in psychoanalytic technique.

Transference is a pathological process that occurs frequently in the acting out of a childhood trauma regardless of the presence of a physician in a therapeutic relationship. It also occurs in therapy as a result of therapeutic efforts. But the latter is something which has to be guided and directed to prevent an intensity which cannot be easily handled either by the patient's ego or by the physician himself.

For the most part, it seems to me, psychotherapy as distinct from psychoanalysis does not have for its goal the working through on a conscious insight level of the childhood traumata. Transference in this form of psychotherapy can be a constructive force when it is not interpreted but when the development of a positive dependent relationship is encouraged which the patient can use but which may never be a part of the patient's insight.

It is a question in my mind whether a psychiatrist who has not been analyzed and therefore never experienced transference from the position of the patient can fully experience the phenomena as they occur from his position as the doctor. However, analysis alone will not accomplish this purpose either, because most young psychiatrists who have had an analysis or are in analysis during the course of their residency training tend to imitate their analyst. They tend to identify with him and to insist upon interpreting their own behavior and the behavior of their patients as if it had the same significance as their behavior with their analyst. Here is an important dilemma for the teacher of psychiatrists. There is a tendency to avoid discussion of transference on the part of some teachers who feel that there should be a sharp line differentiating psychoanalysis from psychiatry, and that the line exists in the area of the technique of handling the transference. I believe this is true, but I do not think this sharp a line can be drawn, or that the topic should be or can be avoided. It seems to me much better to discuss freely the concept of transference and countertransference and to help the resident to differentiate these phenomena so that he can use what factors are of advantage to him in his relationship with the patient and not get involved in a transference situation which he does not understand and does not know how to deal with.

It is only by a thorough discussion of these phenomena and repeated illustration of them in case material that the resident can learn to recognize the difference and know when a transference is something that is part of the patient's pathology and when it is a goal of the therapeutic process for the purpose of working it through with insight and reintegration for the patient.

I have seen many young residents who encouraged the expression of feelings directed toward themselves and who call this transference, failing to recognize their representative position in transference phenomena. They do not look for the significant figure from the past with whom they are being misidentified. Consequently, they enter into the patient's fantasy, unintentionally, to be sure, but nevertheless to the patient they seem to be participating in either an old experience which the patient is repeating or in a fantasy which the patient has always wanted to realize. The latter state of affairs is, of course, the more pernicious and the more difficult to deal with. The resident who finds himself with a clinic patient, perhaps a borderline psychosis, often finds himself in an interminable relationship with the patient. He will not be able to deal with it because he does not recognize the transference elements in the patient's behavior or because the patient's resistance will be too high as a result of the conditions of psychotherapy, namely, less frequent interviews, less structured technique. These conditions are usually less conducive to a thorough working through of transference phenomena.

Psychoanalytic technique, it seems to me, is a different procedure with a different goal, compared to other forms of psychotherapy. The conditions under which psychoanalysis is carried on are more structured and therefore of an advantage both to the patient and to the psychiatrist. The frequency of interviews, the use of the couch, the fundamental rule, are circumstances that facilitate the development of the transference neurosis which can be interpreted and worked through. In the long process leading up to the development of the transference neurosis, the patient has learned many things and has developed the ability to tolerate the loss of contact with present reality which is inherent in the transference without slipping into a more permanent separation from the present reality and continuing irrational interpretation of present events.

For the most part, I believe that the concept of transference is something which should be reserved for second- or third-year residents and that the other aspects of the doctor-patient relationship are the ones which should be emphasized in the first year of teaching. This would include, of course, the attitude of the doctor toward the patient in terms of patience, tolerance, nonjudging, and positive firmness. These attitudes, as differentiated from attitudes of other persons in more usual social relationships, and especially in the developmental experiences of any child with its parents, might include something of the concept of transference, but not the technical handling of it.

To summarize what I have said so far, I would stress in the teaching of beginning psychiatrists the basic concepts of psychoanalysis as regards the development and structure of the personality, the basic concepts of psychodynamics, with principle focus on conflict and anxiety and the mechanisms involved in the handling of these stresses. The third main point in the early training would be the attitude of the physician toward the patient, the importance of the relationship between the doctor and the patient, and something of the idea of the inappropriate repetition of unconscious childhood experiences in the relationship with the physician. It is difficult to separate the material that would be presented at the level of a beginner in psychiatry compared to the material that would be valuable learning for the advanced student either in psychiatry or in psychoanalytic training. The main difference in the teaching of psychiatrists and psychoanalysts, according to my way of thinking, would be in the way in which the theory of therapy was presented.

The utilization of psychoanalytic principles in making a diagnosis and prognosis is again a complicated point. To take a good history is the foundation of the diagnosis and prognosis, and to take a good history one has to know something about the genetic approach and the dynamic factors in the making of a diagnosis. But one also has to know a great many fine points in order to make a good diagnostic formulation and prognosis. This is very difficult to teach beginners. However, I believe that the psychoanalytic principles should form a basis for this psychiatric task.

The line between the teaching of psychoanalytic theory to psychiatrists and to candidates for psychoanalysis: This point has already been discussed to some extent. I think the line should be determined primarily by the elementary level of the learning experience of the psychiatrist. This would indicate more emphasis on observation of phenomena on a descriptive level and practice in diagnosis in its most complete sense rather than the learning of therapeutic techniques. As time goes on the line is determined more by the capacity of the individual psychiatrist. The psychiatric resident, by his second year, and especially by his third year, will have demonstrated a capacity for psychological understanding and for empathic relationships which will indicate whether or not he should go on in psychoanalytic training. This does not mean that the one who goes on in psychoanalytic training is necessarily a better psychiatrist, but simply is equipped or can be equipped to handle psychiatric patients in a different way. The line at this point is a delicate one to deal with because of the status question involved. I think this is something which has to be given much more thought than it has received in the past, both on the point of selection of psychiatrists for psychoanalytic training and on the point of teaching of those psychiatrists who do not go on to advanced training. This question is not a new one in any field of education, and I think the problem has been contributed to by the attitude of psychoanalysts more than by the attitude of psychiatrists who are not psychoanalysts.

I think this state of affairs has tended to make young psychiatrists defiantly rebellious. They tend to feel that they are psychoanalysts or can use psychoanalytic principles without formal psychoanalytic training. I do not believe the recognition from the American Psychoanalytic Association is nearly as important as the local attitude of the teachers of these psychiatrists. In some areas the teaching of residents, especially in a supervisory relationship, has been turned over to very recently trained psychiatrists, some of whom are in psychoanalytic training but not yet finished. This condition has, I believe, tended to foster a very strong spirit of competition, and to make the young psychiatrist feel that his equally young supervisor is in a very superior position with a tendency to depreciate psychiatry as such. I think this is a sad state of affairs and should be studied. Perhaps it can be resolved by study of the learning problems of the student and the teaching techniques best adapted to deal with them.

The supervisory experience is a valuable one for the young residents and a fundamental part of their training, but it involves close personal relationships between the therapist and patient and therapist and supervisor which are difficult for a young person to manage. A recently trained psychiatrist can do a good job in the formal classroom teaching of theory, but I wonder whether it would be better for him to wait to begin the supervisory teaching. His own therapeutic experience is often not rich enough to be able to navigate the complex problems which a student presents to him.

I would advocate in the programs for the training of psychiatrists a setup which would provide for supervisory conferences that would enable younger people to learn something about the teaching of therapy before they are thrown into the middle of the job. So much of the teaching of psychiatry or psychoanalysis has been done in a kind of "do-as-I-do" way or "do-as-I-tell-you-to-do" way. This is not good teaching. The various problems and techniques that can be used in the teaching of psychiatry are a field of study in themselves.

Francis J. Gerty, M.D., Professor and Head of the Department of Psychiatry of the University of Illinois College of Medicine, and Director, Psychiatric Division, Neuropsychiatric Institute:

I shall plunge directly into a statement of my thinking on the matter of teaching psychoanalysis to psychiatrists in distinction from training psychoanalysts, following the outline given in your letter.

I do think it is necessary for every psychiatrist to get theoretical instruction in the basic concepts of psychoanalysis. I think he should receive theoretical instruction in all matters having an important place in his field of specialization. The impression I get from reading your letter is that you mean "main stem psychoanalysis," that is, psychoanalysis coming through the main channel which began with Freud's work through those of his followers who have not departed radically from his essential ideas, particularly as to the constructs concerning the unconscious and the methods he evolved for its investigation with the subsidiary developments concerning psychodynamics, instinct and ego, theory of treatment and its application, and use of the principles derived for the purposes of overall evaluation for diagnostic and prognostic uses. It is my opinion that the psychiatrist should also have formal instruction as to the contributions of Jung, Adler, and others, and in the historical perspective which includes these contributions and enables us to compare one with the other. The chief requirement should be for intensive and thoroughgoing theoretical instruction in the basic concepts of psychoanalysis of the Freudian stream.

I do not know that I am competent to draw the boundary line between teaching psychoanalytic theory to psychiatrists and to candidates in psychoanalysis. Knowledge as knowledge is a province of the inquiring and able mind. Boundaries are to serve the purposes of organizing instruction and to suit certain practical and preconceived aims as to its purpose. Thus, in the organization of the work of the psychoanalytic institute, courses might be offered both as to content and timing so that they would fit in with the requirements of the total program, including personal analysis, specialized seminars and conferences, control analyses, and possibly a good many other matters which would have much less importance, if any, for psychiatrists who were not candidates in psychoanalysis. There would be no difference in the kind of information presented to the two groups or as to the general development of ideas. It would be a matter of degree of utilization, not of a kind or quality of instruction. Individualization of instruction and depth of effect should be expected to be much greater for the candidate in psychoanalysis. We should bear in mind the fact that what might be called a pattern processing is more observable in this group. By this I mean that there are those who, for a number of reasons not of uniform weight and value in different individuals, wish to fit themselves into a kind of preconception of the professional figure of the psychoanalyst. A great many of them seem to have been remarkably successful in accomplishing just this. In other words, they have the seal of approval. This seal by itself probably does not testify to more than minimum qualification. It must not be easy, in fact it is probably impossible, not to have some such result occur when any organized system becomes the subject for a curricular program. There are in the psychoanalytic candidate group a great many who are strong individuals and will dare to depart in theory and practice from the inculcations of their training. If psychoanalysis remains chiefly a system, it will not be tolerated for long in unchanged form in medicine any more than any other system ever has been. Nevertheless, the system has use when it introduces and lends force to important and new ideas which may not otherwise receive ready acceptance. At what point the new ideas no longer need the protection of the system is not easy to say. In medicine, particularly, poaching of ideas is regular and recognized practice. The vested interests in the system will more or less naturally tend to insist that what has been poached and then developed and modified elsewhere is not equal to the system-grown product. With reference to psychoanalysis, we do not know as yet how much of the system protection is needed. It might be very well for the purposes of research and the testing of new ideas to keep a vigorous, pure culture going but this pure culture of analysts will have to be made up of unusual men to whom the support of the system is much less important than the discovery of truth. Obviously, to one who thinks as I do, the *political boundaries* in the field of knowledge have little significance. I am sure that a good many psychiatrists who do not become candidates of a psychoanalytic institute do use in their practice psychoanalytic principles. But to answer your question as to whether they keep within the limitations of the theoretical instruction which they may have received during their residency training is difficult. My belief is that in the main they do. I do not believe that it is possible or desirable to warn them that they must never exceed the limits of this instruction. The same warning should not by any means be given to trained psychoanalysts either. This means that risk is involved here. But it is such a risk that must be taken every time we experiment with any new method of treatment. So many of our advances in knowledge and medicine have been what we call extralegal and at the personal risk of the innovator, that prohibitory manifestoes are not advisable. Good persons on either side of the psychoanalytic-nonpsychoanalytic boundary will generate ideas and perform experiments from which many will profit. While we should use all advisable precautions in training physicians for the future, we should not inhibit development and attempt to keep our children forever children.

In another place Gerty expressed himself on this subject and refers in his letter to parts of this publication (55). After discussing the contributions of biological methods in psychiatry, he continues:

Many patients have been cured or helped; favorable attention has come to medicine and psychiatry; research has been stimulated; the doors of general hospitals have been opened to mentally ill patients, and mental hospitals have become somewhat less forbidding places. Undoubtedly, these and other methods of physical treatment have helped promote the private practice of psychiatry. It is doubtful whether they have changed the state of private office practice greatly, have modified much the teaching of psychiatry to undergraduate medical students, or affected the residency training programs remarkably. They have had some effect on all of these, it is true, but private office practice, education of medical students and specialists in psychiatry, psychosomatic medicine, and pediatric psychiatry have been much more affected by developments connected with the treatment of the psychoneuroses. Explorations to discover the place, value, and technic of elicitation and use of psychologic data (in the broadest meaning of the term) in medical examination, diagnosis, and treatment had been long overdue.

The treatments formerly depended on principally for the treatment of psychoneuroses were physical in nature. One need not be astonished that Freud's determined invasion of the unconscious by the free association method and all the things he drew from that capacious "grab bag" aroused suspicion and provoked antagonism which persists to this day. His methods were unprecedented and his manner not particularly conciliatory. I shall not review the history of the psychoanalytic movement or attempt to elucidate the principles and practice of psychoanalysis. Neither do I need to trace the origins of its early schisms and later subdivision into psychoanalytic groups and schools of thought. This must be said: physicians, and, of course, first among them neurologists and psychiatrists, whether or not they have turned into one or another kind of psychoanalyst, have been forced to think about, read about, experiment with, and discover something about the importance of psychologic data—again giving the widest possible meaning to the term—in medicine. It is this chiefly which has affected the private office practice of psychiatry and made it largely psychotherapy. It is this which recently has changed the kind of undergraduate teaching of psychiatry and has so greatly modified the standards of training of specialists in the field of psychiatry. It is this, too, which has chief responsibility for psychosomatic medicine and much to do with the development of pediatric psychiatry.

The force producing most of these changes was psychoanalysis. Of course, a sustained force of this kind is not easily contained. As it burst through the bounds of psychiatric specialization it is still bursting through the bounds of medicine even as it did in its early days in the case of lay analysis. Proposals have been made that a different degree in medicine, possibly Doctor of Psychological Medicine, be granted after a different type of undergraduate medical course which would omit some of the traditional courses in favor of other courses more suited for the intended purpose. It has been suggested that this might be a means of countering the practice of psychotherapy by unqualified psychologists. Psychoanalysts, perhaps more than others in the field of medicine, tend to move quickly in the direction of offering service in the solution of a great variety of social, governmental, and international problems. As sometimes with Freud, a general philosophy seems to overshadow the more definitely medical concepts and technics. There is evidence that psychoanalysts are settling down into the more usual patterns of medical functioning. They are finding their place in medicine and having their effect on it. As they become more generally accepted the need for a protective autonomy will grow less. . . . The interdependence of psychiatry and the rest of medicine becomes steadily more apparent. One can never tell from what direction the help will come to psychiatry for the solution of some of its problems. I would not expect psychoanalysis to survive as an autonomous system in medicine, but acknowledgment must be made of the tremendous contribution of Sigmund Freud and his followers to psychiatry and to medicine. It is well to honor a master ever and to follow him far enough but not to be dependent on him too much or too long.

Roy R. Grinker, M.D., Director, Institute for Psychosomatic and Psychiatric Research and Training of the Michael Reese Hospital, Chicago:

Your first question poses immediately a problem in semantics. Most of the leading training centers for psychiatrists teach the fundamental principles of psychodynamics. Without this inclusion in the curriculum, psychiatry is flat and unpalatable both to the residents and the teachers and would probably consist of nothing more than descriptive phenomenological data and physical therapy. The semantic difficulty involves the use of the word psychoanalysis. We should hesitate to say that we taught psychoanalysis, for psychodynamics is not limited to the concepts and theories of the psychoanalytic school. However, in practice, especially at an institution like ours, where most of the teachers are psychoanalysts, the psychodynamic concepts are almost exclusively psychoanalytic. We try to include some material which has reference to the historical position of Adler, Jung, Rank, and at times even touch on the contributions of Janet. Inevitably, however, the teaching of psychodynamics becomes almost exclusively the teaching of psychoanalytic concepts. We could not turn out residents as finished psychiatrists without giving them a very wide grasp of such psychodynamics, of the concepts of ego development, of the processes of instinctual development. These all are part of our curriculum and considered absolutely necessary. As a matter of fact by the time the resident reaches his second year, he can discuss almost any case from the frame of reference of these three headings. We do not go very far into the theory of psychoanalytic treatment because we have to struggle, as I shall

speak about later, against the tendency of the resident who is
being taught psychodynamics to use these as if he were practicing psychoanalysis. Of course, we discuss the theories of transference and of resistance and attempt to give some general notion
of the process of uncovering therapy. We try to steer away from
a discussion of the development and meaning as well as the interpretation of the transference neurosis. Unfortunately we cannot
avoid the danger which we recognize because in the Journal Club,
where the resident chooses his own articles to review, he selects
many papers dealing with psychoanalytic therapy. Skipping to
the utilization of psychodynamic or, if you will, psychoanalytic
principles in making a diagnosis and prognosis they must be taught
and are in practice taught very thoroughly. When a resident presents a case at a conference, he gives the results of his history taking and the anamnesis in such a manner that a diagnosis and prognosis can be formulated along psychoanalytic lines. In summary then I consider it absolutely necessary for every psychiatrist to get theoretical instruction in the basic concepts of
psychodynamics which ultimately turns out to be psychoanalysis.

Your second question asks where we draw the line between
teaching psychoanalytic theory to psychiatrists and to candidates
for psychoanalysis. We have never felt impelled to draw a line
largely because we know that all our residents are either candidates for psychoanalysis or hope to become candidates. I know
no way by which one can draw a line between psychoanalytic
theory that is useful to psychiatrists as contrasted with that which
is useful for psychoanalytic candidates. Perhaps the analytic institutes go into considerably more detail and perhaps they practice
the theoretical concepts in greater depth on individual cases. Yet
our students after their psychiatric training find that much of
what they obtain in their theoretical courses at the Psychoanalytic
Institute is repetitious. If one can say anything that characterizes
the difference, it is that in the psychiatric training program there
is a much broader acceptance of doubts and a much more candid
admission of the unknown. (You may think it strange that such a
statement should be made in Chicago. It is true nevertheless that
many of the teachers at the Chicago Institute teach orthodox psychoanalysis quoting line for line from Freud and the early analysts, brooking little in the way of doubts or controversy. It is
sad to say but the Chicago Institute has become stricter, less lib-

eral, as the years have gone by and our students remark on this fact many times.) You ask how much individual consideration is made according to the student. I would say that most students are exposed to the general framework of the same kind of didactic teaching. When it comes to supervision, however, in individual cases, those who have a particular flair for understanding psychodynamics are permitted to go much farther into the unconscious processes of their patients. This has to be done with great caution because with very little encouragement the student will embark on a psychoanalytic form of therapy intending to probe to the deepest level of the genetic factors involved in a neurosis and get himself implicated in transference problems that he cannot handle. On the other side of the picture, we encounter students who are psychologically stupid or so sick themselves that we must soft-pedal any consideration of psychoanalytic theory and try to steer them into administrative psychiatry or descriptive psychiatry or a form of neuropsychiatry with the utilization of physical methods. Regarding those psychiatrists who do not become candidates of a psychoanalytic institute for some reason or other, we find that they continue to practice using psychoanalytic principles. There is a large number of these young people doing psychiatry in Chicago who are on the periphery of psychoanalytic training. Some of them have had their personal analyses interrupted, some of them have been rejected for further psychoanalytic training, yet all of these practice psychiatry utilizing psychoanalytic principles and some of them even do wild analysis and speak about their therapy to their patients as if it were psychoanalysis. In this country, where there are no restrictions on practicing a specialty without certification, there is no way by which we can limit the student's activity once he is out of his training institution. In doing personal analyses of residents in training we find that many of them, certainly not from our institution, are urged by their supervisors to place their patients on couches and to make interpretations as if they were analysts in order to "get different material than that obtained when the patient is sitting up." I think we have a real problem in our community where practically all of the institutions involved in the Associated Faculties have been teaching psychoanalytic theory. We may find ourselves overwhelmed and outnumbered by ex-students doing wild analyses. Dynamic psychiatrists do not need to get formal recognition from the American Psychoanalytic

Association. I would say that the actual experience is that many of these nonanalysts who have been trained in dynamic psychiatry consider themselves as analysts and actually practice it.

George C. Ham, M.D., Professor and Chairman, Department of Psychiatry, University of North Carolina Medical School, Chapel Hill, N.C.

My experience is based on my work at Michael Reese Hospital, in the Chicago Psychoanalytic Institute, and the three and a half years here. We are just now getting to the point where some of our residents are completing training, but there have not been enough to fully test the situation. We do, however, have some 24 residents in training as well as junior staff some of whom have not had analytic training, and on this basis I can give you some of my feelings and impressions.

In regard to your first question, I would answer that psychoanalytic theory should be taught to all residents. I think, however, one has to differentiate between theory and practice. I think theory should be taught, but if the man is to use the technique, he should have a good deal of supervision in its use over a reasonably long time (several years).

In regard to question two, I do not think there is a sharp line. My experience so far has indicated that there is quite an uneven spread when one looks at the courses in a psychoanalytic institute and in a training center like this. In many regards the institute's teaching has ignored areas which I would consider to be extremely important to any good psychiatrist or physician and has taught some other areas rather lightly or haphazardly. The hospital center tends, on the other hand, to emphasize the application of psychoanalytic theory to broader and more varied problems as they present themselves in patients every day. The very nature of the "classical psychoanalytic technique" automatically limits the type of patient that can be dealt with and thus limits the teaching in many institutes to the handling of just the "analyzable" patient. This, I think, is unfortunate in that it tends to limit the studies to one group of patients rather than the application of the theory to the many and varied types of problems that are present in society.

In regard to individual consideration according to the student, it must be pointed out that our Residency Training Program consists mainly of giving the resident responsibility and constant supervision. The amount of supervision that our men get is in a completely different bracket from that given in institutes in that we probably, during a three-year period, would give 10 to 50 times as much supervision. Obviously one has to look for and take into consideration the degree of anxiety which is often manifested by resistance or too enthusiastic acceptance of the concepts presented.

In my experience, almost all psychiatrists who are trained in psychodynamics use it in their practice without overtly transgressing the limits of their instruction. It must be pointed out that the psychiatrists with whom I have been associated and the staff here live in a dynamically oriented psychiatric community which has some condescension toward those psychiatrists of any other credo, and where each psychiatrist is easily surveyed by colleagues and rated according to generally accepted standards. If some of these psychiatrists were to move into professionally less structured communities, the attitude of those who are hostile to analysis might change. It seems to me desirable that psychiatrists use their knowledge without attempting to be psychoanalysts. It is interesting only to note that the young men here, who know that a number of us are members of the 'American' and three of us are teaching at the Washington Psychoanalytic Institute, do not have strong urges for formal training through an institute. They seem to wish at the present time to have a personal psychoanalysis by a person of some experience, and to have their seminars and their training within this situation. It appears that centers such as this are gradually taking over the same content and supervisory techniques for the training of psychiatrists from psychoanalytic institutes although obviously we deal with a much broader spectrum of illness than is dealt with in a psychoanalytic institute. In our opinion the men who wish it and some for whom we think it is indicated should be able to have a rather thoroughgoing personal analysis. This would train them to be excellent psychiatrists not limited to psychoanalysis as it is understood today in the restricted and classical sense on patients for whom this technique alone is fitted.

It is interesting to point out something which I think is quite striking. Our undergraduate medical school curriculum, which when I came here consisted of 25 hours of so-called medical psychology, has now been extended so that we are teaching in all four years of the medical school a total of some 1400 curriculum hours.

This does not include the collaboration with the Department of
Medicine, the Psychosomatic Service, and the Department of
Medicine and Pediatrics. The 1400 hours refers to just that time
which the students actually spend under our direct tutelage. We
begin in the first year with a course in the basic science of human
behavior (Human Ecology and Adaptation) taught by anthropologists, psychologists, psychiatrists, preventive medicine physicians, social workers, etc., and give a combination of didactic
demonstrations and small group sessions. The second year is a
course in the development of personality, and the clinical syn-
dromes, using English and Finch's book and your book on psychosomatic medicine. The third-year students spend seven weeks full
time on our inpatient service where they actually have responsibility for the evaluation and treatment of inpatients under supervision. In the fourth year they spend seven weeks in the outpatient
department doing the same thing. It is striking that our third-year
students often have more competence and more knowledge than
do the men who come here for residency after an internship from
some other medical school. This indicates that the type of material, much of which I did not learn until my second year in the
Chicago Institute and as a resident, is now being assimilated, at
least intellectually, by the end of the second year in medical
school. Obviously, this is not a deep-going understanding, but it
is an opening of eyes and a "horizon stretching" which makes for
a much broader understanding of illness and human adaptation.

In regard to the future, I do feel that eventually the men who
are going to be trained as psychiatrists will want personal analysis,
but that as more and more people are trained in this way there
will be less and less need for psychoanalytic institutes. We envisage here the possibility of setting up a degree course in the
University, which for the usual three years of residency will give
the person a doctoral degree in medical psychology. If they wish
to specialize in and spend more time in either child work or psychoanalysis as a special technique this will require two to three
years more, additional seminars, theses, supervision, and a satisfactory personal analysis after which a doctoral degree of psychoanalytic medicine could be given.

At the present time in regard to psychoanalytic training we
have formal relationships with the Washington Institute but interestingly only very few of our residents wish for formal psycho-

analytic training. They state that they do not wish to be just analysts, they want to be good psychiatrists.

With some notable exceptions the training of psychoanalysts and psychiatrists has been directed toward practice—a highly skilled "trade school" approach. Research and research *discipline* and prestige have suffered. In my opinion the outstanding contribution that training centers can make during the next decade is to bring fundamental and applied research into its proper hierarchical position as a goal for trainees that has proper rewards. Only through this will our field continue to advance.

Our efforts are heavily weighted in this direction.

Lawrence S. Kubie, M.D., Clinical Professor of Psychiatry, School of Medicine, Yale University:

I cannot conceive that a psychiatrist could function intelligently without a vivid awareness of the concurrent interplay between conscious, preconscious, and unconscious processes in every moment of life. This would be true whether his interest is in psychosomatic physiology, pharmaco-dynamics, the impact of electrical currents on central nervous functions (e.g., in shock treatment or in electronarcosis) or in the vagaries of so-called psychosurgery. Psychodynamics is as basic for the psychiatrist as is an understanding of the fundamental principles of chemistry, physics, and mathematics, or of comparative morphology and embryology in general biology.

Therefore the problem becomes not *whether* but *how* this firsthand awareness is to be inculcated. This after all is an area to which we bring deep resistances, resistances which make it possible even for trained psychoanalysts to give lip service to the concept of an interplay between psychological processes which operate on different levels or systems, yet without real conviction about it; resistances which often reveal themselves in the ability to talk freely about psychodynamic phenomena, "the unconscious," etc. (since what one distills through one's own head always enjoys a special kind of reality for the speaker), while remaining unable to listen to anyone else using the same words, unable to grant the same words any validity when someone else uses them. (Most of our students go through this phase; and some never get beyond it.) There are resistances which make it pos-

sible for us to recognize the role of unconscious and preconscious processes in everybody else's life, but not in our own. In
other words, this is a quite special problem in education. Consequently it is one thing to keep it before us as a goal for everyone
in the field; it is another to understand clearly how to help everyone to reach this goal.

You may think that after these introductory statements I am
about to plump flatly for analysis for everybody; but I am going
to fool you. Certainly analysis is a deeply important experience;
and one which helps a certain percentage of people to penetrate
this sonic barrier; but, unfortunately, it does not achieve this for
all. There are plenty of "licensed," esteemed, and even distinguished practitioners of psychoanalysis who do not really believe
in unconscious or preconscious processes, although they talk
about them all the time; and this despite one or two or even three
so-called training analyses. That, however, is another story.

The next issue concerns the categories of data which may be
necessary for the training of the psychiatrist. You mention six:
(1) psychodynamics (which I have already discussed); (2) ego
development; (3) instinctual development; (4) theories of therapy; (5) utilization of psychoanalytic concepts in practical
therapy; and (6) utilization of these concepts in diagnosis and
prognosis. These are not coequal subdivisions. Nor are they
equally basic. As I have said, an understanding of *psychodynamics*
is in essence the understanding of the concurrent interplay of
conscious, preconscious, and unconscious processes in every moment of life. The developmental concepts consist of an understanding of the role of individual history in ego development, in
superego development, and in instinctual development. Together
all of these help to determine the role that conscious, preconscious, and unconscious processes will ultimately play in life in
general. Furthermore, integral to an understanding of psychodynamic development is an understanding of the evolving phases
of identifications, since the integrity of the various ego systems
within every personality depends on this (with its derivative
manifestations, such as role diffusion, larval multiple personalities,
etc.). The understanding of these psychological processes is impossible without the ability to recognize the symbolic representation of unconscious processes in dreams, in symptoms, and in so-
called "sublimations," a term which I deplore. Finally, the psychiatrist must also understand the operation of those opposing forces

which obstruct his own view of unconscious processes: to wit, resistance and defensive mechanisms. Anyone who wants both to understand and influence human psychology must understand all of these things.

Yet for teaching purposes and for research as well, all of this can be put in simple terms. We do not need one tenth of our cluttered baggage of psychoanalytic terminology.

The above list omits two other essential items: one is the study of *all* techniques by which preconscious and unconscious processes can be explored; the other is the study of that interaction between investigator and subject which we call transference and countertransference. This is as important in research into behavior as it is in therapy. Therefore it must be part of the equipment of all who wish to study behavior, sick or well.

Research psychiatrists should be trained much as the *clinical psychologist* is trained (i.e., without any orientation toward therapy yet deeply concerned with the study of the comparative physiology of sick and healthy human organisms). On the psychological level this would involve a study of the dynamics of all human behavior, without any of the value judgments which are implied by such loaded concepts as normal or abnormal, adjusted or unadjusted, sick or well, productive or destructive, etc. Therefore, on the experimental frontier I would envisage psychiatrists whose training would include an understanding of all basic aspects of psychoanalysis, but with little or no training in psychotherapy, diagnosis, or prognosis.

In a sense the answer to your second question is implicit in what I have already said. I do *not* think that there is an important distinction between the *theory* which we should teach to the candidates in psychoanalytic institutes and the *theory* which we should teach to any other psychiatrist, particularly if by theory as distinct from technique we have in mind all fundamental premises, preconceptions, concepts, and derivative hypotheses, and the data derived from psychoanalytic observations.

Certainly any psychiatrist who has been exposed to instruction which is colored by psychoanalytic principles will forever after use this in one form or another, clearly or vaguely, in his approach to patients. You and I know that most of our colleagues, analyst and nonanalyst alike, fall into cliché-thinking. They bandy terms around which have long since ceased to have vivid, concrete, or sharply defined meaning. Such terms become as worn as old coins, until they lose their original clear imprint; yet we still use them, and delude ourselves that they adequately describe or even explain the psychological phenomena which we are studying.

In general, they do not do any more harm in this way than they would if they were free of this clouded psychoanalytic verbiage, except for those who are under a strong inner compulsion to rub the noses of their patients in premature and painful confrontations. This we sometimes dignify by the term of "interpretation." Yet this again is an error which depends more on the personality of the "therapist" than on the kind of training that he has had. I have known psychiatrists who are far more gentle and more subtle in their interpretive processes than are many analysts.

If you were to ask me to give you my impression of the statistical frequency of any of these phenomena, I am afraid it would be impossible for me to do this. Indeed, I think it is impossible for anyone to do so. I do not know how many psychiatrists engage in "psychoanalytic therapy" after exposure to partial psychoanalytic teachings. I suspect that this depends largely on the temper of the community in which each lives. Where there is a lot of chitchat about analysis, many such men may call themselves "analysts." Where there is no such receptive attitude, they call themselves by other names; yet do about the same things as before.

Maurice Levine, M.D., Professor and Head of the Department of Psychiatry, University of Cincinnati College of Medicine:

Let me give you some of my impressions about the questions that you raised in your recent letter, about the teaching of psychoanalysis to psychiatrists in distinction to the training of psychoanalysts.

My answer to your first question approaches this problem from a number of vantage points. One is to call attention to the fact that present-day psychiatrists must function in a number of directions, some emphasizing some aspects of psychiatry and others emphasizing other aspects of psychiatry. Pertinent to this is the fact that the Cincinnati training center has to think not only in terms of producing future teachers of psychiatry in medical schools but also must think in terms of producing psychiatrists for the State Hospital System of Ohio and other states, and also in terms of providing people who can function as psychiatrists and neurologists in towns of 25,000 to 200,000 in the Midwest. Further a number of our people are trained with the idea that they will become directors of mental-hygiene clinics. Others will go on to training in a psychoanalytic institute, etc. With this variation in psychiatric functioning in our current culture and with the variations in the plans of those in training, it becomes necessary to avoid a simple answer to the types of question that you raise. In other words, in the training process, as in psychotherapy, one has to consider goals as well as the techniques. When a man in training in our clinic is to have a career in the State Hospital System, or as a psychiatric or neurologic consultant and therapist in a small center, his training must have more emphasis on diagnostic work, shock therapy, hospital management, etc., than would be true of a man whose career probably will involve a large emphasis on psychotherapy. With this difference in goals, there must be differences with respect to the amount of instruction in the basic concepts of psychoanalysis.

Another relevant point is the fact that your question rotates around "theoretical instruction." In this connection I have to emphasize the fact that to an extraordinary degree our theoretical instruction arises out of case material rather than out of organized courses of theoretical instruction. During the course of any one week each resident is likely to see 15 to 20 patients in continued therapy plus the study of several new patients, which adds up to the fact that over the course of a year he will have direct contact with 50 to 250 or more cases of his own. In addition, he will have indirect contact with several hundred patients of his contemporaries, when he takes calls for them, or when he is the ward-management supervisor of a ward on which other residents' patients are included. In addition to this, during the course of a week he attends two to five ward rounds or case seminars in which his own or others' patients are discussed. (This is in addition to individual supervision.) The end result is that we have an extraordinary opportunity to have theoretical instruction arising spontaneously, naturally, and organically out of current and actual case material. This makes for a much better learning process and lessens the need for organized lecture instruction. Further it permits the kind of emphasis in the theoretical instruction about psychoanalytic material that I think is most suitable for those who are to practice as general psychiatrists, in that the emphasis is constantly on immediate and active problems. For example, transference and countertransference phenomena can be taught in a way that is most valuable. During the course of a year the residents will hear 20 to 25 other residents-in-training present their case material and consequently will see firsthand in over 200 cases how the way in which patients are responding to individual residents' personality influences their therapy for good or bad. He will also hear the leader of the seminar bring in transference and countertransference material. The emphasis here, of course, would not be on the genetic roots of the residents' countertransference, but rather on the ways in which some current attitude or defense or temptation or whatnot of the resident in relationship to the patient is influencing the therapy. For example, he will be able to see repeatedly the ways in which an overly authoritarian resident has certain types of success with patients who need that kind of approach and the ways in which the authoritarian resident will produce a chaotic situation or a stymied situation in other types of patients. This is essentially one form of the teaching of a major chapter of psychoanalytic understanding, but it does not include an attempt at a thorough understanding of the genetics or dynamics of the authoritarian attitude of the other residents.

With the above preliminary comments, I can say that we do have a certain amount of theoretical instruction in the basic concepts of psychoanalysis in the form of lectures and literature seminars, etc., in addition to the teaching I mentioned above, and that I can answer your question clearly in the affirmative that we do consider it necessary for every psychiatrist to have instruction in the basic concepts of psychoanalysis.

In terms of the fact that this discussion is concentrated on the training of the general psychiatrist, I should mention some other relevant aspects of our teaching. One is that we stress tremendously the importance of adequate clinical diagnosis, since it is urgent that the group that we are training be able to do an adequate job in that direction in view of their future areas of responsibility. However, there is another reason for such an emphasis on clinical diagnosis: our center stresses a psychoanalytic orientation in the general practice of psychiatry, and this raises the immediate danger that our residents-in-training will be so fascinated by the drama of love and hate, guilt and shame, murder and sex, and all of the other intrapsychic phenomena which are the basis not only of psychoanalysis but of all great literature and art, that they may easily have the temptation to devote too much of their attention and interest and fascination to this aspect of their understanding and so may neglect the need to understand clinical diagnosis. I do not overestimate clinical diagnosis, and I know that until the psychoanalytic influence became a dominant force, psychiatrists generally tended to have their security and competence be in the field of clinical diagnostic thinking, but I have become deeply concerned at the swing in the opposite direction. I have seen graduates of psychoanalytic institutes who failed to recognize schizophrenic developments or psychotic nuclei, or suicidal depressive states and the like, and I have seen the same thing happen in analytically oriented centers in which the new and fascinating emphasis on psychodynamics was not counterbalanced by an emphasis on clinical diagnosis. I use my leadership quite strongly in this direction in this department. This provides for some fascinating possibilities since I think that in certain ways psychodynamic understanding can add important material in the practice of the average psychiatrist in the making of a clinical diagnosis, as well as in dynamic formulations and therapy.

Another factor, which was sharply brought to my attention by the great good luck of the structure of this department, is pertinent here. Theoretical instruction in psychoanalysis often tends to emphasize the intrapsychic dynamics of patients and in a sense to neglect interpersonal problems. I think this in part is responsible for some of the confused reactions against this emphasis by some of the culturalists in our field. But it is my conviction that theoretical instruction in psychoanalysis has to have many facets and must include material in which the interplay between the biological and the cultural is dealt with quite directly rather than as a to and fro theoretical controversy. In some ways this is more important in the training of the general psychiatrist than in the training of the person who will spend most of his time functioning as a psychoanalyst. Consequently I have the feeling that in our training of the general psychiatrist we must pay a great deal of attention to the interplay of forces which can be, for simplicity, subsumed under the two headings—intrapsychic and interpersonal. In our own center this becomes a very spontaneous and natural thing to do, since one of our major responsibilities is to function as the psychiatric consultation and treatment service for some 80 social agencies (part of the budget of the department comes from the Community Chest). The end result is that not infrequently we have a seminar in which a resident presents a patient whom he is seeing in individual psychotherapy and in which his discussion is focused chiefly on the intrapsychic dynamics of the patient and on transference-countertransference problems in the therapy; with high frequency then one of our social workers who is seeing a member of the family, or a representative of one of the referring or collaborating social agencies, will pipe up with a comment about the pressures on this patient from the neighborhood, the religious group, the members of the family, or others. The attempt then is made by the group to see the interrelationship of these interpersonal factors and the psychodynamics, in the fluctuations in the therapy, etc.

For example, we are able not infrequently to see that an apparent therapeutic improvement is actually based on the fact that the wife in recent weeks has been more aggressive and hostile and perhaps more satisfying to the patient's need for punishment.

Still another point which has to do with the teaching of psychoanalytic understanding to psychiatrists in training has to do with our type of case material. We have the responsibility as part of a city hospital to take any disturbed patient if we have a vacant bed. In this area of our work we are not able to pick and choose our case material. Consequently we have many borderline psychotic patients and many overt psychotic patients, and it is my experience that it is often far easier to teach psychoanalytic material on the basis of what one sees with psychotic patients than it is to teach psychoanalytic material on the basis of uncovering and the reconstructive formulations necessary in the psychoanalytic work with fairly well-defended neurotic patients. It is not difficult, for example, to teach a resident the reality of castration anxiety when he has a patient admitted in a psychotic panic who holds on to his genitalia for hours because of his conviction that it is to be amputated, after he had had such-and-such an experience or fantasy.

Another point to mention is that we, for very practical reasons as well as for reasons stemming from conviction, insist that our residents be given adequate training in the somatic aspects of their work. I am proud of the fact, for example, that our autopsy permission rate is higher than that of any other department in this hospital. Also I am proud of the fact that the only diagnosis of typhoid fever made in the City of Cincinnati last year was made by one of our residents on a patient who was admitted as having a hysterical type of confusional state. I think that this is of the utmost importance for a number of reasons. One is that our people will be functioning in such a way that the need to have a strong feeling for somatic disease is urgent. Another is that it gives them a real capacity for thinking in terms of a variety of psychosomatic and somatopsychic sequences which are deeply fundamental to the theoretical understanding of psychoanalysis.

In your letter you ask the very difficult question of where to draw the line between teaching psychoanalytic theory to psychiatrists and to candidates for psychoanalysis. I am far from having the answer to this question, of course. In part my answer would have to do with the fact that we teach that kind of material which seems to arise inevitably out of consideration of the dynamic and therapeutic aspects of a case under our local circumstances. The usual patient is seen in our clinic once a week. Consequently there inevitably will be some limitation to the productivity and depth of the material and therefore the type of emphasis in the instruction is somewhat different. Further in this type of therapy there is very little of the spontaneous development of a far-reaching infantile neurotic type of repetition and consequently our teaching about genetics tends to be more limited. Further with the kind of focusing that arises out of our case material we tend to emphasize current realities rather than childhood fantasies. We tend to emphasize dynamics rather than genetics. We tend to emphasize countertransference phenomena as they affect the interpersonal relationship with a patient rather than to stress the roots of countertransference. We stress conscious and preconscious conflict more than we do unconscious. We tend to stress the manifest content of the dream rather than the latent content of the dream. I should of course put in at this point that by stressing one more than the other we do not eliminate the other from consideration, but that our material calls for this kind of emphasis and that further I think that in view of the level of training of the individuals concerned these are the safer emphases. Obviously we do not limit the amount of reading or interest that our residents may have in any kind of case material or theoretical discussion in the literature. But the line you mention develops naturally, in that a resident is not able to see much direct usefulness to him of an extensive interest in a dream screen or in dream symbolism (except in a limited way), but is able to see a great deal of pertinence to him in the development of a capacity to pick up indications of hidden resentment, indications of unconscious homosexual stirring when the resident is too warm and friendly with a patient, and matters of that sort.

In answer to another of your questions, I can say that I have the feeling that those psychiatrists who do not become candidates of a psychoanalytic institute do actually use psychoanalytic principles of the sort that we teach, in their later practice, and do keep within the limits of their instruction. As a matter of fact, I think that this is an easier goal to reach than is the comparable goal of teaching practitioners and internists and others. I cannot offhand recall a situation in which our psychiatric residents misused the psychoanalytic aspects of their training, but I can remember several instances in which internists and general practitioners did make such mistakes. For example, I know one physician who is disturbing to his patients by interpreting their symptoms on a symbolic basis.

Your next question is whether many of our residents consider themselves something like dynamic psychiatrists although they do not get formal recognition from the Psychoanalytic Association. The answer is that none of them uses the word psychoanalyst for himself after finishing his training with us, and that many of them frequently do use the term dynamic psychiatry for the kind of thing that they are likely to do, and many of them will see patients in psychotherapy on a once a week or twice a week basis with a continuation of the same sort of psychotherapy that they learned with us, viz., with a greater emphasis on support rather than the arousal of anxiety, on relationship rather than on insight, with a recognition of the fact that they are using limited psychoanalytic understanding and techniques.

All in all we do not have many problems of people who overstep bounds and go in for the kinds of therapy for which they are not suitably trained or personally capable. I am not sure that this would be true in all comparable centers. We have a group of psychiatrists on our faculty in Cincinnati who are deeply interested in the well-being of the resident group and evoke from them a very healthy set of responses. I could imagine a training situation in which the faculty would evoke a great deal of competitiveness or rebellious hostility from its residents; under those circumstances the residents might well step beyond bounds. In this connection it should be mentioned that our people who do not have training in psychoanalytic institutes recognize that we really do not regard them as second-rate citizens and consequently they are saved from some of the need to go beyond limits in proving that they are as good as psychoanalysts.

My point in these last comments, and in some of the previous paragraphs of this letter, is that I would not want to generalize from our local situation in my answers to your questions. This is a new field, and the end result of the training programs (and so the answers to your questions) is determined not only by educational plans and concepts, but also by the training facilities, the emotional interplay of faculty and residents, etc., in the individual centers of training.

Sandor Lorand, M.D., Professor and Head of the Department of Psychiatry, State University of New York College of Medicine:

I would consider it essential for every psychiatrist to know something about the basic concepts of psychoanalysis, whatever these concepts include, so that they will be able to utilize these concepts in their work. I think that we analysts who have the job of teaching should be aware that we do a great service not only to the potential psychiatrist but also to the community which needs the services of psychiatrists. All psychiatrists need to improve their skill in diagnosis, in interviewing the patient, and in appraisal of the patient's difficulties, which appraisal will be quite different if they have some knowledge of psychoanalytic concepts. Not only in the area of diagnosis and appraisal of the patient's condition will they gain a great deal through proper teaching of analytical principles, but also their approach to the patient and their initiating psychotherapy and carrying it out will be quite different. Naturally, we are all aware of the fact that proper diagnosis itself is a start in initiating treatment.

It is very difficult to draw a sharp line between teaching psychoanalytic theory to psychiatrists and to candidates who are being analyzed. However, it must be done and I think it is up to the experienced teacher to know how to streamline the teaching of psychoanalytic theory and technique, etc., for psychiatrists who will utilize this knowledge to improve their psychotherapeutic work, and where to stop. I think this can best be done if the psychiatrist who is not analytically trained gets little theory in

the teaching but rather clinical demonstration of how the dynamics of psychoanalytical principles can be applied in general
psychotherapy.

The line must be drawn also because if you teach them exactly
the same stuff that you teach analytical students or even close to
the same material, they will very quickly consider themselves to
be analysts. My experience in our clinic at the Division of Psychoanalytic Education at the State University taught me to draw
the line and not to teach the same material to residents in psychiatry as we teach to the candidates in psychoanalysis. We don't
mix them in classes and even the Brief Therapy supervision is
given separately. Senior and junior members of the psychoanalytic faculty give lectures in the general residency program (not to
candidates in analytical training) about dream theory and interpretation, instinct theory, psychopathology of the neuroses, psychotherapy with psychotics. These courses, as I mentioned before, are all streamlined according to the capacity and the ability
of the residents. They are concentrated and simplified as compared to the courses given in analytical training. Even so, I am
sure that many of these residents who are not in analytical training, after they leave the residency program will regard themselves as having been trained in analysis, which is very widespread
and cannot be helped. Even medical practitioners in New York
City call themselves specialists in psychosomatic medicine and tell
their patients that they are doing analysis.

I think that we analysts who are teaching analytical candidates
and psychiatrists cannot be very much concerned with the individuals' own character and what they call themselves. Our job is
teaching and trying to make them better therapists, even if many
are going to misuse their knowledge.

Sandor Rado, M.D., D. Pol. Sc., Clinical Professor of Psychiatry, Director of the Columbia University Psychoanalytic
Clinic, New York:

After more than thirty years of teaching experience, I welcome
this opportunity to express once again my views on psychiatric
education. May I begin by quoting one sentence from a paper
presented in 1946 in a symposium in the training of psychiatrists
[83]:

The physician specializing in psychiatry should be given the opportunity to absorb all available knowledge on the psyche, and the main body of this knowledge is psychodynamics and the techniques of psychoanalysis.

The intervening years have only fortified this conviction. I shall review here the argument and add one more suggestion.

The psychiatrist's job is (1) to explore human behavior, and (2) to prevent and remedy its disorders.

To be properly equipped for these functions, he must above all be firmly grounded in psychodynamics. Based on Freud's psychoanalytic method, this science has now reached the state of development where it can be defined as the systematic adaptational analysis of human motivation. We view adaptational psychodynamics as the basic component of an anticipated *comprehensive dynamics of human behavior* that will include its physiology and genetics as well.

Next, the psychiatrist must be a sound and skilled psychotherapist. It should be clearly understood that in psychiatry treatment is always psychotherapy, even if it is supported by pharmacologic agents or electric or surgical procedures. Psychotherapy is applied psychodynamics. Its current forms are profoundly influenced by, if not directly derived from, Freud's psychoanalytic discoveries in therapeutic technique.

In this light, no psychiatric training can be accepted today as adequate unless it is based on courses in the psychodynamic mechanisms of healthy and disordered behavior, and on the elementary adaptational techniques of psychoanalytic therapy. Furthermore, it must include courses in the physiologic (biochemical, biophysical) and genetic mechanisms of behavior and its disorders; and clinical experience with all forms of behavior disorder over a lengthy period of time.

An integrated program of graduate training built upon these principles has been in existence for eleven years at the Psychoanalytic Clinic for Training and Research of Columbia University.

Sigmund Freud had anticipated many of these developments. In 1922, in an encyclopedia article, he had this to say about the relationship of psychoanalysis to psychiatry [51]:

Psychiatry is at present essentially a descriptive and classificatory science whose orientation is still towards the somatic rather than the psychological and which is without the possibility of giving explanations of the phenomena which it observes. Psychoanalysis does not, however, stand in opposition to it, as the almost unanimous behavior of the psychiatrists might lead one to believe. On the contrary, as a *depth-psychology*, a psychology of those processes in mental life which are withdrawn from consciousness, it is called upon to provide psychiatry with an indispensable groundwork and to free it from its present limitations. We can foresee that the future will give birth to a scientific psychiatry, to which psychoanalysis has served as an introduction.

Adaptational psychodynamics is a basic science not merely of clinical psychiatry, but of all clinical medicine. Command of the elementary techniques of human influence, notably in contact with the physically sick, is indispensable to every physician. These phases of psychiatric instruction await their incorporation into the undergraduate medical curriculum.

However, this progress in both graduate and undergraduate medical education is hampered by a serious scientific difficulty. As was pointed out in my article cited above, psychodynamics is a unique science. Its abstractions stem, to a large extent, from the exploration of the *private* phase of behavior. Psychodynamic language refers to feelings, thoughts, and impulses *within us*, rather than to things and events in the physical world *about us*. No one can arrive at a true understanding of a psychodynamic abstraction unless he has first explored his own inner life and thus recognizes its referent in himself. Examination of a psychiatric patient is guided by the physician's emotional resonance which enables him to sense the patient's feelings. Before the student psychiatrist can learn how to observe and interpret in psychodynamic terms the patient's behavior, he must learn how to observe and interpret in such terms his own behavior. These facts are of overriding importance to those student psychiatrists who desire to subspecialize in the practice of psychoanalytic therapy. As is generally known, they are required to undergo a personal analysis as a preparation for psychoanalytic training.

For obvious practical reasons, it would be impossible to extend this requirement to all student psychiatrists, not to speak of all medical students. It is therefore imperative to develop a less extensive procedure of self-exploration that would prepare these groups of students for absorbing and truly assimilating the amount of psychodynamics they will need in their practice. We must, from the outset, distinguish sharply between this envisaged procedure and personal analysis. For want of a better term, the needed new procedure may perhaps be called *psychodynamic sensitization*. By creating and perfecting such a procedure, we shall make the teaching of psychodynamics meaningful for both the psychiatrist who does not desire to specialize in psychoanalysis and the undergraduate student of medicine.

I myself have been grappling with the problem of psychodynamic sensitization for some time, but I feel strongly that the task of evolving such a procedure is a challenge to all of us. Perhaps our professional organizations could help us to pool our resources to make this achievement possible.

F. C. Redlich, M.D., Professor and Chairman, Department of Psychiatry, Yale University School of Medicine:

I think that every psychiatrist should get some theoretical instruction in the basic concepts of analysis. I could include in this certainly psychodynamics, ego development, instinctual development, theory of analytic treatment, individual and social analytic concepts of psychotherapy, as well as utilization of analytic principles in making a diagnosis and prognosis. I think that every psychiatrist should read the most important papers by Freud and his outstanding disciples. They should, if possible, have close contact in this period of training with outstanding analysts. Personally, I think that this should go for all psychiatrists who will engage in the general practice of psychiatry or do research and teaching in clinical psychiatry; the only exception I can think of is that possibly some people will work in a limited area, such as primarily with neurological patients or in the field of electroencephalography where such instruction will be less important.

The problem whether every psychiatrist should get a personal analysis is a much more complex one, and I feel that this particular question I would not answer in the affirmative. In the first place I think there are some personalities who cannot utilize an analysis and possibly can even get worse from it. But apart from such personalities (i.e., some schizoid and obsessive-compulsive personalities) there are exceptions to the general desirability of a personal analysis; for instance, somebody who sees a great many patients and does mostly organic treatments won't profit too much from a personal analysis unless there are definite internal reasons for it. Yet, in general, I have felt that most of our psychiatrists would benefit from an analysis, even if they don't go into analytic practice in the more narrow sense of the word.

Actually we have stuck to these two principles in our practice at Yale; our residents got the basic psychoanalytic theoretical instruction which you mentioned and most of our people have of their own desire, and to a certain extent encouraged by the senior people in our Department, sought a personal analysis if they could not get full analytic training. The real impact, of course, is made in clinical supervision and conferences and individual supervision, but the supervisors are experienced analysts who convey their viewpoint to the students.

I have heard a lot about the narrow and somewhat fuzzy line between the amount and quality of psychoanalytic training (theory) for psychiatrists who don't become analysts and for candidates for psychoanalysis. It seems there are two principles operating. For one thing, if what we are teaching about analytic theory is compared to what a future analyst knows, it is comparatively little. Another difference is that together with what we teach about analysis, we teach a great many other things too and actually try to weave everything into a rather complex pattern, such as, for instance, Norman Cameron tries to do, fusing various concepts of academic psychology with analytic concepts, particularly using some of the knowledge that comes from behavior theory, from social anthropology, from sociology, animal psychology, etc. A line between what we teach to the nonanalyst and what the future candidate of an analytic institute learns, however, is by no means clear.

It is my experience that the people we have trained here and who have not become psychoanalysts have not abused any of what they have learned here. I don't know of any person from our outfit who called his therapy psychoanalysis when *in facto* it was psychotherapy based on analytic principles. However, even here, in my own opinion, the borderline is quite unclear—I know I am not in agreement in this respect with many of my colleagues who feel that a distinction between analytic psychotherapy and psychoanalysis can be made very easily and readily. However, the people we have trained here who have not become psychoanalysts definitely consider themselves dynamic psychiatrists and it may be that their patients occasionally assume that they are getting psychoanalysis while they are getting psychotherapy; yet I have not heard them say that they are doing psychoanalysis when really they are not doing it. You asked me what the desirable situation would be. I hope that some day psychoanalysis and psychotherapy will all be taught in one setup—preferably a university setup because learning and teaching goes on in such setups for a long period of time with reasonably good results—and that the distinctions over which we fuss so much today will disappear. I don't think there will be any difficulties between a good institution that teaches dynamic psychiatry and an analytic institute that teaches good psychoanalysis. The difficulties will come in between institutions that are teaching bad psychoanalysis and bad dynamic psychotherapy, and when we know more about all these things, maybe we will be better equipped to recognize clearly what is good and what is bad.

Norman Reider, M.D., Chief of Psychiatric Division, Mount Zion Hospital, San Francisco:

The first question asks whether I consider it necessary for every psychiatrist to get theoretical instruction on the basic concepts of psychoanalysis. I'm not sure I understand why you should ask this question. There cannot be any doubt in this day and age in anyone's mind how necessary it is for every psychiatrist to understand psychodynamics, the principles of ego development, libido theory, some facets of the theory of analytic treatment, and how to utilize psychoanalytic principles in psychotherapy. Especially is the last point most important. In my opinion one of the great failures of teaching psychodynamics in medical schools and in residency programs is to turn the teaching program into a sort of junior attenuated psychoanalytic training with little effort to make a distinction between what constitutes psychoanalytic technique as such, and what constitutes technical devices derivative out of theory but which are not strictly psychoanalytic.

Perhaps I can enlarge upon this last point by taking up your second question as to where I draw the line between teaching psychoanalytic theory to psychiatrists and to candidates for psychoanalysis. I hold, contrary to a good many people, some of whom have arrived at their opinions quite honestly and sincerely and others who have arrived at them with the aid of their own opportunistic strivings, that the line between teaching psychoanalysis to psychiatrists and to psychoanalysts is a very sharp one. In the first place, there are differences between students. My own feeling is to the effect that there are relatively very few psychiatrists who are gifted enough, psychoanalytically minded enough, or call it what you will, to be psychoanalysts. Many of these can be very good psychiatrists. But I think we have trained entirely too many people in psychoanalysis who are not at all suited to the nature of the work.

You will recall that at a postwar meeting in New York on psychoanalytic training I took sharp issue with you on this point. At that time no one knew what was going to happen, but you and others were hopeful that we would get a different sort of person into analytic training as a result of war experiences, ones who could be trained more easily, having more moral character and not being so neurotically motivated. My own observations seem to bear out my prediction at that time that the situation would get worse if extensive training was indulged in and if concessions were made to men who were attracted to psychoanalysis only because of what they had found out in their war experiences. There have been hosts of people trained with socio-economic motivation who are not making good analysts. For my part I would like to see us go back to training the neurotically and scientifically motivated individuals.

I can cite numerous examples, and so can many another observer, of dynamically trained psychiatrists or candidates rejected from their analytic training, who use psychoanalytic principles which they learned in their training program, but most of them, in my observation, do not keep within the limits of their instruction. The temptation and prestige value of being an analyst (and I do not mean here merely the use of the couch, etc.) is too great for these people to stand. Moreover, their experiences have been such that they have never learned adequately the difference between psychoanalytically oriented psychotherapy and psychoanalysis. It is a confused jumble in their minds and this jumble need not exist if the lines are drawn sharply as I believe they can be drawn sharply on scientific grounds. There are quite a few papers in the literature already that attest to this fact. Permit me to cite papers by Eissler, Gill, Gitelson, Stone, and myself. There are, of course, many others who have written on the subject.

I grant that some psychoanalytic institutes and many accredited psychoanalysts also confuse these issues. Yet, I think it is high time for psychoanalytic teachers, not only in medical schools, in residency training programs, but also in institutes, to start drawing the line sharply between psychoanalytically derived therapies and psychoanalytic techniques which in my opinion have one purpose: the working through and dissolution of pathogenic defenses against instinctual impulses and the working through of the transference neurosis and regression that comes about automatically and not manipulatively in the analytic situation with the use of proper technical devices. It is clear that what I mean by this is classical analysis.

To repeat, I think it is high time for especially institutes to begin teaching to candidates in their first year what constitutes the difference and to provide good instruction in psychoanalytically oriented psychotherapy. Especially do they have the opportunity of showing differences between techniques used in psychotherapies and in analysis. I realize there are many people who disagree with me. There are some who hold that only if a person is analyzed can he do good psychotherapy of any kind. This I hold to be nonsense. It has been my experience that psychiatrists can do excellent psychotherapy without being analyzed. It is my experience also that many people psychoanalytically trained aren't suited for doing anything but analysis. On the other hand the great failure that we have made, wittingly or unwittingly, is to turn our residency training programs into quasi-psychoanalytic training without effort to draw the sharp lines that are possible.

John Romano, M.D., Head of the Department of Psychiatry, University of Rochester School of Medicine and Dentistry, Rochester, New York:

My answer to the first question is yes. My answer is based on experience which includes nine years in Rochester, four years in Cincinnati, and three of the four years I spent in Boston. Our experiences in this matter have been recorded in a number of publications. Actually we would go beyond your question and state that we consider it necessary for others than psychiatrists who are responsible for the understanding and care of the sick also to receive instruction in these basic concepts. Thus we have participated in the communication of these basic concepts to medical students, nursing students, physicians and nurses, psychiatric aides, social case workers, and clinical psychologists.

I believe you took part in the preparatory commission during Ithaca Conference II (graduate training in psychiatry) which was assigned the topic of the role of psychoanalysis in residency training. If you remember, I participated in the discussion of this group when we met in Ithaca in 1952. You have read and studied Chapter 6 of *The Psychiatrist—His Training and Development*, American Psychiatric Association, 1953, which recorded the substance of this meeting and which was specifically concerned with this topic. As I stated then and repeat now, we find it very difficult to draw a definitive line between method and substance of teaching basic concepts of psychoanalysis to psychiatrists as contrasted to teaching the same to candidates for psychoanalysis. You are aware that as a university department we are responsible for the education and training of a selected number of young physicians who have come to us for psychiatric training. Some of them in the latter period of this training, and others when they have finished three or four years of residency training, have become formal candidates and students in psychoanalytic training institutes. What I shall have to say about the differences which exist comes from my knowledge of what we do as compared to my own experience as a student in a psychoanalytic institute and experiences of members of our staff who have been such students in other institutes. I don't believe there is any basic difference in fundamental method or in the content or substance of what is taught. I do believe that the difference exists in factors such as the intensity of the experience, the repetition of material, and the amount of detail. The psychoanalytic candidate as compared to the psychiatric resident is apt to have had more clinical psychiatric experience. He is older and may have a more complete and full backdrop of experience. He is either completing his own personal psychoanalysis; or he may be treating patients in psychoanalytic therapy under supervision; at any rate he probably is pursuing more intensive psychotherapy with his patients. As a result of this, he has a greater body of primary data obtained from his own personal analysis and from his psychotherapeutic work with patients which helps him to materialize, to confirm, or to criticize the operational hypotheses and theoretical substance of the basic concepts of psychoanalysis. Through these clinical experiences, through repetition of material presented to him in the various seminars and through interchange and exchange of ideas with senior and peer colleagues, his experience is more intense than is the experience of the psychiatric resident.

For many years we have utilized tutorial supervision of our psychiatric residents in addition to the traditional administrative and professorial supervision which is afforded each house officer in this university department. Through the individual tutorial supervision, we are able to deal individually with each graduate student so that means are developed and used to communicate with him according to his needs and abilities at varying points in time during his clinical experience and clinical maturation.

It is our experience that the psychiatrists who have had their graduate training with us and who do not become candidates of a psychoanalytic institute do use in their practice basic psychoanalytic concepts which they learned in their residency training. Although we have made no systematic scrutiny of their day to day practice and behavior, it is our impression they have used these concepts wisely in their various functions as clinical psychiatrists, teachers, and administrators. So far as we know, not one of them who has not undertaken formal psychoanalytic training through institute supervision has assumed falsely functions of formal psychoanalytic therapists. The actual destiny of members of our senior and junior staff including the resident staff is as follows:

a. Seven have completed personal didactic psychoanalysis and have either completed or are completing formal psychoanalytic training in a psychoanalytic institute.
b. Nine are in the process of completing their personal didactic psychoanalysis and may or may not go on to complete formal psychoanalytic training in a psychoanalytic institute.
c. Eight intend to obtain personal didactic psychoanalysis and may or may not go on to complete formal psychoanalytic training in a psychoanalytic institute.
d. Five have not had personal didactic psychoanalysis and probably are not interested in obtaining this or going on to complete formal psychoanalytic training.
e. Eight residents left or were not appointed after only one year of resident training with us. Of these, perhaps two will be interested in obtaining personal psychoanalysis and going on to formal psychoanalytic training.
f. In the past nine years we have had nine persons whose initial

basic interest was in internal medicine and who came to us for
liaison experience in medicine and in psychiatry. Of these nine,
three have gone into formal psychiatry, are undertaking personal psychoanalysis, and may go on to complete formal psychoanalytic training. The major interest of one remains in
medicine, but he is undergoing personal psychoanalysis, but
will probably not go on to formal psychoanalytic training. The
remainder have returned to medicine and are either in active
medical practice or occupy professorial posts in medicine in
this country.

g. Six persons have participated in our liaison teaching program
for obstetricians and gynecologists. None is interested in personal psychoanalysis and none will go on to formal psychoanalytic training.

h. You have probably heard of our unique two-year rotating internship which was started in this university hospital in 1949.
In this two-year period each person spends six months in medicine, six months in minor surgery and obstetrics, six months in
psychiatry, and six months in pediatrics. In the past six years,
seven persons (approximately ten percent of the group) have
chosen psychiatry as a career. At the present time, approximately
one half of this number may be interested in obtaining personal
psychoanalysis and formal psychoanalytic training. Other persons who have finished this two-year rotating internship have
gone into medicine, pediatrics, surgery, tuberculosis, general
practice. We learn from them and from others that the experience with us has been most profitable in terms of their emotional
maturity and clinical scholarship in whatever field they have
chosen. For example, the most outstanding chief resident in
pediatrics in one of the eastern university hospitals was a member of our first group of two-year internes. Although he is not
a psychiatrist, other observers have pointed out to us the outstanding nature of his understanding of emotional problems in
his clinical work.

Our experience leads us to state that the teaching of the basic
concepts of psychoanalysis is an integral and indispensable part
of the training of psychiatrists and of physicians in general.
Fundamentally, we believe that knowledge and understanding of
these concepts help inestimably to teach the physician and psychiatrist what he should and should not do, what he can and can-

not do in terms of psychotherapeutic capacities and limitations. Our experience with psychiatrists in this and in other communities who have not had the benefit of such teaching in the basic concepts of psychoanalysis indicates definitely that they err more flagrantly and repetitively in misinterpreting and misapplying psychoanalytic concepts in their therapeutic approaches. We believe this is so because of their uncritical perception of the basic concepts and their relative ignorance of methods of applying knowledge obtained from such concepts.

Leon J. Saul, M.D., Professor of Clinical Psychiatry, Medical School of the University of Pennsylvania, Philadelphia:

I can probably answer your letter briefly by saying that I think that the only difference between psychoanalysis and what is done in all clinics is that in the clinics patients are seen sitting up and rarely over twice a week. There is no longer any substantive difference between analysis and "psychotherapy"—there is only good and bad analysis, and analysis practiced by graduates of institutes and by those who are not.

It is all in the books, and all young men read it. Even the most orthodox analysts participate in teaching analysis to *medical students*, let alone residents; and many of our medical students at the University of Pennsylvania found our first- and second-year teaching too elementary, because they'd had Freud and also Alexander, Horney, and others and my *Emotional Maturity* in college.

In private clinics, in hospitals, and in private practice, almost every psychotherapist tries to do "psychoanalysis," whether he graduates from an institute or not.

Therefore, I think that in most places the effort is to give residents the best supervision possible, so they'll do it as well as possible even if they do not get formal training. The only alternative is for universities to do as Temple has done and only take as residents men who also are in formal analytic training.

Residents who are not candidates of psychoanalytic institutes often arrange to get personal analyses, and this, as you know, the American Psychiatric Association and local societies are trying to control.

I think *most* all the residents in this area want psychoanalytic training, but the institutes can only take a few (about 14 at ours per year). So the others who are not accepted feel terrible about it, but go ahead analyzing as best they can anyway. They were taught the basic concepts in college, medical school, and residencies. Yes, it is necessary to get as much and as good teaching as possible. I think most places use the best, most experienced analysts they can get to teach medical students and residents.

At the Institute of the Pennsylvania Hospital and at the University Hospital there are seminars for residents run by experienced analysts.

Some psychiatrists and psychoanalysts gave less comprehensive answers and did not respond to all of the questions or centered their statement on one or two of the points. These answers are summarized here using as much of direct quotations as appear pertinent.

Frieda Fromm-Reichmann, M.D., Supervisor of Psychotherapy, Chestnut Lodge, Rockville, Maryland, believes without qualification that every psychiatrist should get theoretical instruction in the basic concepts of psychoanalysis, as enumerated in my questions, with the exception of the classical theory of instinctual development. According to her the teaching here should be a historical and critical presentation of psychoanalytical instinct theory and an evaluation of the interpersonal aspects of the instinctual development along the lines of Fairbairn's, Fromm's, and Sullivan's concepts. Attention should be paid to the possible sexual, and much more so to the cultural, significance of the Oedipus complex in our patriarchal culture. Referring to her own teaching practices, she adds the following:

Candidates for psychoanalysis are not only taught what I consider present valid psychoanalytic theory, but also psychoanalytic theory from a historical viewpoint, so that they are able to integrate my teaching with that of those of their other teachers and the authorities of the American Psychoanalytic Association, who hold the difference between the validity of past and present theoretical concepts to be nonexistent or less significant than they appear to me.

Dr. Fromm-Reichmann's answer to the question where to draw the line between teaching psychoanalytic theory to psychiatrists and to candidates for psychoanalysis is that she does not draw any line as far as content is concerned. "Some of method and accents of teaching are determined by the special field of psychiatry in which a student is interested." The question whether psychiatrists who do not become candidates of psychoanalytic institutes do use in their practice psychoanalytic principles which they learned during their residency training and keep within the limits of their instruction, she answers affirmatively. To the question, whether in her experience many engage in psychoanalytic therapy, calling themselves dynamic psychiatrists although they do not get formal recognition from the American Psychoanalytic Association, she replies as follows:

If you call psychoanalytic therapy what Freud originally called it, namely psychotherapy which concerns itself (1) with the dynamic significance of infantile development and childhood history (though not necessarily in Freud's sexual meaning!), (2) the significance of the various levels of awareness (though not necessarily the use in Freud's specific conception!), and (3) of transference (though not necessarily from the Oedipus constellation) and resistance, then: yes. However, the number of MD's who do psychoanalysis according to the definition of the American Psychoanalytic Association without striving for or receiving formal recognition from the American Psychiatric Association is in my experience negligibly small. (However, there is a growing number of social workers and clinical psychologists who establish themselves as psychoanalysts on the basis of their personal analyses, the attendance of courses in institutions [mental hygiene clinics, VA hospitals]. My personal opinion is that our response to this situation which will continue to develop with or without the agreement of the American Psychoanalytic Association should be to see to it that these "lay-analysts" are more carefully selected and get a more adequate training than they do now, instead of fighting their existence. As it is, many members of the American Psychoanalytic Association train such "lay persons" secretly and give lip-service to the fight against them.)

Heinz Hartmann, M.D., of the New York Psychoanalytic Institute, in a brief but succinct statement says that psychiatrists "ought to get instruction in analytical theory, which has become—or, where it has not, should become—the central subject of psychiatry, representing the closest approach to human conflicts man has so far been able to make. Its teaching is basic, exactly as physiology is for the somatic aspect of medicine (a comparison I have often made and, come to think of it, you, too, have made). This teaching should extend from general analytical psychology to the principles of pathogenesis of neurosis, psychosis, and perversion."

He considers it essential to include a course on developmental psychology (which might also be taught in undergraduate teaching of medical schools). He emphasizes that analytical concepts are necessary in order to understand psychotherapy. Their utilization in so-called analytically oriented psychotherapy should be taught, however, in psychoanalytical institutes. He feels that the utilization of psychoanalytic concepts for making diagnoses and prognoses remains with psychiatrists who have not been analyzed "often like a foreign body and may create confusion." He does not think, however, that this can be prevented. Hartmann does not consider it advisable for psychiatrists to be given "the theoretical curriculum of the psychoanalytic candidates, just cutting down every chapter." He continues:

I am afraid Hegel is right in assuming that there is a point where questions of quantity turn into questions of quality, and such a curriculum would probably not be too good. The teaching will have to be centered differently in various respects, and will have to be worked out with its special purpose in mind. Not an easy task and much too complex a problem to be even broached in a letter.

As to the question of whether many psychiatrists who are not trained psychoanalytically will go beyond their competence, he states:

Many psychiatrists with some superficial analytical teaching use techniques that more or less approximate that of psychoanalysis—part of them call it analysis, others don't. There is a continuum from those who just put some more emphasis in their psychotherapy on, let's say, transference, or resistance, to those who try to emulate whatever they happen to know of the technique of analysis. As to "desirability," I feel that this latter procedure, that is, amateurish or "wild" analysis, is far from being harmless.

Karl Menninger, M.D., Chief of Staff of the Menninger Foundation, in the course of our correspondence stated that he "believes that everything we know of psychoanalytic theory can be taught to psychiatric residents except the details of technique." He adds:

I think this is comparable to surgery in medical school. We tell medical students everything there is to know about surgery, generally speaking, except the details of technique, and we even teach them the theory of that but do not let them do it. I don't think it is at all difficult to draw this line similarly with psychoanalysis.

He further states that "all psychiatry is basically psychoanalytic psychiatry" and adds "what candidates in the institute need that residents don't is how to apply psychoanalysis in treatment, and the history of the development of these (psychoanalytic) ideas." He believes that "psychiatrists who do not become candidates of institutes get great value from psychoanalytic concepts which they learn during their residency training."

He continues:

I am not worried about the psychotherapy my graduates give. I am much more worried about some psychoanalytic candidates who have been borderline individuals and who should probably have been forbidden to do psychoanalysis. I don't think we need to worry about the non-psychoanalytically trained psychiatrists.

John C. Whitehorn, M.D., Psychiatrist-in-Chief of the Johns Hopkins Hospital, finds it difficult to answer my questions unequivocally and clearly because "there is much divergence of opinion as to what constitutes the essence of psychoanalytic principles." He continues:

There are two approaches to the discussion of the questions you present. One, which might be called the technological approach, is concerned with the use of free association, the couch, or dream analysis for the specific disclosure of repressed unconscious, and for working through "transference" and "resistances."

From the technological approach, it appears to me that there is quite a definite distinction between Freudian-analytic and other psychiatrists, in that the latter make little if any use of free association on the couch. It is my impression that there has been an appreciable change in this respect during the last two decades, relatively fewer nonanalysts now resorting to such procedures whereas twenty years ago it was not uncommon for them to "try a little free association" at times. (But psychoanalytic patients are not consistently couchbound, either, in these times.) In regard to the study of dreams, I suppose nearly all psychiatrists, analytic or nonanalytic, pay some regard, and respect, to their patients' reports of dreams and try to understand their implications, but psychiatrists differ widely in the amount of attention to dreams and to the study of associations to dreams. Patients, analytic or otherwise, are likely to respond to evidence of interest in dreams by reporting an abundance of them. In general, I would say that psychoanalytic techniques are not much used by psychiatrists without psychoanalytic training.

From the other approach, which might be called the psychobiological approach, one could discuss in a broader way the basic concepts by which one human being seeks to "understand" another, and the influence of psychoanalysis upon such modes of thinking.

Human beings have been accustomed for many millennia to ascribe motivational meaning to behavior. Indeed, the primitive tendency was apparently universal to ascribe motivational meaning to all action, animate or inanimate, and the initiation of the physical sciences required the resolute exclusion of motivational meaning from the interpretation of impersonal events—which meant for the budding scientist some independence from the common sense of his community. It was appropriate and natural for the mid-nineteenth-century workers to think, by analogy, that a scientific study of human behavior also required the exclusion of motivational meaning—especially was this tendency readily understandable in the area "belonging" to the increasingly scientific-minded medical profession, namely in the interpretation of psychopathological behavior. Later Freud and Meyer, among others, challenged this exclusion, and considered it appropriate to concern themselves with what I would call motivational meanings in pathological behavior. Since everyone inevitably thinks in a definite historical and cultural context, the systematic orientation of Meyer or of Freud expressed in large part their historical scientific preoccupations, and therefore reflected only in a cramped and distorted way the significance of their observations. Freud, with bold imagination, tremendous personal ambition, and considerable dramatic talent, constructed the more attention-getting myths, and thereby patterned the new patter.

What I am trying to get to is some way of saying that present-day psychiatry, in its use of concepts of personality, attitude, and motive, inevitably reflects or incorporates much Freudian thinking.

Nearly all psychiatrists, I presume, at this time think in terms of personality and patients' attitudes—some in terms taken directly from the psychoanalytic literature, others with concepts more commonly referred to as derived from "psychobiology" or from sociology or social anthropology. For example, roles, attitudes, trends. It is difficult to disentangle the specifically psychoanalytic contribution from other contributions which have played a part in the development of concepts of personality, roles, and attitudes.

During the thirties, for my own thinking, I decided that instinct hypotheses were not very suitable for actual clinical use. I also thought (and think now) that the psychoanalytic emphasis on drive or instinct was a choice made in error, in the post-Darwinian period, in a mood of dedication to Science (meaning materialistic or energistic causality). Because the drive idea lent itself to pseudo-quantitative quasi-scientific formulation, it fostered the illusion of scientific mastery, but without the substance. Sometimes, in a historical-speculative frame of mind, I have gone so far as to think that Freud in his more mature years would have rejected this early error, and would have preferred to reformulate his experience and thinking in terms like attitude and motive, rather than instinct or drive, had he not become tired and saddled with the leadership role for a dependent group, emotionally committed to his earlier overly mechanized formulations.

I see much similarity, if not identity, between Freud's observations and his stimulating speculations, and the phenomena for which in my teaching I have used the terms attitude, value, pattern of motivation, roles, and personality. I note, with hope, and doubtless with some admixture of personal vanity, an increasing usage of these latter concepts and terms in case studies and in general psychiatric literature.

To orient resident staff members and others of the staff regarding psychoanalysis, he included "selected psychoanalysts in the senior staff to perform visiting and advisory functions and to report case studies alongside other types of psychotherapy." His plan "aims to bring the working principles in different procedures into manifest action, inviting comparison and contrast not likely to arouse hostility or fanatical adherence."

Of special interest is the answer of *C. H. Hardin Branch*, M.D., Professor and Head of the Department of Psychiatry, College of Medicine, University of Utah, which has no psychoanalytic institute in its neighborhood and therefore, in a certain respect, reflects the special problem of residency training in isolated areas, isolated insofar as the possibilities of psychoanalytic training are concerned:

It should be noted that our situation here does not bring us face to face with this problem since we have no psychoanalytic institute and actually have only one psychoanalyst on our staff and no other psychoanalyst in the state. . . . He does take on an occasional psychiatrist for a personal psychoanalysis—for example, he is planning on beginning a personal analysis of a man who is currently a fourth-year Fellow—but this would not in any way constitute psychoanalytic training or accreditation with an institute.

Our training program, therefore, is directed entirely at providing general psychiatric residency training and experience and those of our residents who wish full psychoanalytic training must go elsewhere. Again for purposes of general orientation it might be well to add that we are hoping to work out some sort of program with the University of Colorado so that psychoanalytic training may be a little more available for the residents from both these programs.

I feel that the status of general psychiatric training (which from my point of view now seems to lack glamour and "drawing power" unless it is closely associated with some sort of psychoanalytic training program) will gain appreciably from the recent move in the direction of acquiring American Board accreditation in psychoanalysis *if* this accreditation requires prior accreditation in general psychiatry. My own feeling, as a Director of the American Board of Psychiatry and Neurology, is that I would oppose accreditation in psychoanalysis *unless* it carried this prior certification in general psychiatry.

With this rather long introduction, I shall try to deal with your questions.

I believe it is necessary for every psychiatrist to get theoretical instruction in the basic concepts of psychoanalysis. I feel that this framework is useful in providing him with an orientation which is universally acceptable and has sufficient clinical and theoretical validation to reassure the resident that the field of psychiatry does have a body of knowledge somewhat analogous to that provided in other specialties in medicine. When it comes to psychotherapy, I think there is a slight danger in that there is less real therapeutic responsibility in orthodox psychoanalysis than in other fields of medicine. It seems to me that there is some encouragement to the resident to attach to the patient the blame for not improving if he follows strictly psychoanalytic theory in putting together his own philosophy. I feel this is unwise and that any psychiatrist, whatever his chosen field of therapy, must remember that he is primarily a physician. He may not wish to treat a particular patient but I feel he must accept a good deal of responsibility for unsatisfactory results rather than, as is so often done, blaming the patient for "resistance," "poor motivation," and the like.

There is sometimes another danger, I think, in presenting psychoanalytic theory to residents as though these concepts were fundamental answers to questions regarding the formation of personality, the development of symptoms, etc. I would, of course, agree that psychoanalytic theories provide excellent working bases for communicating with each other regarding many matters in these areas, but I sometimes find that the statement of psychodynamic principles is too readily accepted by the student as a statement of ultimate causality to such an extent that the physiological elements in the problem are depreciated or ignored entirely. I believe this is a point on which you, yourself, have some very strong feelings. For example, I have had in a case discussion a psychoanalyst object to any consideration of the possibility of surgical treatment for focal epilepsy on the grounds that the epilepsy had so many psychogenic elements that they must be regarded as basic causes. I would be the last to be enthusiastic about surgical treatment for epilepsy but I cannot see that psychogenic factors are so exclusive of other pathologies that no consideration should be given to cortical irritability.

As I indicated at the outset, we cannot draw a line between those of our residents who are going into psychoanalysis and those who are not, since we cannot ourselves offer them psychoanalytic training. Generally speaking—though our program has been operating too short a time to tell—I have a feeling that our training is sufficiently oriented in this direction so that most of our residents will get some sort of psychoanalytic experience or training after they leave us. I feel that most psychiatrists use in their practice psychoanalytic principles and I am quite sure a moderate number of them actually use some sort of psychoanalytic technique, including free association, the use of the couch, three to five interviews per week, etc. I have found that some psychiatrists tell patients that they are doing psychoanalysis partly because of the attached prestige but partly, I think, because in the lay mind all psychotherapy seems more closely allied to "psychoanalysis" than to "psychiatry" which is often associated with hospital practice. I think the answer to this particular problem would lie in more rigid definition of what actually is psychoanalysis and perhaps some way in which the APA directory would not designate people as psychoanalysts simply on their say-so.

If we had psychoanalytic training available to our residents (and this statement is based not on our immediate situation but on my experience in Philadelphia and my impression of other training centers), I would like to see psychoanalytic training, i.e., special training for the individual who wants to do psychoanalysis primarily or exclusively, given contingent upon the individual's demonstrated ability to accept his responsibility as a physician. This, I think, could be accomplished by collaboration between the staff members who had observed him on the wards and in clinical relations with patients and the committee who would be selecting candidates for psychoanalytic training.

It seems to me that the situation in residency training has never really been clarified with reference to a comparison between those residents who have had even a personal psychoanalysis and those who have received only supervision. I have seen residents obtain a personal psychoanalysis with no initial motivation other than the training program itself. What neurotic needs there were in addition to this motivation, I do not know, but the amount of time involved in a personal psychoanalysis should actually, it seems to me, be matched by the same amount of time applied to standard supervision before we would be able to be sure that there was anything specifically valuable in the former process as compared to the latter. My completely unscientific impression is that close contact with a mature psychiatrist who has good, broad, clinical orientation is valuable to the resident no matter how the process is labeled.

You may be interested in the fact that we are attempting to inaugurate here a very timid approach to this problem by having our residents take on a limited number of "psychotherapeutic" hours with senior therapists not administratively concerned with the residents assigned to them for this project. We would like to see what the residents could expect in a situation which somewhat approximated the situation of the patient in therapy. We have not yet started it because we are attempting to ascertain the amount of cooperation to be expected from the staff. As you undoubtedly would anticipate, there are strong feelings pro and con. Interestingly enough, the persons who disapprove of the idea have thus far invariably objected on the grounds that (a) the experiment will accomplish nothing, and (b) that it will run a real danger of disturbing the residents. I feel the reasons for these objections are quite obvious.

It is certainly quite confusing to both the resident and to people like myself who are attempting to administer residency programs to see that senior psychiatrists who are good doctors appear to be independent of the "schools" to which they belong. I was particularly impressed by this when I heard your presentation of this in Zurich last summer. One is almost forced to the conclusion that the warm, ethical psychiatrists are innately that way and are neither created nor obstructed by the training programs they have had.

Chapter XI

DISCUSSION OF PREVAILING
PRACTICES AND VIEWS

THE AGGREGATE of these views of leaders in psychiatry reflects well, if not completely, the orientation prevailing in this country toward the role of psychoanalysis in psychiatric residency training. These statements, together with the results of the Ithaca Conference on Psychiatric Education, June 1952 (68), give a fairly adequate picture of present trends in residency training.

The answers represent a spectrum of opinions about the significance of psychoanalysis for psychiatry, particularly psychotherapy. They include the opinions both of practicing psychoanalysts, who participate in the training of psychiatrists, and of psychiatrists who are not members of the American Psychoanalytic Association. *It is, therefore, significant that, without exception, all respondents consider it necessary for every psychiatrist to get theoretical instruction in the basic concepts of psychoanalysis concerning psychodynamics, ego development, instinctual development, utilization of psychoanalytic principles in making a diagnosis and prognosis, theory of psychoanalytic treatment, and the utilization of psychoanalytic concepts in psychotherapy.*

A few of the respondents qualified this overall opinion. Bowman and Grinker mention that they include in their teaching program Adler's and Jung's theoretical concepts. Though they do not state this specifically, I assume most respondents, even those who like myself do not consider these concepts at the present time of particular significance, would agree that it is desirable from the historical point of view to make the students acquainted with the contributions of Jung and Adler.

Frieda Fromm-Reichmann qualifies her statement by singling out the theory of instinctual development as something which should be taught primarily in a critical-historical fashion. Without asking their views in particular, I assume that many of the respondents, if specifically asked, would agree that most of our theoretical concepts, not merely the theory of instincts, should be presented critically in a historical perspective.

It is true that certain of our fundamental views appear better established than others. For example, the phenomenology and theory of ego defenses, the basic mechanisms of repression, projection, overcompensation, reaction formation, turning of impulses from outside objects toward self, identification, the psychology of anxiety and guilt feelings, belong to another category of concepts than those concerning the ultimate nature of the drives. In the theory of choice of neurosis, the relative significance of environmental and constitutional factors is differently evaluated by different authors. There is also a considerable divergence of opinion concerning the quantitative evaluation of the different therapeutic factors. The role of countertransference is not yet a fully clarified issue. Since psychoanalytic training is a truly postgraduate training and not elementary instruction, most authors would agree that it should be taught in a historical-critical vein and that only some portions of psychoanalytic theory should be taught in a pragmatic fashion.

In spite of such qualifying statements, there is almost complete agreement among the respondents, whether or not they are psychoanalysts, that theoretical instruction in psychoanalysis is fundamental in psychiatric residency training.

There is a divergence of opinion as to whether a different kind of instruction in psychoanalytic concepts should be given on the one hand to residents in psychiatry and on the other to candidates of psychoanalytic institutes. Brosin, Gerty, Ham, Menninger, Kubie, Hartmann, Rado, and Romano believe that theory need not be taught on different levels to these two groups, either because, according to Brosin, theory is a "unitary system" or, according to Hartmann, "theory cannot well be taught by cutting down every chapter," or, because as Menninger states, we need not fear that if well taught, theoretical knowledge *will be abused*. Others who agree that theory should be freely taught, as for example Lorand, are willing to take the risk that in some cases it will lead to "wild analysis." Gerty considers this risk something which every field has to take, "when one experiments with any new method of treatment." Saul believes that the quality of basic training is what determines the soundness of a psychiatrist's practice and advocates as thorough a training as possible for every psychiatrist. Romano also stresses this point in saying that abuse of psychoanalytic concepts is less likely to occur with those who received a thorough instruction in theory.

The most basic problem—the relation of teaching to learning—is not explicitly discussed by the respondents. Only Gerty stresses the fact that knowledge has no boundaries; obviously he considers individual ability, initiative, and curiosity more important than "boundaries, which serve the purpose of organizing instruction to suit certain practical purposes."

Others believe that theory can and should be taught on different levels to psychiatric residents and candidates of institutes. Levine and Fleming are the most explicit about how this can be done. Levine teaches theory mainly in connection with the actual clinical problems the residents face in their daily work and believes that one can adjust the amount and content of theoretical instruction to the needs of different residents according to the special field of psychiatry they choose for their later work. Both Levine and Fleming define the main difference between the two levels of teaching—one for psychiatrists in general, one for candidates of psychoanalytic institutes—that in general residency training the genetic aspects of the theory are less important than they are in the teaching of psychoanalysis. Redlich, too, thinks that theory can be taught in degrees, but considers the dividing line fuzzy. Reider, on the other hand, is emphatic in stating that residency training should not turn into "quasi-psychoanalytic" training. Appel hopes that different curricula will be developed for those planning to practice psychoanalysis alone, for those who plan to teach, and for those who want to devote themselves to research.

There is a great deal of divergence of opinion regarding the danger of wild analysis as a result of theoretical instruction of candidates in psychoanalytic concepts. Hartmann does not think that it can be prevented. He speaks of "a continuum from those who just put some more emphasis in their psychotherapy on, let's say, transference or resistance, to those who try to emulate whatever they happen to know of the technique of analysis." Of course, "wild analysis" has existed since the advent of psychoanalysis. Better instruction in the basic principles of psychoanalysis is likely to have a "taming" influence, reducing the wildness of application and contributing to a more systematic exploration of the wider and sounder therapeutic utilization of our basic knowledge.

Grinker, Reider, and Lorand state that many residents who have no opportunity for formal training in psychoanalytic institutes do engage in psychoanalysis, while Appel, Levine, Menninger, Redlich, and Romano report favorably and consider the above an exception.

There is almost complete agreement in regard to the teaching of technique as distinct from theory. All respondents believe that the teaching of psychoanalytic techniques is a special skill and should be taught in psychoanalytic institutes.

Differences of opinion exist, however, about the sharpness of the dividing line between psychoanalysis and psychotherapy based on analytical principles. Fleming and Reider draw a sharp division between psychoanalysis and dynamic psychotherapy. Fleming in detail, and Reider more in a summary fashion, define the difference in the full development of a transference neurosis in psychoanalysis which allows the working through systematically of early conflicts underlying the neurotic disturbance. Redlich believes the dividing line is indistinct. Levine sees the difference more in quantitative terms and defines it as a greater or lesser emphasis on conscious versus unconscious conflicts, and current versus infantile material. He does not, however, eliminate entirely any of these considerations when teaching psychotherapy to his residents. Like Appel, in his teaching he remains closely in touch with the clinical material and seems to call the attention of his students to the relevant material necessary to understand and treat the patient in question. It is noteworthy that in his statement he places greater stress on those aspects of therapy which, according to him, the psychoanalyst neglects, namely the "interpersonal versus the intrapsychic," than on trying to define what the psychotherapist does not need to know.[1]

There is almost full agreement about personal analysis being desirable for all psychiatrists.[2] Some of the respondents, like Reider, emphasize, however, that a psychiatrist may do good psychotherapy without being analyzed. Appel remarks on the temporary disturbing effect of personal analysis upon

[1] See Brosin's statement referring to Grinker, Chapter X.
[2] This coincides with the finding of Klein and Porter "that 75 per cent of analytic teachers and 95 per cent of non-analytic teachers believe all residents should have analytic training to fit them for general psychiatry" (quoted from the report of the Committee on Medical Education of the GAP).

residents, which may last as long as two years. In the Chicago Institute this difficulty was dealt with in the new curriculum by providing for an interruption of the personal analysis at the time when the candidate is ready to begin his supervisory work, the analysis to be continued later.

Rado offers a tentative suggestion as to how to cope with the practical difficulty of offering personal analysis to all residents. This consists in developing a less extensive procedure of self-exploration for which he uses the term "psychodynamic sensitization." Branch of Utah, whose department has no psychoanalytic institute in the neighborhood, makes a similar suggestion.

Bernard Bandler at the Ithaca Conference proposed that "some sort of psychoanalytic training be worked out that would provide a modified personal analysis adapted to the needs of residents as psychiatrists rather than their needs as psychoanalysts" (68). According to Redlich also, the senior analysts of Yale are in favor "of a briefer psychoanalysis for residents who will not take up the specialty of psychoanalysis." There is a widespread apprehension among psychoanalysts that this will dilute psychoanalysis by violating some of its basic principles. The opinion was expressed at the Ithaca Conference that these adverse effects could be overcome if the American Psychoanalytic Association would condone such modified procedures of personal analysis as legitimate and recommend them for psychiatrists in training. Some members of the conference felt that the main difficulty is the prevailing attitude of residents, who attach higher status and prestige to completion of a formal course of psychoanalytic training approved by the American Psychoanalytic Association. It was also felt that the idea should be inculcated into the residents that "to be a psychoanalytically oriented psychiatrist, and also to be qualified in other aspects of this specialty, is the foremost status in prestige and that other considerations such as personal psychoanalysis in the orthodox sense of the term will be of secondary importance." This was expressed in the statement of Bandler (68):

Our residents who are going into psychotherapy will be primarily interested in the treatment of patients. If becoming and being a psychoanalyst loses the terrible overemphasis it has at the present time and its value is altered, it would then be possible to work out a type of psychoanalytic training for residents in connection with the universities and the residency programs that could provide a personal analysis.

There is not sufficient experience to form a final judgment about the value of such individualized personal analyses or personal "psychotherapies" of residents. As has been discussed above, the training analysis of a psychiatrist offers special difficulties which are absent in the usual therapeutic analyses of patients. Yet one cannot lightly dismiss the argument that candidates, like patients, differ in regard to their problems and their capacities to communicate with their own unconscious. Accordingly each training analysis poses an individual problem which can only be evaluated on its own merits. A uniform procedure, therefore, cannot be easily enforced without incurring the danger that such a procedure, particularly its average duration, will be insufficient in one case and longer than necessary in another.[3] The great personality differences of students of psychiatry have been stressed by a number of the respondents (Appel, Brosin, Fleming, and Reider). The flexible adjustment of the training analysis to the candidates' needs appears a logical conclusion. This, of course, requires a great amount of judgment on the part of the training analysts, probably more precise a judgment than is possible to expect today from anyone. Moreover, individualization of training analysis creates that type of practical difficulty which is involved in dealing with large numbers of applicants on a national scale. In spite of such difficulties, a policy of flexibility in training analysis is

[3] See Chapter IX.

a far less radical proposition than experimenting with some type of cursory preparatory psychotherapy to be offered to those residents who will not undertake further training in psychoanalysis. Those who are impressed by the difficulties of bringing about a change in an adult personality at all will be inclined to consider this a poor compromise. Those again who believe that flexible utilization of psychoanalytic principles in psychotherapy of patients as well as of psychiatrists (personal psychotherapy) can be effective in introducing a maturational process, even if not accomplishing immediately far-reaching changes in personality structure, will be more optimistic. This is by no means a closed chapter and only extensive experimentation will provide the final answer.

Chapter XII

SUMMARY AND FUTURE OUTLOOK

SEVERAL conclusions are shared by most leaders in this field. First, that the knowledge of psychoanalytic principles and all that is known about the biology and psychology of personality functions (which in itself is still a greatly limited body of knowledge) should be imparted to all residents in psychiatry who have been carefully selected as to their personal suitability.

Second, that at present psychiatry offers at least three main types of specialization—the psychological approach, the organic approaches, and administrative custodial psychiatry. Consequently selection procedures should take into consideration the fact that different personality types are needed for these three kinds of functions.

Third, that a relative freedom from such personality features as interfere with the understanding of others is the primary requirement for those who will devote themselves to psychotherapy or psychoanalysis. I cannot see any valid reason to differentiate in this respect between these two groups.[1]

And finally, that those who want to apply psychodynamic knowledge for psychoanalytic treatment should undergo the

---

[1] Some authors are inclined to consider different criteria of suitability for analysts and psychotherapists.

type of training which has been developed in psychoanalytic institutes, including personal analysis as a prerequisite.

There is also no reasonable doubt that a thorough personal analysis is an optimal requirement for all psychiatrists who are specializing in the psychological approach to the field. The question whether or not in certain individual cases a "personal psychotherapy" can be substituted for "personal analysis" is an open one which for lack of experience cannot be answered in a dogmatic fashion.

From this perspective, the controversy concerning the relationship of psychoanalysis proper and psychotherapy based on psychoanalytic knowledge appears in a somewhat different light. It is important to know what can and what cannot be accomplished with the one and the other approach. This question, however, cannot be very well decided by dogmatic statements and deductive reasoning. The view is slowly gaining acceptance that these procedures represent a continuum in which the two extremes are radically different but are connected by borderline procedures which blend into one another gradually. There is no doubt that the two extreme sides of this continuum differ radically from each other. On the other hand, profound changes in personality occur sometimes not only through therapy but also spontaneously under the influence of life experiences. They often do occur, but not always, after penetrating, prolonged psychoanalysis and they also occur frequently after so-called transference cures. They also occur under the influence of psychotherapeutic procedures which, quantitatively at least, differ from standard psychoanalysis. We are not yet able to account precisely for all those processes which lead to profound structural changes in personality. Systematic studies, recorded interviews combined with detailed records of the evaluation of each interview by the therapist, observation of the therapy by other trained persons in addition to the therapist who conducts the treatment, are needed to account, step by step, for those changes which take place in a patient during treatment. More-over, it will be necessary to change experimentally, one after the other, the variables which enter into the therapeutic process. For evaluating the different forms of dynamic psychotherapy, treatments must be carefully recorded and observed [2] by several trained persons before these controversial questions can be satisfactorily answered.

Teaching of psychoanalytic theory to all residents of psychiatry will lead occasionally to wild psychoanalysis by those who do not follow up their basic residency training in psychoanalytic institutes. This is a calculated risk which we are taking and have been taking for some time. Knowledge has no boundaries; it can be validly expected that students who are exposed to sound instruction in analytical theory will use their knowledge without transcending their therapeutic competence and, what is even more important, will continually increase their knowledge by learning from their own experience.

One must differentiate between "wild analysis"—that is to say, the unsound application of partial or vague knowledge —and untried and experimental, yet rational, procedures. Considering the fact that, at the present state of knowledge, individual aptitude in all forms of psychotherapy is equally, if not more significant than theoretical knowledge, we need not hesitate to impart all we know about personality to well-screened, carefully selected students.[3] The danger of misuse of this knowledge by those who have no specialized training in psychoanalytic technique can be best reduced not by apportioning knowledge, but by sound and thorough teaching of basic concepts, by improved selection procedures, and by personal analysis. The selection, to be effective, should take place when we admit students to psychiatric residency

[2] Observation does not necessarily mean actual one-way mirror observation but the study by several workers of mechanically recorded interviews, with or without moving pictures, including the notations of the therapist.

[3] See Brosin's statement, Chapter X.

training. The next important measure is the personal analysis of the resident, which can eliminate the reversible impediments in personality and enhance native aptitudes. The difficulty of increasing the number of personal analyses is well known. This is a practical problem and can be met only by practical measures.

Only two respondents, Hartmann and Reider, touched on a crucial point, namely that the utilization of psychoanalytic concepts in psychotherapy should preferably be taught in psychoanalytic institutes. This coincides with the opinion of this author, who considers the application of psychoanalytic knowledge for psychotherapy a more difficult and less explored field than the standard psychoanalytic procedure. This is a step which still has to be worked out. It would appear then that it would be particularly difficult to teach the utilization of psychoanalytic principles in psychotherapy to residents who have no experience in psychoanalytic therapy. Theoretically this conclusion is correct, but it disregards certain practical circumstances. The practice of psychotherapy is one of the major parts of a psychiatrist's practice, and most respondents assert that this practice cannot remain uninfluenced by the theoretical knowledge of psychoanalysis which he obtains during his residency. It appears that we will have to leave this still unexplored and unorganized field to be worked out both by practicing psychiatrists and by practicing psychoanalysts, each group working toward developing techniques of dynamic psychotherapy according to its own background experience and ingenuity. This is obviously the course of events taking place at present. While I agree with Hartmann's remark, I would modify his statement. Exploring and teaching the utilization of psychoanalytic concepts in psychotherapy should be one of the major concerns of psychoanalytic institutes but should not necessarily be restricted to such institutes.

One should not forget that in the not yet formalized applications of psychoanalysis to psychotherapy, psychoanalysts do not have a great head start because psychoanalytic institutes have up to now been mainly concerned with giving instruction in the standard procedure; only recently have a number of psychoanalysts become interested in experimenting *systematically* in their own practice with modifications of the standard procedure.

Therefore, all psychiatrists who are thoroughly acquainted with all that is known of personality functions have a chance to contribute to the development of sound principles of dynamic psychotherapy. I expect that psychiatrists not formally trained in psychoanalysis and not recognized as psychoanalysts will contribute a great deal toward working out a sound theory and practice of dynamic psychotherapy. Their techniques are not yet formalized and consequently not taught anywhere in a uniform manner, as is the case with the teaching of psychoanalytic technique. There can be little doubt that the theoretical principles used in psychotherapy should be the same as those which are the basis of psychoanalysis. The only consistent position is, then, to encourage all psychiatrists who are thoroughly acquainted with all that we know today about personality theory to participate in the pioneering task: working out the different therapeutic techniques by which this basic knowledge can be translated into practice.

Psychiatrists experienced in many forms of therapy have one advantage, namely that of being more flexible in their attitude; because they are less specialized, they are less apt to restrict their practice to patients who fit a special technique which they have mastered. Of necessity they have a greater inclination to experiment and to fit their tool to the variety of unselected patient material. This is borne out clearly in the statements of Brosin, Ham, and Levine, who emphasize the need for teaching residents the broader application of psychoanalytic knowledge to a wide spectrum of patients.

Psychoanalysts, on the other hand, because they have the greatest experience in a most systematic uncovering procedure, will have a special contribution to make, particularly if they will give up a preconceived notion about what psychotherapy can or cannot accomplish.

Psychoanalysts who are interested in such experimentation have a particular opportunity. The vicissitudes of daily practice unavoidably put them repeatedly in a position where they have to change the standard procedure. They have the opportunity to observe closely the different therapeutic factors, the manifestations of transference, countertransference, and the different forms of resistance. They also can study closely the influence of the therapeutic process upon the patient's daily life and, conversely, the influence of daily occurrences in the patient's daily life upon the therapeutic process. In their supervisory activities they have a unique opportunity to observe the influence of the therapist's personality.

To make use of these experiences both for improving the standard procedure and for working out modifications of it appears in this light not only a challenge but well nigh a responsibility.

In this book no radically new principles have been proposed applying either to the theory or the technique of psychoanalysis. Its purpose is to clarify prevailing views and practices, to establish consistently and explicitly underlying observations and assumptions, and furthermore to call attention to the discrepancies existing between our theoretical model of the procedure and what actually takes place in treatment. Such discrepancies in our field, as in any other, indicate the areas where knowledge is deficient and advancements should be expected.

These opaque areas of theory and practice can be reduced to a small number of issues.

First there is the continuous oscillation on the part of past and current authors between the evaluation of psychoanalysis as a primarily cognitive process on the one hand and as a primarily meaningful emotional experience on the other. The accepted formula, that psychoanalysis consists in a gradual extension of the cognitive radius of the conscious ego by re-exposing the ego to mental content which has been excluded from its scope, and that this re-exposition becomes effective only as an emotional experience in the transference, appears unassailable but is incomplete. The cognitive aspect of this process is well understood and is being explored more precisely in recent contributions to ego psychology. Its experiential component, however, is much less clear. One of the emphases of this discussion is that the crucial factor lies in the differences between the past and present (transference) experience. This discrepancy between past and present is introduced by the fact that the analyst's attitude is different from that of the significant persons in the patient's past because it is detached and objective and also because of the therapist's personality. This has been repeatedly stressed by a number of authors; what has not been explicitly formulated is the dynamic effect of this discrepancy. It can be understood only by keeping in mind that one of the ego's basic functions is adaptation to changing external and internal conditions. The discrepancy between the original pathogenic and the transference experience serves as a *natural challenge for the patient's ego to find a new solution.* This is not a simple cognitive act like the solution of a mathematical poser. It consists in a more or less prolonged experimentation in a continued interpersonal setting. It is learning by groping and practice.

It is at this point that the inadequacy of the theoretical model shows up. In the actual interpersonal—patient-therapist—equation the therapist does not figure as a constant factor, a pure intellect or a blank screen, but as a distinct individual. The contrast between the transference experience and the past in each case is also determined by the analyst's countertransference and his total personality. How to include the therapist's personality and the countertransference in our model is a current theoretical issue. The application of the new, improved model to technique is an equally pressing practical problem.

Emphasis upon the analyst's self-awareness and control of his countertransference attitude is the most generally accepted technical recommendation. Previous propositions, such as Ferenczi's active and relaxation techniques, in which the therapist assumes definite roles and attitudes, were not generally adopted. In this book I have tried to elaborate a suggestion I had made previously in other publications, that the therapist's conscious self-control can be more than a negative prescription: it can include within the framework of a basic objective and helpful attitude planfully selected interpersonal climates which appear most suitable for challenging the patient's ego to replace archaic transference patterns with new ones better adapted both to his adult personality and to his present environment. In making this suggestion, I tried to emphasize that inadvertently every analyst actually lends an interpersonal climate to every treatment, not only through his circumscribed countertransference attitude and by virtue of being a person in his own right, but also by intuitively responding to the patient's material while he pursues his therapeutic aims. The knowledge of the patient's past pathogenic experiences can aid this intuition with precise reasoning and reduce the fortuitous effect of the therapist's specific personality. Knowing the patient's past, the analyst does not only sense but *knows* the role into which the patient attempts to cast him and can counteract this purposefully.

The other emphasis in this book is that our advancing knowledge of psychodynamics opens up a vast territory still unexplored in a systematic manner: the application of this theoretical knowledge to different forms of psychotherapy. The different uncovering applications of this knowledge are viewed here as a continuum and the issue of where to draw the line between psychoanalysis proper and other related uncovering procedures, differing in the depth of penetration and in the completeness of the dynamic revival of the past, appears in a different light. The significance of this issue is reduced if the therapist knows what he is doing and understands the differences between the various technical applications of basic knowledge. The fact that such dynamic psychotherapies are based on the same principle as psychoanalysis has important practical consequences both for training and for practice. In this book an attempt is made first to establish the status quo and then to outline a desirable course of future development toward the ultimate unification of all the psychological aspects of psychiatry both in teaching and in practice.

Another point of emphasis of this book is the social significance of the treatment of incipient cases which are therapeutically most hopeful. This implies the view that neurosis is not a static but a developing condition which is subject to general principles prevailing in all organized systems. Once equilibrium is disturbed in such a system, lacking suitable self-controlling feedback mechanisms, the disturbance is apt to follow a spiraling type of disintegrative process. Through imparting emotional insight, therapy supplies an internal self-controlling mechanism: information which is fed back to the source of the original disequilibrating stimulus—in this case, unresolved conflicts. The sooner such a corrective measure is applied the greater is the chance of therapeutic success. Here, in the ambulatory treatment of incipient cases, seems to lie the answer to the most pressing national health problem of our days, our inability to provide adequate custodial and therapeutic aid to advanced cases of psychiatric patients.

This book is on the subject of therapy. Only the first chapter deals with the most significant cultural effect of psychoanalysis, with its influence upon the general outlook of Western man. Psychoanalysis has increased man's awareness of himself and of those current social events which threaten to extinguish his individuality.

Bibliography

ABRAHAM, KARL

1. "Uber eine besondere Form des neurotischen Widerstandes gegen die psychoanalytische Methodik." *International Zeitschrift für Psychoanalyse*, V, 1939. (Translated in *Selected Papers*.)

ALEXANDER, FRANZ

2. *Our Age of Unreason.* (Revised Edition.) Philadelphia, J. B. Lippincott Co., 1951.

3. "Metapsychologische Darstellung des Heilungsvorganges." *Internationale Zeitschrift für Psychoanalyse*, X, 1924, p. 216. (Vortrag auf dem VIII Int. Psa. Kongress in Salzburg, April 1924.)

4. "Psychoanalysis and Medicine." *The Harvey Lectures, 1930–1931.* Baltimore, Williams & Wilkins Co., 1931.

5. Review of "Die Entwicklungsziele der Psychoanalyse," by S. Ferenczi and O. Rank. *International Zeitschrift für Psychoanalyse*, XI, 1925.

6. "Zur Genese des Kastrationskomplexes." *Internationale Zeitschrift für Psychoanalyse*, XVI, 1930. "Concerning the Genesis of the Castration Complex." *Psychoanalytic Review*, XXII, 1, January 1935 (translated by C. F. Menninger, M.D.).

7. *The Psychoanalysis of the Total Personality.* Nervous and Mental Disease Monograph Series, No. 52. New York, Nervous and Mental Disease Publishing Co., 1929.

8. "The Problem of Psychoanalytic Technique." Reprinted from *Psychoanalytic Quarterly*, IV, 1935.

9. "The Quantitative Aspects of Technique." *Journal of the American Psychoanalytic Association*, II, 4, October 1954.

10. "Analysis of the Therapeutic Factors in Psychoanalytic Treatment." *Psychoanalytic Quarterly*, XIX, 4, October 1950.

11. "Psychoanalytic Training in the Past, the Present and the Future." Address given to the Association of the Candidates of the Institute for Psychoanalysis, Chicago, 1951.

12. "Psychoanalysis Comes of Age." *Psychoanalytic Quarterly*, VII, 1938.

13. *Medical Value of Psychoanalysis.* (First Edition.) New York, W. W. Norton & Co., 1932.

ALEXANDER, FRANZ, and FRENCH, THOMAS M.

14. *Psychoanalytic Therapy.* New York, Ronald Press Co., 1946.

BALINT, ALICE and MICHAEL

15. "On Transference and Countertransference." *International Journal of Psychoanalysis,* XX, 1939.

BALINT, MICHAEL, and TARACHOW, SIDNEY

16. "Psychoanalytic Therapy." *Annual Survey of Psychoanalysis,* 1950, Vol. I. New York, International Universities Press, 1952.

BENEDEK, THERESE

17. "Dynamics of the Countertransference." *Bulletin of the Menninger Clinic,* XVII, 6, 1953.

BERMAN, I.

18. "Countertransferences and attitudes of the analyst in the therapeutic process." *Psychiatry,* XII, 1949.

BIBRING, EDWARD

19. "Psychoanalysis and the Dynamic Psychotherapies." *Journal of the American Psychoanalytic Association,* II, 4, October 1954.

BREUER, J., and FREUD, S.

20. *Studies in Hysteria.* Nervous and Mental Disease Monograph Series, No. 61. New York, Nervous and Mental Disease Publishing Co., 1936.

COHEN, ELLIOTT

21. Quoted from *Fortune,* June 1949, p. 170.

COHEN, MABEL B.

22. "Countertransference and anxiety." *Psychiatry,* XV, 1952.

DEWEY, JOHN, HOOK, SIDNEY, and NAGEL, ERNEST

23. "The New Failure of Nerve." *Partisan Review,* January–February 1943.

EHRENREICH, GERALD

24. "A Brief Report on Psychological Testing Experience in the Selection of Candidates for Psychoanalytic Training." Presented to the Faculty Seminar of the Topeka Institute for Psychoanalysis on March 11, 1955.

EISSLER, K. R.

25. "The Chicago Institute of Psychoanalysis and the Sixth Period of the Development of Psychoanalytic Technique." *Journal of General Psychology*, XLII, 1950.

ENGLISH, O. S., and PEARSON, G. H. J.

26. *Common Neuroses of Children and Adults*. New York, W. W. Norton & Co., 1937.

ERIKSON, ERIK

27. *Childhood and Society*. New York, W. W. Norton & Co., 1950.

FENICHEL, OTTO

28. "Zur Theorie der psychoanalytischen Technik." *International Zeitschrift für Psychoanalyse*, XXI, 1935.
29. *The Psychoanalytic Theory of Neurosis*. New York, W. W. Norton & Co., 1945.

FERENCZI, SANDOR

30. "The Further Development of an Active Therapy in Psychoanalysis." *Further Contributions to the Theory of Psychoanalysis*, London, Hogarth Press, 1926.
31. "Relaxationsprinzip und Neokatharsis." *International Zeitschrift für Psychoanalyse*, XVI, 1930.
32. "Child-Analysis in the Analysis of Adults." *International Journal of Psychoanalysis*, XII, 1931.
33. "Gedanken über das Trauma." *International Zeitschrift für Psychoanalyse*, XX, 1934.

FERENCZI, SANDOR, and RANK, OTTO

34. "Developmental Goals of Psychoanalysis." *The Development of Psychoanalysis*, New York, Nervous and Mental Disease Publishing Co., 1925 (translated by Caroline Newton from "Entwicklungsziele der Psychoanalyse," *Internationaler Psychoanalytischer Verlag*, Wien, 1924).

FLIESS, R.

35. "Countertransference and Counteridentification," *Journal of the American Psychoanalytic Association*, I, 1953.

FRENCH, THOMAS M.

36. "A Clinical Study of Learning in the Course of Psychoanalytic Treatment." *Psychoanalytic Quarterly*, V, 1936.

37. *The Integration of Behavior*, Vol. I. Chicago, University of Chicago Press, 1952.
38. *The Integration of Behavior*, Vol. II. Chicago, University of Chicago Press, 1954.

FRENCH, THOMAS M., and ALEXANDER, FRANZ

14. *Psychoanalytic Therapy*. New York, Ronald Press Co., 1946.

FREUD, ANNA

39. *The Ego and the Mechanisms of Defense*. London, Hogarth Press, 1937.

FREUD, SIGMUND

40. "The Dynamics of the Transference" (1912). *Collected Papers*, Vol. II, London, Hogarth Press, 1924.
41. "Recommendations for Physicians on the Psychoanalytic Method of Treatment" (1912). *Collected Papers*, Vol. II, London, Hogarth Press, 1924.
42. "Further Recommendations in the Technique of Psychoanalysis on Beginning the Treatment. The question of the first communications. The Dynamics of the Cure" (1913). *Collected Papers*, Vol. II, London, Hogarth Press, 1924.
43. "Further Recommendations in the Technique of Psychoanalysis. Recollection, Repetition and Working Through" (1914). *Collected Papers*, Vol. II, London, Hogarth Press, 1924.
44. "Further Recommendations in the Technique of Psychoanalysis. Observations on Transference-Love" (1915). *Collected Papers*, Vol. II, London, Hogarth Press, 1924.
45. "The History of an Infantile Neurosis." *Collected Papers*, Vol. III, London, Hogarth Press, 1953.
46. *Totem and Taboo*. London, George Routledge and Sons, Ltd., 1919.
47. *The Ego and the Id*. London, Hogarth Press, 1927.
48. "The Future Prospects of Psychoanalytic Therapy." An address delivered before the Second International Psychoanalytical Congress at Nuremburg in 1910. First published in *Zentralblatt*, I, 1910; reprinted in *Sammlung*, Dritte Folge.
49. *Introductory Lectures to Psychoanalysis*. New York, Boni and Liveright, 1920.
50. "Analysis Terminable and Interminable." *International Journal of Psychoanalysis*, XVIII, 1937.
51. "Psychoanalysis" (An Encyclopedia Article). *Collected Papers*, Vol. V, London, Hogarth Press, 1950.

52. *A General Introduction to Psychoanalysis*. New York, Boni and Liveright, 1920.
53. *An Autobiographical Study*. London, Hogarth Press, 1936.

FROMM-REICHMANN, FRIEDA

54. *Principles of Intensive Psychotherapy*. Chicago, University of Chicago Press, 1950.

GERTY, FRANCIS

55. "The Scope and Relationship of Psychiatry in Medicine." An address read before the Section on Nervous and Mental Diseases at the Ninety-eighth Annual Session of the American Medical Association, Atlantic City, New Jersey, June 9, 1949. Reprinted from *The Journal of the American Medical Association*, CXLIII, June 17, 1950.

GILL, MERTON M.

56. "Psychoanalysis and Exploratory Psychotherapy." *Journal of the American Psychoanalytic Association*, II, 4, October 1954.

GILL, MERTON M., HILGARD, ERNEST, and SHAKOW, DAVID

57. "A Planning Proposal for a Research in Emotional Growth and Mental Health." Privately circulated by the Social Science Research Council, November 1953.

GITELSON, M.

58. "The Emotional Position of the Analyst in the Psychoanalytic Situation." *International Journal of Psychoanalysis*, XXXIII, 1952.

GLOVER, EDWARD

59. "Lectures on Technique in Psychoanalysis." *International Journal of Psychoanalysis*, VIII, 1927.
60. *The Technique of Psychoanalysis*. New York, International Universities Press, 1955.

HARTMANN, HEINZ

61. "The Mutual Influences in the Development of the Ego and Id. Introduction to the Discussion." *The Psychoanalytic Study of the Child*, Vol. VII, International Universities Press, 1952.
62. "Comments on the Formation of Psychic Structure." *The Psychoanalytic Study of the Child*, Vol. II, International Universities Press, 1946.
63. "Technical Implications of Ego Psychology." *Psychoanalytic Quarterly*, XX, 1951.

HEIMANN, PAULA

64. "On Countertransference." *International Journal of Psychoanalysis*, XXXI, 1950.

HILGARD, ERNEST, GILL, MERTON M., and SHAKOW, DAVID

57. "A Planning Proposal for a Research in Emotional Growth and Mental Health." Privately circulated by the Social Science Research Council, November 1953.

HOLT, ROBERT R., and LUBORSKY, LESTER

65. "The Selection of Candidates for Psychoanalytic Training: Implications from the Selection of Psychiatric Residents." Based on paper read before the panel on "Selection of Psychoanalysts" at the Midwinter Meetings of the American Psychoanalytic Association, 1953. The research reported here was carried out at the Menninger Foundation with the financial assistance of the Veterans Administration and the New York Foundation.

66. "The Selection of Candidates for Psychoanalytic Training: On the Use of Interviews and Psychological Tests." Based on paper presented in a panel discussion, "The Selection of Candidates for Training in Psychoanalysis," at the 1953 Midwinter Meetings of the American Psychoanalytic Association.

HOOK, SIDNEY, DEWEY, JOHN, and NAGEL, ERNEST

23. "The New Failure of Nerve." *Partisan Review*, January–February 1943.

HUIZINGA, J.

66a. *Homo Ludens*, London, Routledge and Kegan Paul, Ltd., 1949.

HYMAN, HAROLD T., and KESSEL, LEO

67. "The Value of Psychoanalysis as a Therapeutic Procedure." *Journal of the American Medical Association*, CI, 1933.

ITHACA CONFERENCE, 1952.

68. *The Psychiatrist, His Training and Development.* Report of the 1952 Conference on Psychiatric Education held at Cornell University, Ithaca, New York, June 19–25, 1952. Organized and conducted by the American Psychiatric Association and the Association of American Medical Colleges; published by the American Psychiatric Association, Washington, 1953.

KAISER, HELLMUTH

69. "Probleme der Technik." *International Zeitschrift für Psychoanalyse*, XX, 1934.

KRIS, ERNEST

70. "Ego Psychology and Interpretation in Psychoanalytic Therapy." *Psychoanalytic Quarterly*, XX, 1, 1951.

71. "Comments on the Formation of Psychic Structure." *The Psychoanalytic Study of the Child*, Vol. II, International Universities Press, 1946.

KUBIE, LAWRENCE

72. "The Neurotic Potential and Human Adaptation." Presented at the Dedication of the Psychiatric Wing of the Strong Memorial Hospital, Rochester, New York, March 31, 1949, and printed in *Adaptation*, Edited by Dr. John Romano, Ithaca, Cornell University Press, 1949.

73. "The Independent Institute." *Bulletin of the American Psychoanalytic Association*, VIII, 2, May 1952.

LEVINE, MAURICE

74. "The Impact of Psychoanalysis on Training in Psychiatry." *Twenty Years of Psychoanalysis* (with H. Ross as co-editor), New York, W. W. Norton & Co., 1953.

LITTLE, M.

75. "Countertransference and the Patient's Response to It." *International Journal of Psychoanalysis*, XXXII, 1951.

LOWENSTEIN, R.

76. "Comments on the Formation of Psychic Structure." *The Psychoanalytic Study of the Child*, Vol. II, International Universities Press, 1946.

LUBORSKY, LESTER, and HOLT, ROBERT R.

65. "The Selection of Candidates for Psychoanalytic Training: Implications from the Selection of Psychiatric Residents." Based on paper read before the panel on "Selection of Psychoanalysts" at the Midwinter Meetings of the American Psychoanalytic Association, 1953. The research reported here was carried out at the Menninger Foundation with the financial assistance of the Veterans Administration and the New York Foundation.

66. "The Selection of Candidates for Psychoanalytic Training: On the Use of Interviews and Psychological Tests." Based on paper presented in a panel discussion, "The Selection of Candidates for Training in Psychoanalysis," at the 1953 Midwinter Meetings of the American Psychoanalytic Association.

MANNHEIM, KARL
77. *Ideology and Utopia*, New York, Harcourt, Brace & Co.; London, Routledge and Kegan Paul Ltd., 1953.

MEAD, MARGARET
78. *Male and Female*. New York, William Morrow and Co., 1949.

NAGEL, ERNEST, HOOK, SIDNEY, and DEWEY, JOHN
23. "The New Failure of Nerve." *Partisan Review*, January–February 1943.

NUNBERG, HERMAN
79. "The Synthetic Function of the Ego." *International Journal of Psychoanalysis*, XII, 1931.

OBERNDORF, CLARENCE P.
80. *A History of Psychoanalysis in America*. New York, Grune and Stratton, 1953.

ORR, DOUGLASS W.
81. "Transference and Countertransference." *Journal of the American Psychoanalytic Association*, II, 4, October 1954.

ORTEGA Y GASSETT, JOSE
81a. *Toward a Philosophy of History*. New York, W. W. Norton & Co., 1941.

PEARSON, G. H. J., and ENGLISH, O. S.
26. *Common Neuroses of Children and Adults*. New York, W. W. Norton & Co., 1937.

RADO, SANDOR
82. Reprinted by permission from *Psychiatric Treatment*—Proceedings of the Association for Research in Nervous and Mental Disease, December 14 and 15, 1951, New York, published by Williams & Wilkins Co., Baltimore, 1953.
83. "Psychodynamics as a Basic Science." *American Journal of Orthopsychiatry*, 16, 1946.
84. "Adaptational Psychodynamics: A Basic Science." In *Changing*

Concepts of Psychoanalytic Medicine (Ed. Rado and Daniels), Proceedings of the Decennial Celebration of the Columbia University Psychoanalytic Clinic. New York, Grune and Stratton. In Press.

RANGELL, LEO

85. "Similarities and Differences Between Psychoanalysis and Dynamic Psychotherapy." *Journal of the American Psychoanalytic Association*, II, 4, October 1954.

RANK, OTTO, and FERENCZI, SANDOR

34. "Developmental Goals of Psychoanalysis." *The Development of Psychoanalysis*, New York, Nervous and Mental Disease Publishing Company, 1925 (translated by Caroline Newton from "Entwicklungsziele der Psychoanalyse," *Internationaler Psychoanalytischer Verlag*, Wien, 1924).

REICH, WILHELM

86. *Charakteranalyse.* Wien, privately published, 1933.

RIESMAN, DAVID

87. *The Lonely Crowd.* New Haven, Yale University Press, 1950.

SACHS, HANNS

88. *Freud, Master and Friend.* Cambridge, Harvard University Press, 1946 (copyrighted 1944).

SHAKOW, DAVID, GILL, MERTON M., HILGARD, ERNEST

57. "A Planning Proposal for a Research in Emotional Growth and Mental Health." Privately circulated by the Social Science Research Council, November 1953.

SHARPE, E. F.

89. "The Psychoanalyst." *International Journal of Psychoanalysis*, XXVIII, 1947.

STERBA, RICHARD

90. "The Fate of the Ego in Analytic Therapy." *International Journal of Psychoanalysis*, XV, 1934.

STONE, LEO

91. "The Widening Scope of Psychoanalysis." *Journal of the American Psychoanalytic Association*, II, 4, October 1954.

STRACHEY, JAMES

92. "The Nature of the Therapeutic Action of Psychoanalysis." *International Journal of Psychoanalysis*, XV, 1934.

TARACHOW, SIDNEY, and BALINT, MICHAEL

16. "Psychoanalytic Therapy." *Annual Survey of Psychoanalysis*, 1950, Vol. I. New York, International Universities Press, 1952.

TOWER, LUCIA

93. "The Countertransference." Address delivered before the Chicago Psychoanalytic Society, Spring, 1955.

WEIGERT, EDITH

94. "The Importance of Flexibility in Psychoanalytic Technique." *Journal of the American Psychoanalytic Association*, II, 4, October 1954.

Index

293